MEETING
GLOBALIZATION'S
CHALLENGES

MEETING GLOBALIZATION'S CHALLENGES

Policies to Make Trade Work for All

LUÍS A. V. CATÃO AND
MAURICE OBSTFELD, EDITORS

with a foreword by Christine Lagarde

PRINCETON UNIVERSITY PRESS
PRINCETON AND OXFORD

Published by Princeton University Press
41 William Street, Princeton, New Jersey 08540
6 Oxford Street, Woodstock, Oxfordshire OX20 1TR

press.princeton.edu

ISBN 978-0-691-18893-5
ISBN (ebook) 978-0-691-19886-6

British Library Cataloging-in-Publication Data is available

Editorial: Joe Jackson and Jacqueline Delaney
Production Editorial: Brigitte Pelner
Text and Cover Design: C. Alvarez-Gaffin
Jacket Art: Shutterstock
Production: Erin Suydam
Publicity: Tayler Lord

This book has been composed in ITC Galliard
Printed on acid-free paper ∞
Printed in the United States of America
1 3 5 7 9 10 8 6 4 2

For Elza and Jennifer

Contents

PART III
GLOBALIZATION, DEINDUSTRIALIZATION, AND LABOR MARKET ADJUSTMENT

PART IV
ADJUSTMENT POLICIES

PART V
THE POLITICAL ECONOMY OF TRADE BACKLASH

Acknowledgments

This book collects and expands the various contributions to a conference on "Meeting Globalization's Challenges" that took place at the headquarters of the International Monetary Fund (IMF) in Washington, DC, on October 11, 2017. We take this opportunity to thank all conference participants and, in particular, the staff involved in the organization of that event. That group includes Felicia Belostecinic, Lucia Buono, Tracey Lookadoo, Begoña Nuñez, and Olga Stankova as well as staff from the IMF audiovisual team. We also thank Florian Gimbel, Jeffrey Hayden, Linda Griffin Kean, and Patricia Loo from the IMF communications department, Mahnaz Hemmati and Evgenia Pugacheva from the IMF research department, and James A. John and Alfred Krammer from the office of the IMF's managing director for extensive support in the various phases of this project.

Several academic colleagues helped us track down some of the historical data on globalization trends that this book's introduction uses. We are especially grateful to Laurence Chandy, Michael Clemens, Giovanni Federico, Antonio Tena Junguito, Jonathan Moses, Brina Seidel, Alan Taylor, and Jeff Williamson.

Last but not least, we would like to thank Joe Jackson at Princeton University Press for his consistent encouragement and support of this project as well as Brigitte Pelner, Jacqueline Delaney, and Stephanie Rojas for editorial and marketing work on the book.

Naturally, the usual disclaimers apply. In particular, the views expressed in this book's chapters are those of the respective authors, and not necessarily those of the IMF, its executive board, or its management.

Contributors

Ufuk Akcigit, University of Chicago

Edward Alden, Council on Foreign Relations

François Bourguignon, Paris School of Economics

Luís A. V. Catão, University of Lisbon

Angus Deaton, Princeton University

Rafael Dix-Carneiro, Duke University

Jeffry Frieden, Harvard University

Gordon H. Hanson, University of California, San Diego

Keyu Jin, London School of Economics

Lori G. Kletzer, University of California, Santa Cruz

Anne Krueger, Johns Hopkins University

Paul Krugman, City University of New York

Maurice Obstfeld, University of California, Berkeley

Nina Pavcnik, Dartmouth College

Andrés Rodríguez-Clare, University of California, Berkeley

Dani Rodrik, Harvard University

Michael Trebilcock, University of Toronto

Laura D. Tyson, University of California, Berkeley

Martin Wolf, *Financial Times*

Ernesto Zedillo, Yale University

Foreword

The increasing interconnection between the world's economies has led to something that is truly remarkable: more progress for more people than at any time in human history. This is, in many ways, the story of globalization.

At the heart of this story lies the spirit of openness to trade and technological innovation, which in turn have underpinned the cross-border flow of products, capital, talent, and ideas.

These interconnections have transformed our world, especially over the past generation. They helped reduce by half the proportion of the global population living in extreme poverty. They have boosted per capita incomes and living standards across a broad set of countries, and created millions of new jobs with higher wages.

In addition to being more prosperous, human lives are longer and healthier. Back in 1900, the average life expectancy around the world was thirty-one years. It is now seventy-two years, and this reflects in part our ability to harness the power of trade and innovation.

Communities around the world have felt these gains. According to international opinion surveys, most citizens in both advanced and developing economies perceive global trade as good for themselves and their countries.

But that is not the whole story. While the overall gains to society are large and growing, trade and technological change have come with negative side effects: from job losses in shrinking sectors to social challenges in some communities.

Indeed, many countries are experiencing high economic inequality, and some are facing increased political polarization. These problems are not new, nor are they solely due to trade, but trade openness can bring them into sharper relief. The current trade disputes are, in fact, a symptom of these underlying challenges.

The best policy response is not to turn our backs on trade. Instead, we need to redouble our efforts to create a more inclusive global trading system that works for all.

In these efforts, we can take inspiration from this impressive collection of essays by leading economists, political scientists, journalists, and former policy makers. Their analyses and recommendations are part of a much-needed debate on how to meet the challenges of globalization in the twenty-first century.

FRESH POLICY IDEAS

So what can be done? For a start, all governments need to ensure that policies help those affected by dislocations, whether from trade or—what is likely to be even more important down the road—technological advances.

The good news is that the aggregate employment effect of increased import competition tends to be neutral to positive because there are *more*, higher-paying jobs in expanding sectors.

In the United States, for example, new studies show that job gains related to increased exports largely offset job losses linked to import competition from China (Feenstra and Sasahara 2017). Germany had a similar experience: import competition from China and central Europe led to *greater* export growth and *net job creation* (Dauth, Findeisen, and Südekum 2017).

The key challenge is to increase the ability of displaced workers to find better opportunities in expanding sectors.

Many countries could combine the various forms of unemployment insurance that they already offer with other tools. In the United States, for instance, there is scope to offer temporary income assistance and health benefits as workers upgrade their skills.

There is also room in most countries to expand and improve worker training programs. Experiences in Canada and Sweden show that on-the-job training can be even more effective than classroom learning.

But there are still many unresolved issues. Is it possible—and if so, effective—to focus on specific dislocations, whether from trade, technology, or other factors? Should governments prioritize retraining, job search assistance, or broader labor market reforms? And how can countries strengthen their social safety nets while mitigating disincentives to work?

These are only some of the issues that this book discusses. A common theme is the urgent need for fresh ideas, more effective policy mixes, and the sharing of expertise across borders. Of course, while safety nets and labor market policies are important, they are not enough.

All countries need to reinvent their education systems for the digital age. This imperative is not just about adding a few more coding lessons. It is about fostering critical thinking, independent problem solving, and lifelong learning that can help people adapt to change.

As policy makers and others seek to respond to these challenges, we at the IMF are supporting our member countries in our areas of expertise through analysis, advice, and capacity development, and by offering a platform for dialogue and cooperation.

At the global level, of course, we analyze exchange rates and monitor global economic imbalances. And our surveillance and crisis lending promote more stable international markets. At the country level, we work with *all* our 189 members on a broad palette of policies to help remove trade and investment barriers—encouraging more open economies in which the private sector can thrive and create jobs.

BETTER INTERNATIONAL COOPERATION

To achieve these objectives, trade needs an infusion of more and better international cooperation.

In the first instance, this means working together to resolve the current trade disputes, which have the potential to hurt everyone, especially poorer consumers. Longer term, it means going further to eliminate unfair trade practices, and developing "new rules" for trade that disincentivize protectionism and better reflect the changing structures of our economies.

Further multilateral trade promotion is certainly possible within the World Trade Organization (WTO) framework. We have already seen new or expanded WTO agreements in recent years, including on government procurement, information technology, and trade facilitation.

But many governments are struggling with major issues that do not currently fall squarely within the WTO rules. These include various state subsidies, restrictions on data flows, and intellectual property protection.

To address these issues, we could use "plurilateral" trade agreements—that is, deals among like-minded countries that agree to work within the WTO framework. This would allow a subset of the WTO membership to move forward, while others can join later. There is also room to negotiate new WTO agreements on e-commerce and digital services.

Indeed, we now have an opportunity to create new rules for a world in which data flows are becoming more important than physical trade. Consider the role of data in making services more tradable, from engineering to communications to transportation.

According to some estimates, digital technology already drives half the global trade in services. But trade barriers in this area are still extremely high—equivalent to tariffs of as much as 30 to 50 percent.

We at the IMF believe that by *reducing* these barriers and *increasing* digitalization, *services could become the main driver of global trade*. Who would be the main beneficiaries?

Certainly, the United States and other advanced economies would benefit because they are globally competitive in many service sectors, especially the financial, legal, and consultation sectors. But so would developing economies such as Colombia, Ghana, and the Philippines because they are promoting growth in tradable services, such as communication and business services.

On these issues, one can take heart from the new Comprehensive and Progressive Agreement for Trans-Pacific Partnership (TPP-11). For the first time in a broader trade agreement, TPP-11 countries will guarantee the free flow of data across borders for service suppliers and investors.

Likewise, the design of new twenty-first-century trade deals should facilitate data flows while protecting online privacy, promoting cybersecurity, and ensuring that financial regulators can access data as needed without stifling innovation. The new deals should also take account of labor and environmental concerns.

These challenges can be addressed only in a multilateral setting — where rules are respected, countries work in partnership, and everyone is committed to fairness.

This book is a powerful reminder that better economic integration is not an easy task. Nor is it a uniquely modern challenge.

More than two hundred years ago, Adam Smith wrote in *The Wealth of Nations*, "Commerce, which ought naturally to be among nations, as among individuals, a bond of union and friendship, has become the most fertile source of discord and animosity."

Today's generation of policy makers will be measured by their ability to turn tension into agreement. I believe that with the right policy mix, we can help create a lasting bond of union and friendship—a globalization that works for all.

Christine Lagarde, IMF managing director

REFERENCES

Dauth, Wolfgang, Sebastian Findeisen, and Jens Südekum. 2017. "Trade and Manufacturing Jobs in Germany." *American Economic Review: Papers and Proceedings* 107, no. 5(May): 337–42.

Feenstra, Robert C., and Akira Sasahara. 2017. "The 'China Shock,' Exports, and US Employment: A Global Input-Output Analysis." NBER Working Paper 24022. Cambridge, MA: National Bureau of Economic Research.

MEETING GLOBALIZATION'S CHALLENGES

Introduction

LUÍS A. V. CATÃO AND MAURICE OBSTFELD

"Globalization"—defined as worldwide interdependence through trade in goods, services, and assets as well as the flow of people, information, and ideas—has experienced an unprecedented ascent over the past two hundred years. Using the ratio to world gross domestic product (GDP) of global goods exports as a gauge of interdependence in goods markets, figure I.1 shows that globalization has risen dramatically since the early 1800s, on the back of unprecedented declines in transportation and communication costs and lower tariffs.[1] Using the share of foreign asset holdings relative to countries' GDP as a gauge of interdependence in asset markets, one observes an eightfold increase since 1870 for large currently advanced economies and a tenfold increase for all countries since 1970. By comparison, advances in international labor market integration since the nineteenth century—as measured by the share of foreign-born residents in the total population—have lagged behind, albeit becoming also significant in a few land-abundant

---

[1] In the first wave of globalization in the nineteenth century, the economic hegemon country at the time (the United Kingdom) reduced average tariffs on imports from a peak of 60 percent in the mid-1820s to between 5 to 10 percent just prior to World War I. During the same period, French tariff rates nearly halved to just above 10 percent (see Nye 2007, figure 1.1). Even in the United States—which remained a high-tariff country through World War I—tariffs also fell from a peak of some 60 percent around 1830 to about 40 percent by 1913 (Carter et al. 2006, table Ee430). While this century-long trend toward lower trade protection was not monotonic—being episodically reversed in response to low import prices from poorer countries and globalization backlashes in advanced ones already in the nineteenth century (see O'Rourke and Williamson 2001, chapter 6), and more dramatically in the 1930s—it continued through the second half of twentieth century. By the dawn of the twenty-first century, average tariff rates on imports fell below 5 percent in advanced economies. For further discussion of the role of trade protection and transportation costs in the pace of world trade, see Krugman 1995.

Figure I.1. Global Trade in Goods, Services, and Assets

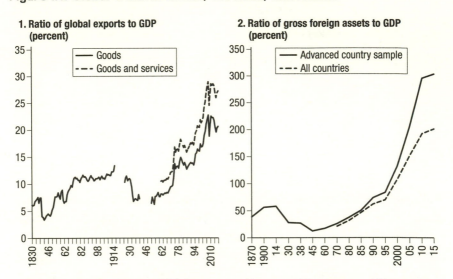

1. Ratio of global exports to GDP (percent)

2. Ratio of gross foreign assets to GDP (percent)

Notes: In panel 1, the pre-1950 data spanned between thirty-seven and fifty-one countries, and are estimated to account for around 90 percent of world trade at the time. In panel 2, the advanced country sample included Canada, France, Germany, Japan, the Netherlands, the United Kingdom, and the United States before 1950, adding other European advanced countries thereafter.

Sources: Federico and Tena-Junguito 2017; Obstfeld and Taylor 2004; Lane and Milesi-Ferretti 2007; IMF *World Economic Outlook*; International Financial Statistics and International Investment Position databases; authors' calculations. Exports and GDP measured in nominal values due to the unavailability or poor reliability of price deflators for earlier years.

New World countries prior to World War I but has typically not surpassed those levels in recent years. In other advanced economies such as those of Europe, international labor-market integration has risen since the 1960s to match the current US level (figure I.2).

As is also apparent from figures I.1 and I.2, the progress of globalization has not been unidirectional; instead, it has followed a stylized U-shaped pattern. Between the two world wars, all three globalization indicators fell. In the case of trade and capital flows, tariff hikes and widespread controls over international transactions took a heavy toll, reinforced by a reversal of the pre-1914 decline in maritime freight rates relative to merchandise prices (see Estevadeordal, Frantz, and Taylor 2003; Krugman, n.d.).[2] In the case of labor flows, strict immigration

---

[2] As shown in Krugman (n.d., table 3), between 1913 and 1938, international real transport costs increased by some 40 percent, after having declined by 20 percent between 1870 and 1913.

Figure I.2. International Movement of Labor

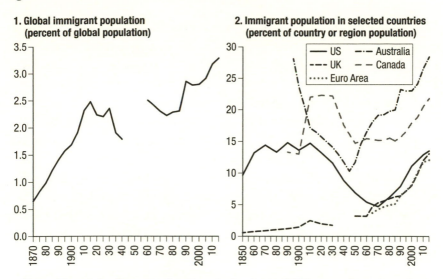

1. Global immigrant population
(percent of global population)

2. Immigrant population in selected countries
(percent of country or region population)

Notes: Figures for German migration stock prior to 1990 were adjusted to take account of border changes associated with the German unification. Specifics of this adjustment are available from the authors on request. No corresponding adjustment could be made to border changes associated with the breakdown of the Union of Soviet Socialist Republics due to lack of data.
Sources: United Nations 2017a, 2017b; World Bank WDI database; Chandy and Seidl 2017; various national data sources; authors' calculations.

quotas starting in 1921 in the United States, and later followed by other countries, were the key culprits (see Hatton and Williamson 1998).[3]

Following World War II, however, reconstruction of the multilateral trade system proceeded under the General Agreement on Tariffs and Trade (GATT), which spearheaded concerted tariff reductions, and restoration of currency convertibility for current account transactions in line with the mandate of the newly created IMF. As a result, world trade recovered spectacularly (see figure I.1).[4] Further reductions in

[3] According to Joseph Ferrie and Timothy Hatton (2015), less strict restrictions began earlier in the main host countries, such as the White Australia Policy of 1901, and dictation tests introduced in Cape Colony and Natal in 1897, New Zealand in 1899, and British Columbia in 1907, followed by the literacy tests for immigrants to the United States in 1917. Other factors, such as the progressive withdrawal of subsidized passage for immigrants, also played a role already in the two decades prior to the collapse of employment and wages in host countries during the Great Depression of the 1930s.

[4] While figure I.1 reports the ratio of nominal trade to nominal GDP, which relative price changes such as the oil price increases of the 1970s can distort, it nonetheless

tariffs and capital controls in the 1990s, together with expanded membership of the WTO (the GATT's successor), promoted the rise of global value chains and set the stage for a further climb in globalization to its peak just before the 2008–9 global financial crisis. Starting in the mid-1990s through the crisis, trade growth further outpaced GDP growth and gross international capital flows rose about three times faster than trade growth.[5] Some have characterized the resulting trade and investment environment as "hyperglobalization" (Rodrik 2011; Subramanian and Kessler 2013). Yet the advance of globalization has stalled since the global financial crisis—a reflection of, among other factors, the financial sequelae of the crisis as well as tensions in the multilateral trade system. There has been growing skepticism about the benefits of free trade and multilateralism in some countries, most notably in the United States—ironically, the chief architect of the postwar global economic order. Ongoing stresses in the multilateral trading system owing to new tariffs, retaliatory measures, and growing protectionist discourse—notably in the tensions among the United States. China, and Europe—have clearly weighed on global trade. Having grown about twice as fast as global GDP in the five decades through the eve of the 2008–9 global financial crisis, global trade grew only slightly faster than GDP in 2018 (actually shrinking in the final quarter of that year) and seems likely to slow even further in the near term (WTO 2019). These developments make it unwise to rule out the risk of an outright reversal in the postwar globalization trend.

As seen in the interwar period, however—and also (albeit less dramatically) during the belle epoque leading up to World War I—threats to globalization in the form of tariff hikes, immigration restrictions, and nationalist-populist politics are not new.[6] As in the past, today's

---

gives a reasonably accurate picture of trends in global trade openness. Douglas Irwin (1995) describes trends in global trade volume and real GDP since 1950 and their connection with tariff cuts following GATT negotiation rounds. Because construction of a fuller historical span of data on real trade relative to real GDP is fraught with price deflator issues, we chose to use nominal trade and nominal GDP data in figure I.1. For a breakdown of more recent trade volume trends between advanced countries and emerging and developing economies, see IMF/WB/WTO 2017, figure 1.

[5] According to OECD (2011) estimates, gross cross-border capital flows rose from about 5 percent of world GDP in the mid-1990s to an all-time high of 20 percent in 2007.

[6] On the anatomy of pre–World War I backlashes, see Williamson 1998; O'Rourke

threats are rooted in the fact that globalization's full economy-wide benefits may take time to materialize and are almost always unevenly distributed anyway, thus necessarily producing winners and losers. As the literature documents, discontent among the losers tends to rise with income inequality, large trade imbalances, slower productivity growth, and mounting unemployment. Thus, it is no surprise that perceptions of free trade as a zero-sum game rise precisely during periods of uneven or weak economic gains as well as import competition, feeding antiglobalization politics (see O'Rourke and Williamson 2001; Hays 2009). This historical regularity does not make the risks less important this time, however. Rather, parallels with the past bring the risks of the present economic context into sharper relief. How policy makers manage the benefits and downsides of globalization is therefore as critical as ever.

Against that background, this book provides an up-to-date appraisal of the benefits and costs of globalization and its current challenges, seeking to shed new light on how policies can tip such a cost-benefit balance so that the proglobalization "economic calculus" is better aligned with the "political calculus" that makes globalization viable. Building on an October 2017 conference titled "Meeting Globalization's Challenges" at the IMF in Washington, DC, the book brings together eighteen essays by leading thinkers on the anatomy of globalization. They address the following main questions:

- How big are the aggregate gains that globalization offers to countries that embrace it, and what are the sources of the gains?
- Why have globalization's aggregate benefits been high for some countries, but seemingly lower for others, with the most fortunate ones achieving impressive income convergence with richer peers while others have been less successful?
- Why have income gains been especially uneven within some countries over the past three decades?
- To what extent (and how) have rising inequality and other developments contributed to antiglobalization politics and policies?

---

and Williamson 2001. For an early and influential study of German agricultural protection in this period and its political consequences, see Gerschenkron 1943.

- What types of policies can mitigate the downsides of globalization, and to what extent?
- What are the main challenges to globalization lying ahead?

Because the phenomenon of globalization is multifaceted, some narrowing of focus is inevitable. This book concentrates on trade and technology, and the various economic and sociopolitical challenges that exposure to them poses. The focus is appropriate and timely for several reasons. First, international trade has been the key engine of global economic (and political) integration since time immemorial, and dramatically so over the past two hundred years. Second and importantly, challenges to the multilateral trading system have increased sharply in prominence among other challenges to globalization, and a better understanding of how to meet them clearly warrants urgent attention. Third, trade and technology have historically underpinned the internationalization of capital and labor, and continue to do so via offshoring and the spread of global supply chains, rather than the other way around.[7] Fourth and more practically, given the space already needed for an adequate treatment of trade, to go meaningfully beyond the limited coverage of financial globalization and immigration in this volume would require another book (or two) altogether.[8]

The book contains five parts. Part I offers a foundation for subsequent analyses with technically accessible and up-to-date synopses of research on two main mechanisms through which trade delivers welfare gains: global production efficiency, and technology promotion and diffusion. Part II turns to some of the downsides of globalization. One of them is the unevenness of trade gains across countries. The essays in this part ask how export-led development policies have worked, what sets their limits, and what dangerous imbalances might be generated. No less

[7] Absent trade, international financial transactions are impossible (as there would be no way to transfer real resources between countries in payment of net financial obligations). In addition, history has witnessed periods of rising trade globalization without substantial capital mobility (as during the Bretton Woods system of 1945–71) as well as periods of rising globalization with impaired labor mobility (as in much of the twentieth century). Thus, a process of economic globalization necessarily must encompass as its sine qua non lower trade barriers and rapidly expanding trade.

[8] Moreover, several other surveys of globalization challenges take up financial globalization. See, for example, Rodrik 2011; Wolf 2015; Ostry, Loungani, and Berg 2019; Clausing 2019.

important, the discussion in part II also touches on the timely issue of how far globalization has been shaping both within-country and cross-country income inequalities.

Part III extends the scope of the analysis by taking up a much-discussed source of wage inequality within countries—namely, the deindustrialization associated with the greater penetration of manu-facturing imports from low-wage countries. Building on recent insights into employment and wage responses to "shocks" in trade exposure, part IV looks at policy options to facilitate the economy's adjustment at the lowest possible economic and social cost. It does so by exploring the practical problems in discerning the various ways that factors ad-ditional to trade can cause job and wage-income losses, and reappraising the performance of past adjustment assistance policies. Part V explores the political background to trade backlashes. Finally, part VI concludes the book with an overview of pending challenges due to health care needs, regulation, automation, job uncertainty, and the task of recon-ciling globalization with national sovereignty and democratic political processes.

In what follows, we summarize the main takeaways.

GAINS FROM TRADE AND INNOVATION

Estimating the full gains from trade in macroeconomic models is not easy. In chapter 1, Andrés Rodríguez-Clare explains why this is an important endeavor and where the current literature stands. He first posits a parsimonious framework in which trade gains depend on only two key parameters: how much a country trades (its openness) and the price elasticity of substitution between traded goods (a measure of how much consumers gain from having access to a broader variety of traded goods). In general equilibrium models with multiple sectors and input-output relationships, this formula yields gains that, while not quanti-tatively trivial, are still short of being empirically realistic. Trade gains can, however, reach more realistic levels once one extends the simplest models to include some key imperfections in market functioning to allow for complementarities between trade and foreign investment, and encompass substitution elasticities with a sounder empirical basis. These alternative gains turn out to be especially high for smaller open economies as well as those that cannot produce primary inputs essential to production and consumption. A paradox, though, is that while poorer open economies stand to gain the most from trade, they often forgo those gains because they trade far less than predicted by theory. Possible reasons include high exporting costs, which may owe, not only to protectionism, but also to distance from final markets, infrastructure bottlenecks, and currency controls (at times leading to an overvalued currency and excessive spending on non-tradable goods). Thus, policy improvements on all these fronts seem crucial for poorer countries to benefit fully from globalization, thereby closing more of their income gap with richer countries.

From the very foundation of classical economics in the eighteenth century, a much-touted benefit of globalization has been its promotion of technology and productivity gains through specialization along with the spread of best practice. Yet productivity and output gains from trade have been disparate across countries. An uneven international dispersion of new productive processes and ideas, as well as diverse capacities to absorb and bring them into practice, are at play. This heterogeneity raises the central question of the determinants of innovation, its impact on economies, and the roles of globalization and national policies and institutions in the generation and transmission of technological progress across borders.

In chapter 2, reporting novel research based on data for US regions and sectors since 1840, Ufuk Akcigit highlights the existence of positive causal relationships under which innovation drives both growth and social mobility. He shows that these relationships are stronger in more globalized regions, defined as those with cheaper transportation costs and higher labor mobility vis-à-vis the outer world, including through the inflow of migrant investors. Chapter 2 also asks what governments can do to foster innovations within their national borders and benefit from them. Tariffs appear to have at best only short-lived positive effects on innovation, whereas research and development (R & D) subsidy policies are far more effective in the longer term. Akcigit also demonstrates how innovation responds positively to schooling and household income. Overall, chapter 2 thus establishes the existence of a virtuous circle connecting globalization, innovation, and income growth, while also positing an important role for human capital-enhancing policies in strengthening these connections.

TRADE AS A DEVELOPMENT TOOL:
WHAT HAVE WE LEARNED?

Mounting evidence on the effectiveness of international trade as an engine of economic growth led many emerging market and developing economies (EMDEs) that pursued inward-looking development policies before the 1990s to open their economies. Yet growth outcomes have been mixed across different countries. This mixed record suggests that lower trade barriers and greater trade openness can be facilitators of rapid economic growth, but may well not be sufficient by themselves to produce it. Dani Rodrik argues in chapter 3 that *how* countries open up matters. This dependency is apparent from the recent success of Vietnam—as well as the earlier successes of China and other Asian EMDEs—compared with the disappointing outcomes in much of Latin America, despite much of that region having lowered trade barriers dramatically. To understand the contrast, Rodrik posits a model economy comprised of high-productivity, middle-tier, and low-productivity occupations. Asian countries opened up aggressively on the export side, but only gradually on the import side, thereby protecting incomes and mitigating job losses in the middle-tier sector. In contrast, Latin America's liberalization was sweeping and swift on the import side, leading to abrupt employment losses in the middle-tier sector and pushing jobs into the low-productivity informal sector. A highly dual economy emerged, bringing aggregate productivity down despite higher productivity at the top tier. *When* a country opens up also matters—that is, whether it does so when global trade is expanding faster or slower. The bottom line is that successfully deploying the foreign trade engine to promote income convergence toward richer economies requires the right strategy at the right time. But what else do we know about what strategies are likely to work best?

China's impressive export-led growth experience could obviously provide some clues, along with cautionary lessons. In chapter 4, Keyu Jin stresses the role of extensive state control of the financial system in mobilizing household saving, and directing it at below-market interest rates to infrastructure and capital formation in export industries. Coupled with capital account controls that have often helped the authorities to limit currency appreciation as well as foreign direct investment regulations that fostered technology transfers, this strategy has been successful in lowering exporting costs and producing higher trade surpluses, thereby boosting overall economic growth. But such state interventions have also generated enormous resource allocation distortions that have been slowing productivity growth, creating an economy more dependent on nonmarket stimuli. Moreover, this growth model generates large global trade imbalances that make China more vulnerable to protectionist reactions from its trade partners—impulses that are exacerbated by the perception that China's distinctive economic framework and policies have created an uneven playing field for trade and investment. That said, some ingredients of the Chinese export promotion strategy—if combined with sensible exit strategies from intervention, better social safety nets, and concern to avoid negative spillovers on trading partners—could still produce better domestic outcomes than precipitous unilateral import liberalization. In some EMDEs, the latter has too often led to greater incentives for conspicuous consumption at the expense of capital accumulation, and thus to unsustainable current account deficits and financial excesses likely to trigger financial crises (see Gourinchas and Obstfeld 2012; Catão and Milesi-Ferretti 2014).

DO TRADE AND GLOBALIZATION BREED INEQUALITY?

Recent years have seen much debate on the extent to which globalization has bred income inequality, and through which channels. To answer these questions, it is useful to distinguish between inter- and intracountry inequality—with *global* inequality (the income difference between any two persons anywhere on the globe) being a combination of inter- and intracountry inequality. Figure I.3 depicts trends in global inequality since 1990, together with the respective inter- and intracountry components, according to the standard Gini coefficient metric.[9]

Start with *across-* or intercountry inequality (depicted by the higher dashed line in the figure below). While some EMDEs have shown only limited convergence toward advanced economy income levels despite

[9] We choose the 1990 starting point owing to limited data availability, particularly for emerging markets. The post-1990 data used in the figure cover no less than 90 percent of world income and population.

Figure I.3. Global Inequality Measures

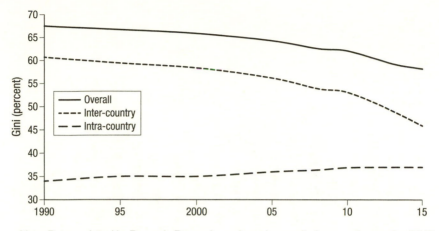

Note: Data updated by François Bourguignon based on preliminary estimates for 2013 and 2015.
Source: Bourguignon 2015.

opening to world markets, as noted above, the good news is that several large and populous EMDEs have scored impressive income gains (China and India most notably). Their successes pushed down the intercountry Gini coefficient, thus helping reverse the secular trend toward greater intercountry inequality lamented by some economists in the past when looking at pre-1990 data.[10] Importantly, income convergence by these large EMDEs, because of both their low initial per capita incomes and enormous populations, has led to a dramatic fall in the share of world population living below the poverty line. And as Angus Deaton points out in his chapter, even in countries where income convergence has been more limited, other welfare indicators—for example, child mortality and longevity—have improved dramatically over the past decades, reflecting the international diffusion of new products and knowledge that globalization has allowed.

The bad news, though, is that average *within-* or intracountry income inequality has risen (as measured by the Gini coefficient and shown by

[10] For documentation of the secular trend toward global divergence and cross-country inequality prior to the 1990s, see, among others, Pritchett 1997; Bourguignon and Morrison 2002; Baldwin 2016. It is, however, important to bear in mind that considerable convergence in per capita incomes did occur within some country groups prior to the 1990s (notably within the group of then-OECD members; see Williamson 2005).

Figure I.4. Share of Top 1 Percent Earners in National Income

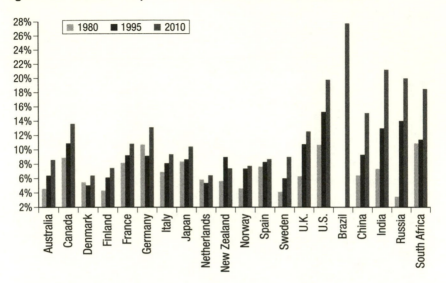

Sources: World Inequality Database (https://wid.world/) and authors' calculations.

the lower dashed line in figure I.3). Further, it has been accompanied by a startling and nearly universal rise in the national income share held by the top 1 percent of income earners—that is, the extremely rich (figure I.4). While high-income concentration at the top of the distribution has been historically common in EMDEs, it has been a striking new development in the modern history of advanced democracies.

Is globalization to blame? A popular answer is affirmative: by fostering the shift in low-skilled jobs from the rich world to labor-abundant, low-wage countries, globalization drove down the between-country component of global inequality while driving up within-country inequality in advanced economies. Many economists point to skill-biased technical change as another contributor to higher within-country inequality—in emerging as well as advanced economies—although trade policy and changes in production technologies often interact (Acemoglu 2003; Goldberg and Pavcnik 2007; IMF 2017). Some recent research (Egger, Nigai, and Strecker 2019) suggests that since the mid-1990s, globalization has induced a redistribution of tax burdens away from high earners, and toward middle and lower incomes. In chapter 5, François Bourguignon challenges this generalization by noting that trends in intracountry inequality have been quite diverse over the past three decades, notwithstanding countries' common exposure to globalization and technology. In Bourguignon's telling, domestic policy reforms that strengthened the power of capital relative to labor seem to be a main culprit. Even though external competitiveness concerns may have motivated these domestic policies in the first place, the evidence is suggestive of a subtler link between globalization and intracountry inequality than is frequently portrayed. Bourguignon's discussion also highlights the striking decoupling between the relatively mild and nonmonotonic increase in *overall* inequality in many advanced economies, and the popular perception that inequality has been rising dramatically everywhere. He suggests that such public reactions may reflect higher aversion to inequality when it manifests as income concentration at the top of the distribution. Other factors may have added to the growing public sensitivity to top-income inequality in recent years: financial sector bailouts, fiscal austerity, and a legacy of higher unemployment and compressed real wages in much of the advanced world following the global financial crisis of 2008–9 (Tooze 2018). Recent evidence points to the emergence of "superstar" firms as a correlate of the fall in labor's share and, presumably, more extreme top incomes (see Autor et al. 2017). While globalization may provide more scope for superstars to emerge, technology (for example, through network effects) is clearly an essential factor.

Globalization, Deindustrialization, and Job Losses: A New Consensus?

Notwithstanding the heterogeneity of intracountry inequality trends that Bourguignon's chapter documents, it remains a fact that inequality has risen in some systemically important countries, most notably in the United States and other Anglo-Saxon advanced economies over the past thirty years or so. This rise has coincided with massive losses of industrial jobs and a falling share of manufacturing output in GDP—what some have called "deindustrialization" for short—the flip side of which has been the growing significance of the manufacturing sector in manufacturing-exporting EMDEs, notably Asia and eastern Europe (figure I.5). So, it is crucial to probe into what role trade may have played in deindustrialization and wage inequality (see also IMF 2018).

Figure I.5. Changes in the Manufacturing Share in GDP (1995–2016, constant prices)

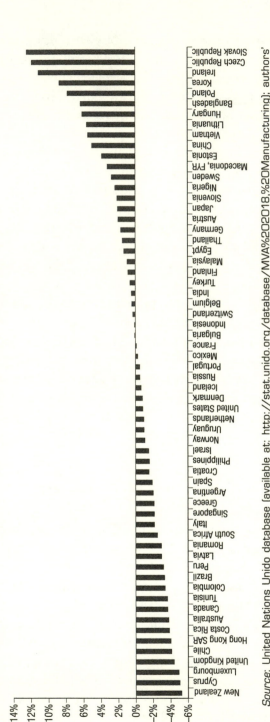

Source: United Nations Unido database (available at: http://stat.unido.org/database/MVA%202018,%20Manufacturing); authors' calculations.

A standard analytic tool to explore the link between trade and the gains and losses of some sectors and production factors relative to others is the famous Stolper-Samuelson theorem. This theorem shows how trading with a relatively labor-abundant, low-wage economy can reduce real wages in the import-competing sector (like manufacturing) of a capital-abundant country (like most advanced economies), and that this can happen even if national income grows owing to expanded trade. As Paul Krugman notes in chapter 6, many studies using this analytic framework and pre-1995 data found only a modest *economy-wide* effect of trade in explaining the sharp rise in income inequality in the United States starting in the 1970s. Skill-biased technical change was seen to have played a much larger role. A main basis for this reasoning was the still relatively small size of manufacturing imports from EMDEs compared with the sizes of advanced economies, even as late as the mid-1990s (around 2 percent of the GDP of advanced economies). As import penetration of cheaper manufactures from EMDEs nearly tripled (relative to advanced countries' GDP) between the mid-1990s and 2008, however, the consequences became far more significant. The proliferation of global supply chains (which ensured that some of the value-added of imports continued to be generated within advanced economies) may have had a dampening effect. Nonetheless, the net adverse effects on employment, wages, and income distribution could no longer be ignored, and they would naturally be felt more strongly in advanced economies with more accommodating trade policies as well as lower job and social protection.

The United States provides perhaps the leading case study in the disruptive effects of advanced economy trade with EMDEs, not only because of the sheer magnitude of the manufacturing trade deficit and attendant job losses, but also because of the comparatively early start of manufactured import penetration.[11] In chapter 7, Gordon Hanson dissects the impact of the so-called China shock on US regional labor markets. Unlike competition from higher-wage manufacturing powerhouses like Japan and Germany through the early 1990s, the China shock was more concentrated in terms of time and felt more widely across manufacturing subsectors. With manufacturing being a source

[11] Prior to about 1982, the United States posted surpluses in its manufacturing trade balance, averaging about 1 percent of GDP after the early 1960s. See Rowthorn and Ramaswamy 1997, chart 2b.

of relatively high-paying jobs to lower-skilled and longer-tenured middle-aged segments of the US male labor force, the social and political reverberations were more readily felt. Hanson cites the key quantitative finding of a cumulative decay in earnings of displaced workers, averaging about 20 percent over a decade, and further magnified for workers dismissed during the 2008–9 recession. In their influential work, Hanson and coauthors also document a powerful income multiplier effect at the level of local communities: geographically concentrated job losses depress local government revenue, undermining public services and raising unemployment even in sectors not directly affected by trade. The ripple effects therefore extend far beyond manufacturing, and include depressed home prices, higher male mortality, and broken families—hence feeding social malaise and antitrade politics (see, for example, Autor and Dorn 2013; Autor, Dorn, and Hanson 2013, 2018; Autor, Dorn, Hanson, and Majlesi 2016a, 2016b).

While the effects of trade shocks on advanced economies have dominated attention recently because of the domestic trade backlash they have provoked, economic theory suggests—and the data bear out—that trade liberalization could similarly have disruptive effects in EMDEs. As figures I.4 and I.5 make apparent, deindustrialization and the potentially inequality-generating effects of trade and technology are not the exclusive preserves of advanced economies. Yet trade is not usually seen as the main driver of income inequalities in EMDEs. This is partly because EMDE income inequalities are high to begin with (due to colonial heritage and highly skewed land ownership), and partly because intra-EMDE inequality is often masked by faster growth and Stolper-Samuelson effects that tend to lift the wages of low-skill workers (the more abundant production factor in poorer economies). Both considerations possibly help to explain the more favorable attitudes toward trade in EMDEs relative to advanced economies according to comparable public opinion surveys across countries (figure I.6).[12]

Despite the diversity of country-specific trends, however, Nina Pavcnik argues in chapter 8 that we should not ignore the unequalizing effects of trade openness in EMDEs. Slicing the evidence by sectors

---

[12] Econometric analyses of data sets on individual workers corroborate a generally less favorable attitude toward trade among the lower skilled in advanced countries (Scheve and Slaughter 2001; Mayda and Rodrik 2005; Walter 2017).

Figure I.6. Perceived Impact of Trade on Jobs and Wages in Surveyed Countries

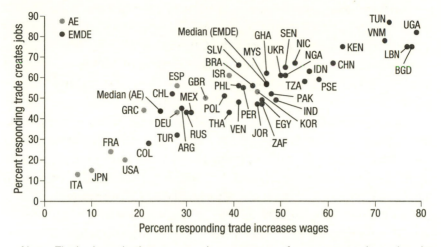

Notes: The horizontal axis measures the percentage of survey respondents choosing "trade increases wages" out of a set of four possible responses including also "trade decreases wages," "trade does not make a difference," and "I don't know." The same applies to the trade and jobs question as measured on the vertical axis. Survey results for 2018, albeit spanning fewer countries, display a similar pattern.

Sources: IMF/WB/WTO 2017, based on Pew Foundation data and IMF staff calculations.

and firms, Pavcnik shows that easier access to external markets has allowed the most productive firms and sectors to take better advantage of export possibilities, increasing revenue and the wages they pay to their workers too. Trade thus widens within- as well as across-sector wage inequality. The significance of this wage effect depends on skill level, education attainment, and location, and as regional mobility remains strikingly low in EMDEs, regional trade shocks to job and wages have had a much greater effect on economy-wide inequality than previous research has acknowledged.

In chapter 9, Rafael Dix-Carneiro presents evidence on Brazil that echoes Pavcnik's conclusions. The chapter focuses on the dynamics of manufacturing wages and jobs in Brazil following a trade liberalization round in the 1990s. This policy change was virtually a controlled experiment in that the decision to liberalize was deliberate and unilateral, and trade protection was high to begin with, making attendant labor market effects clearly discernible as manufacturing output and employment shrank relative to other sectors (as well as other manufacturing-exporting EMDEs; see figure I.5).[13] That episode is also informative for policy makers going forward, as the scope for further trade liberalization in Brazil and many other EMDEs remains considerable—in contrast to the one-off nature of the China shock for advanced economies. Strikingly, much as in the United States, manufacturing jobs and wages in Brazil took a prolonged dive, with the effects taking about a decade to die out, and the earnings of displaced workers stabilizing then at significantly lower levels. As with the China shock in the United States, the effects were geographically concentrated. But unlike the US case, the informal job market played a key role in absorbing redundant labor, possibly mitigating the kind of sociopolitical backlashes seen in the United States. Yet growing informality also contributed to labor market dualism (as productivity and product wages are typically lower in informal jobs) and had other adverse social effects, including higher crime rates in affected regions. Importantly, once one accounts for the effects of slow transitions into more precarious jobs, the economy-wide welfare gains from trade liberalization are lower by up to a quarter.

Compensation and Labor Market Adjustment Policies

Economists have long known that trade can increase the dispersion in domestic incomes: it creates winners and losers, and hence more inequality if the losers are not better off to begin with. Mindful of the social welfare consequences of unequalizing effects from trade reforms, economists have long invoked principles whereby compensatory transfers ensure that no one ends up worse off. But those principles are notoriously difficult to implement in practice.[14]

This difficulty raises two questions. First, if compensation is imperfect or itself costly in practice, and especially if adjustment to trade shocks has costs, then what is the trade-off between market efficiency and equity? Second, given that policy makers decide to embrace trade liberalization, what compensation and adjustment assistance mechanisms might be available and effective?

---

[13] As shown in figure I.5, Brazil was not unique in losing manufacturing jobs to other EMDEs, as there was also a massive reallocation of manufacturing out of EMDEs with apparent comparative advantage in commodity production, including most notably Chile and much of Latin America. For further discussion, see Wood 2017.

[14] For a review of the utilitarian criteria and other social justice principles that could justify compensation/redistribution policies, see Trebilcock 2015, 9–30.

On the first question—the trade-off between the gains from freer trade and the challenge of compensating losers—much may depend on the starting point, as Rodrik (2018) has pointed out. At high tariff levels, a move to free trade (or low tariffs) tends to yield big efficiency benefits for both producers and consumers. While it also leads to a large income loss for the factor that the import-competing industry uses more intensively (think of it as low-skill labor in advanced economies), the political and economic (deadweight) costs of compensating those losers may be small relative to the aggregate efficiency gain. On the other hand, small tariff reductions may yield quite trivial efficiency gains compared with the cost of transferring resources from the winners to compensate losers. Rodrik (2018) argues on this basis that once trade barriers are low enough, the aggregate efficiency benefits from reducing them further may well fail to justify the costs of shielding the losers from harm.

Figure I.7 illustrates a situation in which tariff reduction yields net overall benefits to the economy but reduces the real wages paid to low-skill labor, as indicated by the upward sloping dotted line. The wage loss is the amount of compensation low-skill workers must receive to avoid being worse off: the bigger the tariff reduction is, the more the winners must be taxed to compensate the losers. The situation with initially high (40 percent) tariffs corresponds to the figure's southeast corner. There, the net aggregate efficiency benefit of tariff elimination covers much of the real wage loss (which at this point is at its maximum of just under 10 percent of GDP). In fact, the aggregate gain will exceed the wage loss for a sufficiently high price elasticity of imports. A favorable ratio of net benefit to gross wage loss becomes increasingly less likely as the initial tariff declines, however. This is because the incremental efficiency benefit of eliminating tariffs declines very rapidly as tariffs near zero, while the absolute cost of the compensation (equal to the decline in the low-skill wage times the share of low-skill employment in GDP) does not fall toward zero nearly as fast. This finding therefore suggests that trade liberalization might well go too far when compensating losers is costly relative to the additional efficiency gains of further tariff cuts.

To be sure, the simple model and numerical computations underlying figure I.7 omit important benefits of full trade liberalization. One is to reduce wasteful rent seeking of tariff revenues and other lobbying

Figure I.7. Size of Compensation of Low-Skilled Workers Due to Tariff Elimination

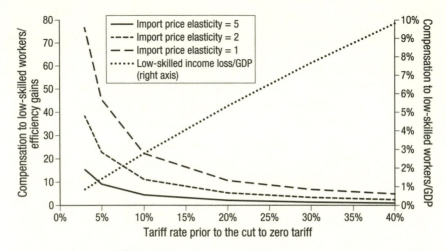

Note: Authors' calculations based on a standard two-sector trade model with the import-competing sector intensive in unskilled labor, as in Rodrik 2018.

costs (see, for example, Krueger 1974). Indeed, it is precisely *because* the redistributions that trade policies can cause are significant, that it is worthwhile for lobbyists to expend considerable resources on seeking protection. The other cost of protection missed by this model is that tariff rates are rarely (if ever) applied uniformly across product varieties. Protection can entail prohibitive tariff rates for certain varieties, limiting consumers' choices and weighing heavily on consumer welfare (Feenstra 1992). This simple model and the Rodrik argument also abstract from dynamic gains. Moreover, when offshoring is extensive, so that the production of a final good in one country depends on multiple border crossings by intermediate inputs, even relatively low tariffs can be quite costly (Yi 2003). Finally, the Rodrik setup has a powerful but perhaps less obvious implicaton: if tariffs are initially high, and the policy choice is between full and partial tariff elimination, full elimination will be preferred. In other words, if it is worth cutting tariffs at all, it is worth cutting them immediately to zero (Catão and Obstfeld 2019).

Nonetheless, the Rodrik assertion lays bare how compensation costs can loom large. Coupled with the problem of *how* to transfer resources from winners to losers—especially if government revenues shrink with globalization—the end result is possibly to make full compensation

Figure I.8. Expenditure on Active and Passive Labor Market Policies and Import Penetration (Percent of GDP)

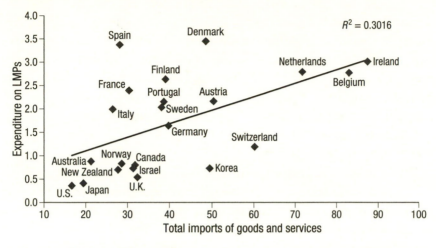

Sources: OECD and IMF World Economic Outlook database; authors' calculations.

prohibitively high. This difficulty perhaps helps explain why compensation in the form of "active" or "passive" labor market policy remains a relatively small fraction of GDP (uniformly below 4 percent and as low as 0.5 percent), even in rich countries. Figure I.8 shows a conspicuously positive cross-country correlation between openness and spending (as a share of GDP) on labor market policies, which is surely a reflection of two-way causality: the social safety net facilitates policies to promote openness, while less trade protection generates the political demand for more social protection.

Disaggregated econometric analyses certainly support the first of these mechanisms: countries (and regions within countries) that devote more resources to compensation and reemployment policies seem to fare significantly better in sustaining protrade attitudes (see Rodrik 1998; Hays 2009; Margalit 2011). Indeed, the symbiosis between elements of the welfare state and trade liberalization goes back to the late nineteenth century (Huberman 2012; Williamson 2005; O'Rourke 2018).

Against this background, we return to the second question raised earlier—how to maximize the effectiveness of policies that compensate trade's losers. One approach is to promote labor market adjustment. As

Anne Krueger notes in chapter 10, it can be difficult or impossible to discern which job and wage losses owe purely to trade, as opposed to technology changes or other causes (like macro policies, business mismanagement, or bad luck). Krueger argues that the desire to qualify for trade-specific compensation programs can incentivize unsuccessful workers and managers to collude and misleadingly blame business failure on trade. Moreover, subsidizing firms and jobs that would otherwise be lost to import competition is often simply to delay the inevitable. Krueger concludes that general labor market policies that do not single out trade-related job and wage losses are preferable. A better approach is to protect people, not jobs.

While other authors subscribe to this view, the evidence in chapters 7 to 9 that trade-related losses could be distinct in important respects leads some to see a case for special treatment, as argued by Lori Kletzer in chapter 11. The case may be especially strong when a trade shock arises from specific, easily identifiable government policy changes—for example, the United States' grant to China of permanent normal trade relations status, or US entry into the North American Free Trade Agreement (NAFTA). Still, it seems to be the case that those advanced economies with more extensive social safety nets have suffered less backlash against trade per se (though clearly immigration has been another matter).

If general labor market policies—targeted or not—are a necessary complement to sustaining trade openness, the next question is: How effective have they been in practice? A first obstacle to answering this question is the diversity of these policies.[15] A second is that performance evaluations are far from foolproof, partly because they are so dependent on the choice of statistical methodology (Heckman, Lalonde, and Smith 1999). One illustration comes from Benjamin Hyman's (2018) recent work using more convincing identification than in some previous studies of the effects of the US Trade Adjustment Assistance (TAA) program. He finds that TAA has perhaps been more successful in the short

[15] The OECD (2018) classifies them as training, employment incentives, sheltered and supported employment and rehabilitation, direct job creation, start-up incentives, out-of-work income maintenance and support, and early retirement. The latter two categories encompass so-called general or passive labor market policies, whereas the others are usually labeled active labor market policies, with all categories including sector-targeted and untargeted programs.

to medium term in raising earnings than earlier assessments indicated (see the discussions in Krueger's, Kletzer's, and Hanson's chapters), but acknowledges that its success in raising human capital and earnings has been rather modest in the long run. This perception is reinforced by recent results of quasi-controlled experiments on regional training programs using detailed US data (Manolli, Michaelides, and Patel 2018). The latter are more optimistic about outcomes than were earlier studies, but that said, one must still be prepared to accept that the weight of the evidence to date points to the *economic* cost-benefit balance of such programs being less favorable than one might wish in the longer term.

There is nonetheless some agreement that to maximize the effectiveness of compensation, governments should combine passive with active labor market policies, as they complement one another by offsetting potential moral hazards through reskilling and job-search incentives (IMF/WB/WTO 2017). Existing evidence also supports calibrating the intensity of support to business cycle conditions and macro stabilization policies, given that wage losses tend to be higher and more persistent when job losses occur during downturns (as noted in Hanson's and Kletzer's chapters). Finally, and consistent with the evidence that trade-related income losses may be special in their geographic and sectoral concentration as well as through spillovers to other sectors, there is a case for fine-tuning active labor market policies to those specificities.[16] Such fine-tuning could include redirecting assistance toward small communities and regions rather than individuals, fostering spatial labor mobility, and possibly giving wage subsidies to those who lose jobs to import penetration (as Kletzer advocates in chapter 11).

Overall, part of the answer to Rodrik's challenge about the cost of compensation is to expand the range of social safety nets to make them more automatic and therefore less costly, at least with respect to the transaction costs of repeated political decisions to help the losers from trade. In any case, other structural shocks to labor markets—for example, due to technology change—already provide ample justification for such expansion. The latter are set to intensify due to developments

[16] One criticism of the US TAA program lies in its failure to target spillover effects on communities, which often are more clearly visible than effects on individuals, who must show direct harm from imports. Jeffry Frieden makes this point in chapter 12.

already on the horizon, such as the proliferation of future technologies based on artifical intelligence.

The Political Economy of Trade Backlash

As noted above, we know from history that the losers from trade have at times succeeded in mobilizing the political process to stop or even reverse aspects of integration with world markets. Mancur Olson (1965) offered a key reason why: gains from trade openness in many cases are spread widely and thinly across agents, and thus may be relatively small or less visible for most individuals, while losses tend to be concentrated in distinctive groups that are better able to organize to pressure the government. Added to that, there is a widespread perception that trade dislocations emanate from trade agreements designed by corporate elites and mainstream politicians, sealed in countries' capitals, far from the immediate concerns of working people. (The perception prevails even though, in reality, much of the actual trade displacement would probably have taken place even in the absence of any such agreements).[17] As Jeffry Frieden argues in chapter 12, this perceived failure of the political establishment to represent the interest of broad segments of the electorate—as he calls it, a *failure of representation*—once combined with the *failure of compensation* accumulated over decades, makes many voters more likely to support populist and extreme political parties (or extreme candidates within mainstream parties). This tendency has been extensively documented for the United States (Autor, Dorn, Hanson, and Majlesi, 2016a and 2016b) as well as some other advanced economies (Becker, Fetzer, and Novy 2017; Clarke, Goodwin, and Whiteley 2017; Colantone and Stanig 2018), and certainly lies behind the United Kingdom's Brexit travails. Whereas immigration rather than import penetration has been the relatively stronger trigger for such reactions in continental Europe and the United Kingdom, recent research (surveyed by Frieden in his chapter) also shows that UK areas hit harder by trade competition, and particularly from Chinese import penetration, were more likely to vote for Brexit. Importantly, job losses connected with trade appear to have an adverse impact on incumbent politicians that is about twice as large as the impact of job losses due to other factors.[18]

---

[17] Alan Blinder (2018) also makes this point.

[18] In many of the UK regions where majorities supported Brexit, however, there was long-standing industrial decline, predating China's rise and driven also by the

Anger at a failure of representation also applies, of course, to the *cultural* aspect of globalization backlash. Cultural backlash channels a resentment of global forces, and "elite" groups seen to threaten traditional values and the sense of community self-identity, which can add to welfare (Grossman and Helpman 2018). It is unclear what compensation would look like in this case—although nationalism and populism, including resistance to immigration, and in some extreme cases, demands for the expulsion of foreigners, can result. While this form of backlash goes far beyond economics, it is intimately tied to the economic forces that trade helps to unleash, which promote production agglomeration, and thereby a more pronounced urban–small town gradient in productivity and opportunity (Eichengreen 2018; Velasco 2018).

The potential for backlash against trade, however, seems to be considerably lower in countries with more organized and arguably more balanced bargaining between labor and management—as in the small, open economies of Scandinavian countries, which also spend far more (as a percentage of GDP) on labor market programs (recall figure I.8). This response to trade compares unfavorably with countries where labor-capital bargaining is fragmented and governments lack a tradition of working consensually with social partners. In those cases, the political system seems to offer greater latitude for policies that seek to shift the cost of globalization to foreigners through the pursuit of beggar-thy-neighbor trade policies—as opposed to policies that internalize the cost of adjustment. As Edward Alden observes in chapter 13, it is thus unsurprising that many US voters saw their endorsements of Donald Trump in 2016 as a unique opportunity to send a message on import penetration and globalization in general, given Trump's long-standing views about the United States being a victim of its trading partners. In a highly integrated trade system, such political developments are clearly

---

overall shift in the British economy toward services, notably financial services based in London. The Blackburn with Darwen district in Lancashire, the subject of Robert Dore's (1982) study of adjustment in a onetime textile town, favored leaving the European Union by 56.3 percent—actually a slimmer margin than for Lancashire as a whole (where all fourteen districts favored Brexit). Of course, the rise of London has had the side effect of exacerbating regional income inequalities and fueling resentment toward "elites." Echoing the US experience discussed in Hanson's chapter and the various references cited above, Eleonora Alabrese and coauthors (2018) find that one could also successfully predict Brexit voting based on voters' low education background, employment status, age, and overall life dissatisfaction.

not just a matter of national concern. As recent events show, the domestic repercussions of globalization can reshape a country's foreign economic policies around the question of which governments bear most of the burden of adjustment to trade and technological change. As Alden notes, relative to previous US administrations since Franklin Delano Roosevelt's, the emphasis in US policy shifted starting in 2017 from trade policies aiming to expand the global pie to those seeking to grab a larger slice for the United States. That shift, in turn, implies a turn away from the post–World War II focus on a rule-based multilateral system under the GATT and then WTO, to a preference for serial bilateral trade negotiations—in which bigger economies have more bargaining power. A move toward more flexible multilateral trading rules can be welcome—as Michael Trebilcock argues in chapter 14—but a zero-sum stance on trade negotiations will clearly undermine the gains from trade on a global basis and possibly reverse cross-country value chain linkages, with sizable deadweight losses (as also pointed out by Krugman in chapter 6). At a minimum, US bilateralism would confront other countries—as Peterson Institute economist C. Fred Bergsten pointed out at the conference—with a fundamental question of how far to proceed with trade liberalization without the cooperation of a key founding member and leader of the postwar global trading system. Some countries outside the United States could build their own rules-based trade arrangements without it—witness the Comprehensive and Progressive Agreement for Trans-Pacific Partnership covering eleven of the twelve original TPP countries, or the European Union (EU) pacts with Japan and Canada. Alternatively, some countries might be pushed to strike exclusive bilateral deals with the United States. The global trading system could evolve into a fragmented patchwork of both bilateral and plurilateral arrangements.

In short, the failure to represent politically and compensate economically the losers from globalization and other long-term structural changes has placed the postwar global trading system in peril.

Other Challenges and Policies

Income growth and its distribution are widely used measures of welfare, yet their correlations with other relevant metrics of social well-being are imperfect, and those metrics may have an important story of their own to tell. In chapter 15, Deaton shows that economic growth in the

United States over the past three decades has been accompanied by worse performance along several dimensions compared with other advanced economies: stagnant median wages, low workforce participation, and for non-Hispanic, non-college-educated whites, sharply deteriorating quality-of-life indicators relative to other social groups.[19]

What role has globalization played? Deaton argues that import penetration and job migration to low-wage EMDEs are not likely major culprits, as developments in the United States have been distinct compared with other rich countries that have been similarly exposed to global economic forces. While globalization has been correlated with a long-term decline in the pretax/pretransfer share of labor in national income in other advanced economies (IMF 2017), social outcomes have been distinctively worse in the United States.

Policies that have increased the cost of the US health care system well above international comparators, while also degrading its quality, have been important. So have policies that have further shifted the power balance from labor to capital (including a lower tax burden on capital, erosion of real minimum wages, and business-friendly deregulation)—a point that applies across a broader set of countries, as argued by Bourguignon, but that is especially relevant for the United States. Deaton maintains that rectifying the imbalance in worker power would go a long way toward creating an economic environment in which the benefits of globalization and technology are more widely shared, in turn raising political support for globalization in the United States.

How to manage the labor market effects of automation poses another critical challenge to globalization going forward, as noted above. For decades, economists have debated how much "pure" technology versus "pure" trade effects contribute to growing inequality and structural transformation—a distinction increasingly difficult to draw, as discussed earlier, and also evident from the large variance of existing estimates on the relative contributions. There is some consensus that automation has been no less important than trade in explaining job and wage losses in advanced economies, particularly in manufacturing (see Lawrence and Edwards 2013; IMF 2017; DeLong 2017; Helpman 2018; Krugman's chapter in this volume). One implication is that trade restrictions

---

[19] For a striking illustration of the long-term stagnation of median household income, see US Census Bureau 2015.

can have only limited mitigating effects on job and wage losses as labor-saving technologies advance. Nonetheless, trade is certain to remain central to debates over automation's effects, if only because trade and technology are intimately intertwined, and moreover, the same policies that promote adjustment to trade shocks are needed to respond to new technologies.

Against this background, Laura Tyson addresses two important questions in chapter 16:

1. What patterns of wage and employment change should be expected as automation advances?
2. What can policy do to mitigate the likely adverse job market consequences?

Regarding the first question, Tyson reminds us that both theory and historical experience support the view widely held by economists that automation is unlikely to produce mass unemployment over the long term. As with any technical progress, automation raises productivity, incomes, and hence demand for new products and jobs, so that job losses in some sectors should eventually be compensated by job creation in others. Yet massive changes in employment composition can still be economically disruptive in real time, particularly if much of the labor force has skills that do not match well with those demanded in emerging areas of employment. The result could be substantial and prolonged frictional as well as structural unemployment.

Absent effective policy intervention, Tyson expects labor market changes to evolve along two dimensions. First, as automation continues to eliminate routine tasks typically performed by low- and medium-skill labor, further economic and political polarization may ensue: workers will continue to face stagnating real median wages, while non-college-educated workers in particular will see declines in real earnings relative to workers with college or higher educations. Overall income inequality would accordingly rise further.

Second, the varying pace of automation and the spread of artificial intelligence raise uncertainty about the scope of employment changes—uncertainty that is already borne out by the wide range of new estimates.[20] Especially disturbing is the feasibility of artificial-intelligence-

---

[20] In addition to the references cited in Tyson's chapter, specific country studies are included in Acemoglu and Restrepo 2018; Dauth et al. 2017.

driven automation extinguishing many higher-skill jobs, which are traditionally a sizable share of middle-class occupations.[21]

What can policy do? As always, macro policies to sustain aggregate demand and job growth are important. Macro policies, however, can do only so much to counter automation-driven unemployment. Policy makers must seek other policies. It is useful to group these into labor supply, labor demand, and enhanced risk-sharing policies. On the labor supply side, policies that improve education and increase the supply of high-skill labor can help counter the effects of skill-biased automation on inequality (see, for example, Goldin and Katz 2009).[22] On the labor demand side, policies that expand investment in infrastructure, alternative energy, and paid care for the aging can help absorb low- and middle-skill workers displaced by automation. To deal with greater uncertainty about the future nature and sectoral composition of employment, better risk sharing through broader social safety nets and reemployment programs seems key.[23] In addition, Tyson notes, because the rapidly changing nature of technology demands greater adaptability of skills, lifelong learning needs to become a reality. This change, in turn, calls for the redesign of some workforce training programs and other changes at all levels of education. Finally, because tax and compensatory transfer policies are costly, politically contentious, and susceptible to wasteful lobbying, it is important that such risk-sharing arrangements be institutionalized and rules based. All these goals make for an ambitious policy agenda going forward.

---

[21] According to artificial intelligence expert Vivienne Ming (2018), "The global professional middle class is about to be blindsided." She cites the result of a recent competition at Columbia University between human lawyers and their artificial counterparts, in which both read a series of nondisclosure agreements with loopholes in them. "The AI found 95 per cent of them, and the humans 88 per cent," she says. "But the human took 90 minutes to read them. The AI took 22 seconds."

[22] Such supply policies include better and more accessible university education, wider and better mid-career training programs, and immigration policies geared to high-skill workers.

[23] A question in this connection is why risk sharing is not more effectively done by the private sector. For instance, more efficient and solid financial systems can greatly aid risk sharing. Empirical evidence that risk sharing across US households has been much higher than usually thought (Schulhofer-Wohl 2011), despite a limited social welfare network, is suggestive of this possibility. In most circumstances and in particular for shocks that are more long lasting (like technological unemployment), there is a clear case, however, that governments need to take a hand in achieving more efficient risk pooling.

GLOBALIZATION, DEMOCRACY, AND NATIONAL SOVEREIGNTY

The rise of populism and political extremism in the new millennium imparts a sense of urgency to the policy agenda outlined above and further elaborated in the remainder of this volume.[24] Given that populism thrives on antiglobalization discourse, economic and other forms of nationalism, and more autocratic governance, its gain in traction precisely during hyperglobalization raises two questions. Does globalization itself weaken liberal democracy by sowing the seeds of political backlash? And is there really an inherent conflict between globalization and national sovereignty, as populist manifestos seem to indicate? The influential work by Rodrik (2000, 2011, 2018) offers one unified answer. It postulates a trilemma involving globalization, democracy, and sovereignty: a country can combine any two of the three, but never have all three simultaneously and in full force.

Martin Wolf and Ernesto Zedillo discuss this hypothesis in the last two chapters of the book. They contend that such a trilemma is not typically binding—the more so if countries pursue the right policies.

To understand their reasoning, consider first the relationship between globalization and democracy. Wolf argues that both, ideally, give everyone equal opportunities: to achieve economic success in the market regardless of national boundaries (in the case of economic globalization) or have a voice in public affairs (in the case of democracy). Like democracy, globalization depends on the rule of law (national and international). But in other key respects, the similarity breaks down. Critically, democratic authority is defined on a national basis and rests on citizenship, while global business is transnational. Globalization erodes the

---

[24] Rodrik (2018, figure 1) shows that the share of votes going to populist parties (defined as those with electoral strategies emphasizing cleavages between in- and out-groups, which include anti-immigrant parties in Europe, Trump in the United States, and left-wing nationalists in Latin America) trended up worldwide from about 10 percent in 1996–2000 to 25 percent in 2011–15. David Autor, David Dorn, Gordon Hanson, and Kaveh Majlesi (2016a) show that vote polarization in the United States has been on the rise since the 2002 midterm elections. Our own calculations based on international survey data from the Pew Foundation (for specifics, see IMF/WB/WTO 2017, 16–18) also show a worldwide deterioration about the perceived benefits of free trade starting around 2002.

accountability of global firms and investors to national authorities and indeed national polities.

Thus, globalization and democracy can be mutually supportive, but they can also come into conflict. In practice, historical data indicate a net positive long-term comovement, reflecting that globalization propels growth through trade and innovation, while growth, in turn, tends to breed democratic stability.[25] As the latter in turn helps spur productivity, growth, and support for further globalization, a virtuous circle can ensue.

Such a benign outcome presumes, of course, that globalization's net economic benefits are not so unevenly shared as to become themselves a destabilizing political force. In general, a favorable alignment of globalization and democracy requires that domestic policies and institutions align voters' interests broadly with globalization. The increasing perception that this has not been the case has contributed to the recent backlash.

Globalization and sovereignty, likewise, may be mutually supportive, or not. Clearly, if the former entails some commitment to multilateral rules by all countries, it actually could enhance the sovereignty of smaller ones seeking to embrace globalization. Smaller countries typically have less bargaining power in bilateral negotiations, so multilateral agreements on trade, immigration, and financial and environmental regulations can protect them from potential "bullying" by mightier nations, thereby empowering—rather than weakening—their sovereignty. More generally, mutual supportiveness will depend on consistency of the sovereign's preferences with the need for economic openness and institutions that encourage an efficient international allocation of production. If the sovereign's preferences are derived from a democratic process, however, the previous discussion suggests that the result will be sensitive to the domestic policy environment. A noninclusive policy

---

[25] On the long-term association between globalization (measured by trade openness) and democracy, see figure 17.1 in chapter 17. For documentation of the positive association between democracy and growth, see Friedman 2006; Acemoglu et al. 2019. Friedman's discussion also speaks to a related and recent literature on the effects of economic prosperity on happiness, trust, and the stability of democratic institutions. On this, see Algan and Cahuc 2014; Brueckner, Chong, and Gradstein 2015. For an early argument that openness and democracy can be mutually consistent, see Garrett 1998; for a recent one, see Iverson and Soskice 2019.

setting will more likely lead to voter rebellion against the constraints that globalization places on national sovereignty. On the other hand, effective inclusive policies can make this outcome less likely.

Thus, the constraints imposed by globalization can potentially bind preferred sovereign policies. But this result is not predestined; the right policies—policies that reliably compensate those hurt by trade—could create an environment in which the three elements of the trilemma can be reconciled.

Reconciliation is of course facilitated if trade partners can commit credibly to international rules that prevent national free riding, and if voters see those rules as promoting their best interest. In addition to sound domestic policy frameworks, the other key element to make globalization work is therefore a globally comprehensive multilateral system that allows nations to contain the greater potential for negative externalities that globalization brings. Cooperation on trade rules, financial stability, immigration spillovers, climate change—the key area of international taxation—and a host of other issues is an essential complement to national action to ensure that economic growth is inclusive. Michael Huberman (2012) argues that in the latter part of the pre–World War I era, reciprocal international ageement to enhance labor protections sometimes promoted market opening. Such standards (as well as other safeguards) can also be part of the picture, as they are in a number of current trade agreements, including within the European Union.

The difficulty with this mode of reasoning is that in democratic societies, the domestic policies and international commitments that could ease trilemma trade-offs must *themselves* result from the democratic process, and be permanent enough that they are a reliable foundation for economic and political stability. Put another way, conditions favorable to navigating the trilemma have to emerge *endogenously*, with success dependent on initial, historically determined conditions. In some situations, it could unfortunately be the case that as in the old New England saying, "You can't get there from here." One can think of at least four different political equilibriums that could emerge from democratic processes (figure I.9), with only two of them favorable to globalization, and the second of those possibly politically unstable (as some would argue the recent US experience shows):

Figure I.9. Political Ideologies and Trade Policy

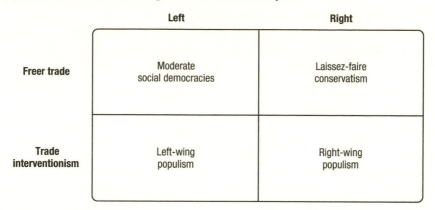

	Left	**Right**
Freer trade	Moderate social democracies	Laissez-faire conservatism
Trade interventionism	Left-wing populism	Right-wing populism

Source: Authors.

1. Voters embrace egalitarian policies (high progressive taxation financing an extensive social safety net), which can then facilitate trade and financial openness, and even some immigration (for example, classic European social democracy).

2. Voters do *not* want policies to address inequality directly (through higher progressive taxes and extensive social transfers), but economic openness is still the chosen policy. The latter could occur because of voter beliefs or ideologies positing the superiority of free market resource allocation—for instance, a belief that trade benefits trickle down to everyone even in the absence of redistributive policies. (More cynically, openness may be chosen despite a lack of redistributive fiscal policies when trade's winners can use their resources to guide political outcomes, including by influencing the electorate's views). Examples of voters choosing such laissez-faire approaches include Reaganism in the United States and Thatcherism in the United Kingdom.

3. Voters do not demand policies to address inequality directly, and government successfully deflects blame for inequality toward other countries, rolling back globalization and trying (insofar as possible) to extract rents from foreigners through higher import tariffs, the discouragement of offshoring, and tighter immigration rules, both to raise domestic employment as well as wages and possibly to appease xenophobic sentiment. This is the pattern under right-wing populism. In

this model, trade restrictions rather than explicit redistributive policies are the tool of choice to support the political base.

4. Voters do want policies to address inequality directly, and the government choses to redirect resources, both through taxation that is more progressive and taxes on foreign trade as well as business, and by restricting immigration to raise domestic employment and wages (the case of left-wing populism).

Of the first two, globalization-friendly outcomes, the second may well be politically unstable, as losers from globalization become progressively disillusioned. In either case, however, both Wolf and Zedillo agree that globalization can backfire if not managed well. For them, a salient destabilizing force is the unwillingness or inability of governing elites to adopt policies that reverse current inequality trends and mitigate concentrated losses from structural change. As Zedillo reminds us, policy failures leading to growing inequality, economic crises, and streamlining pressures on the welfare state were already apparent in many countries prior to hyperglobalization (see also Berger 2000). The roots of political outcomes, as noted above, run deep. But such failures are potentially much costlier today because globalization raises the downsides from bad policies and governance. This factor, in turn, makes it easier and more tempting for political leaders to make globalization the scapegoat for their own shortcomings—resulting in a transition from the second outcome above to the third or fourth outcomes.

The bottom line is that globalization can bring enormous benefits to all citizens, but their realization is strongly dependent on having the right complementary policies. Whether governments do enact those policies, however, will depend on electorates' choices. The big question must be, "How can we get there from here?" One part of the answer, however partial, must be an informed and rigorous analysis of globalization's effects along with the policy options for addressing dislocations and spreading benefits more widely. We hope that this volume helps readers to identify where and why policy upgrades are needed, and how political leaders should go about making them.

REFERENCES

Acemoglu, Daron. 2003. "Patterns of Skill Premia." *Review of Economic Studies* 70, no. 2 (April): 199–230.

Acemoglu, Daron, and Pascual Restrepo. 2018. "Automation and New Tasks: The Implications of the Task Content of Technology for Labor Demand." Unpublished manuscript, November.

Acemoglu, Daron, Suresh Naidu, Pascual Restrepo, and James A. Robinson. 2019. "Democracy Does Cause Growth." *Journal of Political Economy* 127, no. 1 (January): 47–100.

Alabrese, Eleonora, Sascha O. Becker, Thiemo Fetzer, and Dennis Novy. 2019. "Who Voted for Brexit? Individual and Regional Data Combined." *European Journal of Political Economy* 56 (January): 132–50.

Alden, Edward. 2017. *Failure to Adjust: How Americans Got Left Behind in the Global Economy.* Lanham, MD: Rowman and Littlefield.

Algan, Yann, and Pierre Cahuc. 2014. "Trust, Growth and Happiness: New Evidence and Policy Implications." In *Handbook of Economic Growth*, edited by Philippe Aghion and Steven Durlauf, 2: 49–120. Oxford: North Holland.

Autor, David H., and David Dorn. 2013. "The Growth of Low Skill Service Jobs and the Polarization of the U.S. Labor Market." *American Economic Review* 103, no. 5 (August): 1553–97.

Autor, David H., David Dorn, and Gordon H. Hanson. 2013. "The China Syndrome: Local Labor Market Effects of Import Competition in the United States." *American Economic Review* 103, no. 6 (October): 2121–68.

———. 2018. "When Work Disappears: Manufacturing Decline and the Falling Marriage Market Value of Young Men." NBER Working Paper 23173. Cambridge, MA: National Bureau of Economic Research.

Autor, David H., David Dorn, Gordon Hanson, and Kaveh Majlesi. 2016a. "Importing Political Polarization? The Electoral Consequences of Rising Trade Exposure." NBER Working Paper 22637. Cambridge, MA: National Bureau of Economic Research.

———. 2016b. "A Note on the Effect of Rising Trade Exposure on the 2016 Presidential Election." Unpublished manuscript, November.

Autor, David H., David Dorn, Lawrence F. Katz, Christina Patterson, and John Van Reenen. 2017. "The Fall of the Labor Share and the Rise of Superstar Firms." NBER Working Paper 23396. Cambridge, MA: National Bureau of Economic Research.

Baldwin, Richard. 2016. *The Great Convergence: Information Technology and the New Globalization.* Cambridge, MA: Harvard University Press.

Becker, Sascha, Thiemo Fetzer, and Dennis Novy. 2017. "Who Voted for Brexit? A Comprehensive District-Level Analysis." *Economic Policy* 32, no. 92 (October): 601–50.

Berger, Suzanne. 2000. "Globalization and Politics." *Annual Review of Political Science* 3 (June): 43–62.

Blinder, Alan S. 2018. *Advice and Dissent: Why America Suffers When Economics and Politics Collide.* New York: Basic Books.

Bourguignon, François. 2015. *The Globalization of Inequality.* Princeton, NJ: Princeton University Press.

Bourguignon, François, and Christian Morrisson. 2002. "Inequality among World Citizens: 1820–1992." *American Economic Review* 92, no. 4 (September): 727–44.

Brueckner, Markus, Alberto Chong, and Mark Gradstein. 2015. "Does Economic Prosperity Breed Trust?" CEPR Discussion Paper 10749. London: Center for Economic Policy Research.

Carter, Susan B., Scott Sigmund Gartner, Michael R. Haines, Alan L. Olmstead, Richard Sutch, and Gavin Wright. 2006. *Historical Statistics of the United States: Millennial Edition.* New York: Cambridge University Press.

Catão, Luís A. V., and Gian Maria Milesi-Ferretti. 2014. "External Liabilities and Crises." *Journal of International Economics* 94, no. 1 (January): 18–32.

Catão, Luís A. V., and Maurice Obstfeld. 2019. "Trade Liberalization: Aggregate Gains versus Sectoral Losses, and the Perils of Partial Reform." Unpublished manuscript.

Chandy, Laurence, and Brina Seidl. 2016. "Is Globalization's Second Wave about to Break?" Global View Paper 4. Washington, DC: Brookings Institution.

Clarke, Harold D., Matthew Goodwin, and Paul Whiteley. 2017. *Brexit: Why Britain Voted to Leave the European Union.* Cambridge: Cambridge University Press.

Clausing, Kimberly. 2019. *Open: The Progressive Case for Free Trade, Immigration, and Global Capital.* Cambridge, MA: Harvard University Press.

Colantone, Italo, and Piero Stanig. 2018. "Global Competition and Brexit." *American Political Science Review* 112, no. 2 (May): 201–18.

Dauth, Wolfgang, Sebastian Findeisen, Jens Suedekum, and Nicole Woessner. 2017. "German Robots—The Impact of Industrial Robots on Workers." CEPR Discussion Paper 12306. London: Center for Economic Policy Research.

DeLong, J. Bradford. 2017. "Where US Manufacturing Jobs Really Went." *Project Syndicate,* May. https://www.project-syndicate.org/commentary/manufacturing-jobs-share-of-us-economy-by-j--bradford-delong-2017-05?barrier=accessreg.

Dore, Robert. 1982. "Adjustment in Process: A Lancashire Town." In *Import Competition and Response,* edited by Jagdish N. Bhagwati, 293–320. Chicago: University of Chicago Press.

Egger, Peter H., Sergey Nigai, and Nora M. Strecker. 2019. "The Taxing Deed of Globalization." *American Economic Review* 109, no. 2 (February): 353–90.

Eichengreen, Barry. 2018. *The Populist Temptation: Economic Grievance and Political Reaction in the Modern Era.* Oxford: Oxford University Press, 2018.

Estevadeordal, Antoni, Brian Frantz, and Alan M. Taylor. 2003. "The Rise and Fall of World Trade, 1870–1939." *Quarterly Journal of Economics* 118, no. 2 (May): 359–407.

Federico, Giovanni, and Antonio Tena-Junguito. 2017. "A Tale of Two Globalizations: Gains from Trade and Openness, 1800–2010." *Weltwirtschaftliches Archiv* 153, no. 3 (August): 601–26.

Feenstra, Robert. 1992. "How Costly Is Protectionism?" *Journal of Economic Perspectives* 6, no. 3 (Summer): 159–78.

Ferrie, Joseph, and Timothy Hatton. 2015. "Two Centuries of International Migration." In *Handbook on the Economics of International Migration,* edited by Barry Chiswick and Paul Miller, 53–88. Oxford: Elsevier, 2015.

Friedman, Benjamin. 2006. *The Moral Consequences of Economic Growth.* New York: Random House.

Garrett, Geoffrey. 1998. "Global Markets and National Politics: Collision Course or Virtuous Circle?" *International Organization* 52, no. 4 (Autumn): 787–824.

Gerschenkron, Alexander. 1943. *Bread and Democracy in Germany.* Berkeley: University of California Press.

Goldberg, Pinelopi K., and Nina Pavcnik. 2007. "Distributional Effects of Globalization in Developing Countries." *Journal of Economic Literature* 45, no. 1 (March): 39–82.

Goldin, Claudia, and Lawrence F. Katz. 2009. *The Race between Education and Technology*. Cambridge, MA: Harvard University Press.

Gourinchas, Pierre-Olivier, and Maurice Obstfeld. 2012. "Stories of the Twentieth Century for the Twenty-First." *American Economic Journal: Macroeconomics* 4, no. 1 (January): 226–65.

Grossman, Gene, and Elhanan Helpman. 2018. "Identity Politics and Trade Policy." Unpublished manuscript, Harvard University, December.

Hatton, Timothy J., and Jeffrey G. Williamson. 1998. *The Age of Mass Immigration: Causes and Economic Impact*. Oxford: Oxford University Press.

Hays, Jude C. 2009. *Globalization and the New Politics of Embedded Liberalism*. Oxford: Oxford University Press.

Heckman, James, Robert Lalonde, and Jeffrey Smith. 1999. "The Economics and Econometrics of Active Labor Market Programs." In *Handbook of Labor Economics*, edited by Orley C. Ashenfelter and David Card, 3: 1865–2097. Oxford: Elsevier.

Helpman, Elhanan. 2018. *Globalization and Inequality*. Cambridge, MA: Harvard University Press.

Huberman, Michael. 2012. *Odd Couple: International Trade and Labor Standards in History*. New Haven, CT: Yale University Press.

Hyman, Benjamin G. 2018. "Can Displaced Labor Be Retrained? Evidence from Quasi-Random Assignment to Trade Adjustment Assistance." Unpublished manuscript, University of Pennsylvania, January.

IMF (International Monetary Fund). 2017. "Understanding the Downward Trend in Labor Income Shares." *World Economic Outlook*, chapter 3. Washington, DC: International Monetary Fund.

———. 2018. "Manufacturing Jobs: Implications for Productivity and Inequality." *World Economic Outlook*, chapter 3. Washington, DC: International Monetary Fund.

IMF/WB/WTO (International Monetary Fund, World Bank, and World Trade Organization). 2017. "Making Trade an Engine of Growth for All: The Case for Trade and for Policies to Facilitate Adjustment." Washington, DC: International Monetary Fund.

Iversen, Torsten, and David Soskice. 2019. *Democracy and Prosperity: Reinventing Capitalism through a Turbulent Century*. Princeton, NJ: Princeton University Press.

Irwin, Douglas A. 1995. "The Gatt in Historical Perspective." *American Economic Review* 85, no. 2 (May): 323–28.

Krueger, Anne. 1974. "The Political Economy of the Rent-Seeking Society." *American Economic Review* 64, no. 3 (June): 291–303.

Krugman, Paul. 1995. "Growing World Trade: Causes and Consequences." *Brooking Papers on Economic Activity* 1: 327–62.

———. n.d. "The Interwar Trade Decline." https://www.princeton.edu/~pkrugman/interwartrade.pdf.

Lane, Philip, and Gian Maria Milesi-Ferretti. 2007. "The External Wealth of Nations Mark II: Revised and Extended Estimates of Foreign Assets and Liabilities, 1970–2004." *Journal of International Economics* 73, no. 2 (November): 223–50.

Lawrence, Robert Z., and Lawrence Edwards. 2013. "US Employment Deindustrialization: Insights from History and the International Experience." Policy Brief PB 13-27. Washington, DC: Peterson Institute for International Economics.

Manolli, Dayanand S., Marios Michaelides, and Ankur Patel. 2018. "Long-Term Effects of Job-Search Assistance: Experimental Evidence Using Administrative Tax Data." Cambridge, MA: NBER Working Paper 2442.

Margalit, Yotam. 2011. "Costly Jobs: Trade-Related Layoffs, Government Compensation, and Voting in U.S. Elections." *American Political Science Review* 105, no. 1 (February): 166–88.

Mayda, Anna Maria, and Dani Rodrik. 2005. "Why Are Some People (and Countries) More Protectionist Than Others?" *European Economic Review* 49, no. 6 (August): 1393–430.

Ming, Vivienne. 2018. "The Professional Class Is about to Be Blindsided by AI." *Financial Times*, July 27. https://www.ft.com/content/3aac2330-8f38-11e8-b639-7680cedcc421.

Nye, John V. C. 2007. *War, Wine, and Taxes: The Political Economy of Anglo-French Trade, 1689–1900.* Princeton, NJ: Princeton University Press.

Obstfeld, Maurice, and Alan M. Taylor. 2004. *Global Capital Markets: Integration, Crisis, and Growth.* Cambridge: Cambridge University Press.

OECD (Organization for Economic Cooperation and Development). 2011. "International Capital Flows: Structural Reforms and Experience with the OECD Code of Liberalisation of Capital Movements." Report from the OECD to the G20 Sub-Group on Capital Flow Management. Paris: Organization for Economic Cooperation and Development. https://www.oecd.org/economy/48972216.pdf.

———. 2018. "The Scope and Comparability of Data on Labour Market Programs." Paris: Organization for Economic Cooperation and Development. https://www.oecd.org/els/emp/ALMPdata-Scope-and-Comparability.pdf.

Olson, Mancur. 1965. *The Logic of Collective Action: Public Goods and the Theory of Groups.* Cambridge, MA: Harvard University Press.

O'Rourke, Kevin H. 2018. "Economic History and Contemporary Challenges to Globalization." NBER Working Paper 25364. Cambridge, MA: National Bureau of Economic Research.

O'Rourke, Kevin H., and Jeffrey G. Williamson. 2001. *Globalization and History.* Cambridge, MA: MIT Press.

Ostry, Jonathan D., Prakash Loungani, and Andrew Berg. 2019. *Inequality: How Societies Can Choose Inclusive Growth.* New York: Columbia University Press.

Pritchett, Lant. 1997. "Divergence, Big Time." *Journal of Economic Perspectives* 11, no. 3 (Summer): 3–17.

Rodrik, Dani. 1998. "Why Do Open Economies Have Bigger Governments?" *Journal of Political Economy* 106, no. 5 (October): 997–1032

———. 2000. "How Far Will International Economic Integration Go?" *Journal of Economic Perspectives* 14, no. 1 (Winter): 177–86.

———. 2011. *The Globalization Paradox: Democracy and the Future of the World Economy.* New York: W. W. Norton.

———. 2018. "Populism and the Economics of Globalization." *Journal of International Business Policy* 1, no. 1–2 (June): 12–33.

Rowthorn, Robert Eric, and Ramana Ramaswamy. 1997. "Deindustrialization: Causes and Implications." IMF Working Paper 97/4. Washington, DC: International Monetary Fund.

Scheve, Kenneth F., and Matthew J. Slaughter. 2001. "Labor Market Competition and Individual Preferences over Immigration Policy." *Review of Economics and Statistics* 83, no. 1 (February): 133–45.

Schulhofer-Wohl, Sam. 2011. "Heterogeneity and Tests of Risk Sharing." *Journal of Political Economy* 119, no. 5 (October): 925–58.

Subramanian, Arvind, and Martin Kessler. 2013. "The Hyperglobalization of Trade and Its Future." Working paper WP 13-6. Washington, DC: Peterson Institute for International Economics.

Tooze. Adam. 2018. *Crashed: How a Decade of Financial Crises Changed the World.* New York: Penguin Random House.

Trebilcock, Michael. 2015. *Dealing with Losers: The Political Economy of Policy Transitions.* Oxford: Oxford University Press.

United Nations. 2017a. "International Migration Flows to and from Selected Countries: The 2015 Revision." UN Department of Economics and Social Affairs, Population Division. http://www.un.org/en/development/desa/population/migration/data/empirical2/migrationflows.shtml.

———. 2017b. "World Population Prospects 2017." UN Department of Economics and Social Affairs, Population Division. https://population.un.org/wpp/Download/Standard/Migration/.

US Census Bureau. 2015. "Real Household Income at Selected Percentiles: 1967 to 2014." September 16. https://www.census.gov/library/visualizations/2015/demo/real-household-income-at-selected-percentiles--1967-to-2014.html.

Velasco, Andrés. 2018. "Policymaking in the Time of Populism." Presentation at the London School of Economics. http://www.lse.ac.uk/school-of-public-policy/assets/Documents/Professor-Andr%C3%A9s-Velasco-SPP-Launch-Speech-.pdf.

Walter, Stefanie. 2017. "Globalization and the Demand-Side of Politics: How Globalization Shapes Labor-Market Risk Perceptions and Policy Preferences." *Political Science Research and Methods* 5, no. 1 (January): 55–80.

Williamson, Jeffrey G. 1998. "Globalization, Labor Markets and Policy Backlash in the Past." *Journal of Economic Perspectives* 12, no. 4 (Fall): 51–72.

Williamson, Jeffrey G. 2005. "Winners and Losers over Two Centuries of Globalization." In *Wider Perspectives on Global Development*, edited by UNU-WIDER, 136–74. London: Palgrave Macmillan.

Wolf, Martin. 2015. *The Shifts and the Shocks: What We Have Learned—and Have Still to Learn—from the Financial Crisis.* New York: Penguin Random House, 2015.

Wood, Adrian. 2017. "How Globalisation Affected Manufacturing around the World." Vox: CEPR Policy Portal. March 18. https://voxeu.org/article/how-globalisation-affected-manufacturing-around-world.

WTO (World Trade Organization). 2019. "Global Trade Growth Loses Momentum as Trade Tensions Persist." Press Release 837, April 2. https://www.wto.org/english/news_e/pres19_e/pr837_e.htm.

Yi, Kei-Mu. 2003. "Can Vertical Specialization Explain the Growth of World Trade?" *Journal of Political Economy* 111, no. 1 (February): 52–102.

PART I

TRADE AND THE GAINS OF GLOBALIZATION

1

The Gains from Trade in Rich and Poor Countries

ANDRÉS RODRÍGUEZ-CLARE

Over the postwar period, the world has experienced a rapid process of globalization. A simple way to measure this process is by looking at worldwide imports and exports relative to world GDP. From 1960 to 2016, this measure of globalization increased from around 25 to 60 percent. As we face a backlash against this process, exemplified most notably by Brexit and the election of Trump in the United States, it is useful to pause and reflect on what the trade literature has to say about the welfare implications of trade. Trade is of course not the only dimension of globalization—multinational production, capital flows, and migration are also important—but in this chapter, I will focus exclusively on trade.

The trade literature has made significant progress over the last decades in mapping trade models to data to provide more credible quantitative answers to crucial questions in the field, such as the welfare effects of trade. There was certainly an important literature starting in the late 1970s on computable general equilibrium that had the same goals, but for various reasons the computable general equilibrium program was somewhat divorced from the academic literature. Spurred in large part by Jonathan Eaton and Samuel Kortum (2002), there has been an ongoing effort to use standard trade theories for quantitative analysis. Costas Arkolakis, Arnaud Costinot, and I (2012) have shown that under standard (although strong) assumptions, and conditional on the magnitude of trade flows and value of the *trade elasticity*—a parameter governing the sensitivity of trade flows to trade costs that can be estimated using the gravity equation (see Head and Mayer, 2014)—several different trade theories ranging from the Ricardian to the Melitz (2003) model actually lead to equivalent implications for the welfare effects of trade.

MEASURING THE GAINS FROM TRADE

The quantitative analysis that emerges can best be illustrated with the answer to a simple question: What are the overall gains from trade for some given country? Defining the gains from trade as the negative of the real income losses associated with a move to autarky, the analysis in Arkolakis, Costinot, and Rodríguez-Clare (2012) shows that the gains from trade can be computed by a simple formula that depends on two sufficient statistics: how much the country trades and the trade elasticity. This simple formula implies that the gains from trade range from around 2 percent for the United States to around 8 percent for Hungary (see Costinot and Rodríguez-Clare 2014). Adding some realistic features to the framework, such as multiple sectors and an input-output structure that maps onto the input-output matrix of each country (as in Caliendo and Parro 2015), the gains increase significantly. For example, the gains for the United States increase to 8 percent. If one follows recent empirical findings and allows for inputs to be strong complements in production, then the gains from trade would be even larger (see Baqaee and Fahri 2019).

The same mode of analysis can illuminate counterfactual scenarios more realistic than a return to autarky. For example, what are the implications of a tariff war (Ossa 2011), removing all remaining import tariffs in the world (see Caliendo et al. 2017; Kucheryavyy, Lyn, and Rodríguez-Clare 2017), or Brexit (see Dhingra et al. 2017)?

It is important to acknowledge that the results from this analysis come from calibrating a standard gravity model to be consistent with the observed cross-section of trade flows in the data, and so there are strong parametric assumptions needed for the extrapolation necessary to infer welfare under the counterfactual scenario. Clearly much more work is needed to test the validity of these extrapolations. Ideally, we would exploit quasi-natural experiments with trade policy and check actual effects against those predicted by the calibrated models, but this is obviously challenging. Two papers by Jim Feyrer (2009a, 2009b) have received a lot of attention in this regard. He used the differential growth of trade by air and sea along with the closing of the Suez Canal to construct instrumental variables for the variation in trade exposure over time so that the regression of real income on trade could be run as a panel with country fixed effects. The estimated welfare gains from trade in these papers are significantly higher than those implied by the quantitative analysis in Costinot and Rodríguez-Clare (2014). As discussed at length by Dave Donaldson (2015), this gap between empirics and quantitative analysis could be due to an upward bias in Feyrer's empirical analysis. But it could also owe to a problem in the way that the trade elasticity is normally estimated and/or the theory's failure to capture the different channels through which trade raises welfare. I discuss these possibilities next.

Standard quantitative analysis evaluates the size of the trade elasticity by relying on the gravity equation to estimate how trade flows respond to trade costs via a cross-section regression across country pairs (with origin and destination fixed effects). That method relies mostly (and often uniquely) on the variation in an importer's demand across different supplier countries, with little (or none) of that variation capturing the way in which trade costs affect substitution between imports and domestic purchases. And yet as discussed in Costinot and Rodríguez-Clare (2014), it is this last elasticity (i.e., between domestic and foreign goods and services) that matters for the gains from trade. A recent paper by Robert Feenstra and coauthors(2018) uses cross-section and time-series variation to estimate the elasticity for domestic versus foreign goods and services as well as the more standard elasticity across alternative import sources estimated from the gravity equation. The results imply that the former elasticity is significantly lower than the latter, which in turn implies that the gains from trade are three times higher (at least) than those estimated in the standard cross-section gravity approach. This alone could close the gap between the empirical and quantitative estimates of the gains from trade discussed by Donaldson (2015).

Over and above this issue of a potential mismeasurement of trade elasticities, standard calibrated trade models may be overlooking important transmission channels. One stems from the complementarity between trade and multinational production, as argued by Natalia

Ramondo and I (2014). We conclude that such complementarity could lead to a doubling of the gains from trade relative to standard models with no multinational production. Moreover, as formalized most recently by Francisco Buera and Ezra Oberfield (2016), trade may serve as a conduit for flows of ideas that increase productivity in the recipient countries (see also Ufuk Akcigit's chapter in this volume). Although in principle this channel may help in closing the gap, one concern is that the timing may not work: whereas the large gains estimated by Feyrer take place in a matter of a few years, the dynamic gains studied by Buera and Oberfield are likely to materialize only after decades of integration.

GAINS FROM TRADE IN POOR COUNTRIES

I now turn to a more practical question: Do poorer countries gain less or more from trade? There is a simple theoretical reason for why they should be expected to gain more: since poorer countries are economically smaller, then they should be more open, and more open countries generally gain more from trade. Thus, among the countries included in the analysis by Costinot and I (2014), Denmark and Belgium have gains from trade of 41 and 54 percent, respectively, and Slovenia has gains of 58 percent—all of which are much higher than the 8 percent gains of the United States or 21 percent gains of Germany. Michael Waugh (2010) explores this question directly with a much larger sample that includes many poor countries. Surprisingly, he concludes that poor countries do not systematically gain more from trade. This finding implies that poor countries must also systematically have larger barriers to trade. In principle, this could be because they are more remotely located relative to the large markets of North America, Europe, and East Asia, but Waugh's analysis suggests that the problem arises because of the high costs that poor countries face in exporting their products to rich countries. These costs could partly be explained by the higher tariffs that rich countries impose on the agricultural and labor-intensive goods that poor countries tend to export, but it could also come from the problems of infrastructure that lead to high export costs in poor countries. An alternative explanation that does not rely on higher trade barriers is that, because of nonhomothetic preferences, poor countries devote more of their income to spending on less tradable goods (see Fieler 2011), implying lower trade shares and lower gains from trade.

Are there reasons besides differences in trade shares that would imply larger or smaller gains from trade in poorer countries? A restrictive assumption of the quantitative analysis in the piece by Costinot and I (2014) is the assumption that the production possibilities frontier across multiple sectors is linear. Thus if the economy moves to autarky, it can simply start substituting domestic production for imports without suffering from increasing marginal costs. The associated losses come only from the fact that domestic goods are imperfect substitutes for imports, but not from the classic theoretical story about the increasing opportunity cost of producing a good as its sector expands. As an illustration, consider the case of the oil sector. The trade elasticity in this sector is obviously high, as this is a simple commodity, and hence the standard quantitative analysis implies that the losses from not being able to import oil are not that big, even in a country that only produces a small share of the oil it absorbs. In fact, increasing the production of oil may be extremely costly and could lead to huge losses for oil-importing countries that move to autarky.

Thibault Fally and James Sayre (2017) explore the implications of extending the gravity model at the heart of the quantitative analysis discussed above, but now allowing for the importance of natural resources and commodities (e.g., oil). Consistent with the logic above, they find that the gains from trade are higher for countries that have uneven endowments of natural resources; such countries would suffer more from moving to autarky than implied by the standard model with a linear production possibilities frontier. In other words, trade openness measured as in the simple model is no longer a sufficient statistic for the gains from trade. We also need to know how diversified that trade is across different commodities. Importantly, since poor and small countries tend to have uneven resource endowments, they tend to have production structures highly specialized in a few commodities, implying higher gains from trade than large or rich countries reap, even conditioning on the degree of openness.

The conclusions emerging from this analysis by Fally and Sayre line up with those discussed above in connection to the paper by Feenstra and coauthors (2018). Indeed, allowing for natural resources is likely to lower the trade elasticity for domestic versus imported goods below that prevailing across different sources of foreign goods, just as found by Feenstra and coauthors. In future research, it would be important to test whether the implications emerging from Fally and Sayre, in particular a lower implied trade elasticity between domestic and foreign goods in poor and small countries, is something that can be detected directly in the data through the estimation procedure used by Feenstra and coauthors.

Another complication that may matter for the computation of the gains from trade is the presence of domestic distortions. We know from basic trade theory that if such distortions are present, the gains from trade may be higher or lower than those computed in a first-best environment, and they could in principle even be negative. An interesting recent paper in this regard is by Tomasz Swiecki (2017). This paper studies the implications of a wedge preventing labor from moving from agriculture to manufacturing to equalize the value of the marginal product of labor across the two sectors. Thus, since in autarky the economy is already devoting too much labor to the agricultural sector, countries that specialize in agricultural exports would be exacerbating that distortion, leading to lower gains from trade. In contrast, countries specializing in manufacturing goods would have larger gains from trade. One complication here is that it is difficult to measure the agriculture-manufacturing wedge, and there are in fact authors who argue that it does not exist (see, for example, Young 2013). Swiecki computes the wedge by looking at the ratio of value added per worker (adjusting for labor shares) across sectors and finds that the gains from trade are systematically lower in poor countries than in rich ones—again because these countries tend to specialize in sectors with lower marginal productivity of labor. For example, the gains from trade for Ethiopia, a country heavily specialized in agriculture, are 6.4 percentage points lower than the 28.1 percent gains implied by the standard model.[1]

---

[1] Another reason why poor countries may gain more from trade than richer ones is that these countries are farther from the global frontier and hence have more to grow as they converge to that frontier. Thus if trade facilitates convergence, then it should lead to larger gains than for poor countries. For a discussion of the case for such "dynamic gains from trade," see Harrison and Rodríguez-Clare 2010; Costinot and Rodríguez-Clare 2018.

Importantly, the existence of such distortions or wedges implies that trading economies may obtain large benefits from policies designed to correct them. Whereas in closed economies the welfare gains derived from such interventions are limited by the negative feedback arising from domestic demand, in a trading economy such feedbacks are naturally weaker. This implies that policies to neutralize domestic distortions may be complementary to trade liberalization, as discussed by Roberto Chang, Linda Kaltani, and Norman Loayza (2009) and Ann Harrison and I (2010).

CONCLUDING REMARKS

Several broad points are crucial to emphasize in closing. First, the gains from trade may be quite large once we take into account that the relevant trade elasticity is lower than the one estimated from a gravity equation, which is the one that is commonly used in quantitative analysis. Second, such gains from trade miss complementarities between trade and multinational production or the flow of ideas, implying an even larger understatement of potential trade gains. Third, since poor countries tend to have less diversified endowments of natural resources, they are likely to gain more from trade than rich countries do (at least compared with the gains implied by the standard quantitative analysis), except if they end up specializing in sectors that have relatively low productivity due to the domestic distortions.

Finally, the discussion above has ignored distributional considerations that empirical research has shown to be important. In the case of poorer countries, the empirical evidence is discussed by Nina Pavcnik in chapter 8 of this volume. Simon Galle, myself, and Moises Yi (2017) offer a recent study extending the quantitative analysis of Arkolakis, Costinot, and I (2012) to allow for distributional implications, but their findings apply exclusively to the gains from trade and welfare effects of the China shock (as conceptualized in Autor, Dorn, and Hanson 2013) in the United States. This paper finds that overall trade and events like the China shock may increase inequality a bit in the United States, so if social welfare is decreasing in inequality, then the gains from trade or from the China shock would be lower than those that the standard analysis implies. For reasonable degrees of inequality aversion, however, the downward adjustment is small. More generally, finding a way to understand and deal with income distribution effects is an important task in that it may help mitigate the backlash against globalization that we have seen across the United States and some other advanced economies in recent years (for a broad theoretical treatment of this question, see Costinot and Werning 2018).

REFERENCES

Arkolakis, Costas, Arnaud Costinot, and Andrés Rodríguez-Clare. 2012. "New Trade Models, Same Old Gains?" *American Economic Review* 102, no. 1 (February): 94–130.

Autor, David H., David Dorn, and Gordon H. Hanson. 2013. "The China Syndrome: Local Labor Market Effects of Import Competition in the United States." *American Economic Review* 103, no. 6 (October): 2121–68.

Baqaee, David Rezza, and Emmanuel Fahri. 2019. "Networks, Barriers, and Trade." Mimeo, University of California, Los Angeles, and Harvard University.

Buera, Francisco J., and Ezra Oberfeld. 2016. "The Global Diffusion of Ideas." NBER Working Paper 21844. Cambridge, MA: National Bureau of Economic Research.

Caliendo, Lorenzo, and Fernando Parro. 2015. "Estimates of the Trade and Welfare Effects of NAFTA." *Review of Economic Studies* 82, no. 1 (January): 1–44.

Caliendo, Lorenzo, Robert E. Feenstra, Fernando Parro, and Alan Taylor. 2017. "Tariff Reductions, Entry, and Welfare: Theory and Evidence for the Last Two Decades?" NBER Working Paper 21768. Cambridge, MA: National Bureau of Economic Research.

Chang, Roberto, Linda Kaltani, and Norman Loayza. 2009. "Openness Can Be Good for Growth: The Role of Policy Complementarities." *Journal of Development Economics* 90, no. 1 (November): 33–49.

Costinot, Arnaud, and Andrés Rodríguez-Clare. 2014. "Trade Theory with Numbers: Quantifying the Consequences of Globalization." In *Handbook of International Economics*, edited by Gita Gopinath, Elhanan Helpman, and Kenneth Rogoff, 4: 197–262. New York: Elsevier.

———. 2018. "The US Gains from Trade: Valuation Using the Demand for Foreign Factor Services." *Journal of Economic Perspectives* 32, no. 2 (Spring): 3–24.

Costinot, Arnaud, and Iván Werning. 2018. "Robots, Trade, and Luddism: A Sufficient Statistic Approach to Optimal Technology Regulation." NBER Working Paper 25103. Cambridge, MA: National Bureau of Economic Research.

Dhingra, Swati, Hanwei Huang, Gianmarco Ottaviano, João Paulo Pessoa, Thomas Sampson, and John Van Reenen. 2017. "The Costs and Benefits of Leaving the EU: Trade Effects." *Economic Policy* 32, no. 92 (October): 651–705.

Donaldson, Dave. 2015. "The Gains from Market Integration." *Annual Review of Economics* 7 (August): 619–47.

Eaton, Jonathan, and Samuel Kortum. 2002. "Technology, Geography, and Trade." *Econometrica* 70, no. 5 (February): 1741–79.

Fally, Thibault, and James Sayre. 2017. "Commodity Trade Matters." Mimeo, University of California at Berkeley.

Feenstra, Robert, Philip Luck, Maurice Obstfeld, and Katheryn N. Russ. 2018. "In Search of the Armington Elasticity." *Review of Economics and Statistics* 100, no. 1 (March): 135–150.

Feyrer, Jim. 2009a. "Distance, Trade, and Income: The 1967 to 1975 Closing of the Suez Canal as a Natural Experiment." NBER Working Paper 15557. Cambridge, MA: National Bureau of Economic Research.

———. 2009b. "Trade and Income: Exploiting Time Series in Geography." NBER Working Paper 14910. Cambridge, MA: National Bureau of Economic Research.

Fieler, Ana Cecília. 2011. "Nonhomotheticity and Bilateral Trade: Evidence and a Quantitative Explanation." *Econometrica* 79, no. 4 (July): 1069–101.

Galle, Simon, Andrés Rodríguez-Clare, and Moises Yi. 2017. "Slicing the Pie: Quantifying the Aggregate and Distributional Effects of Trade." NBER Working Paper 23737. Cambridge, MA: National Bureau of Economic Research.

Harrison, Ann, and Andrés Rodríguez-Clare. 2010. "Trade, Foreign Investment, and Industrial Policy for Developing Countries." In *Handbook of Development Economics*, edited by Dani Rodrik and Mark Rosenzweig, 5: 4039–214. New York: Elsevier.

Head, Keith, and Thierry Mayer. 2014. "Gravity Equations: Toolkit, Cookbook, Workhorse." In *Handbook of International Economics*, edited by Gita Gopinath, Elhanan Helpman, and Kenneth Rogoff, 4: 131–96. New York: Elsevier.

Kucheryavyy, Konstantin, Gary Lin, and Andrés Rodríguez-Clare. 2017. "Grounded by Gravity: A Well-Behaved Trade Model with Industry-Level Economies of Scale." Mimeo, University of California at Berkeley.

Melitz, Marc J. 2003. "The Impact of Trade on Intra-Industry Reallocations and Aggregate Industry Productivity." *Econometrica* 71, no. 6 (November): 1695–725.

Ossa, Ralph. 2011. "Trade Wars and Trade Talks with Data." NBER Working Paper 17347. Cambridge, MA: National Bureau of Economic Research.

Ramondo, Natalia, and Andrés Rodríguez-Clare. 2013. "Trade, Multinational Production, and the Gains from Openness." *Journal of Political Economy* 121, no. 2 (April): 273–322.

Swiecki, Tomasz. 2017. "Intersectoral Distortions and Welfare Gains from Trade." *Journal of International Economics* 104, no. 1 (January): 138–56.

Waugh, Michael. 2010. "International Trade and Income Differences." *American Economic Review* 100, no. 5 (January): 2093–124.

Young, Alwyn. 2013. "Inequality, the Urban-Rural Gap, and Migration." *Quarterly Journal of Economics* 128, no. 4 (November): 1727–85.

2

Globalization and Innovation

UFUK AKCIGIT

Productivity isn't everything, but in the long run it is almost everything. A country's ability to improve its standard of living over time depends almost entirely on its ability to raise its output per worker.
—*Paul Krugman, Age of Diminishing Expectations, 1994*

These words by Krugman, a Nobel Laureate economist, summarize why it is so important to understand the drivers of long-run growth. A recent study (IMF 2018) documented one more time that open economies receive positive international spillovers, thus suggesting that more open economies can innovate and grow more thanks to them. What are the exact channels through which globalization might affect innovation? More generally, what are the economic impacts of innovation on society and its income growth in the long run? Despite their importance, it has been hard to answer these questions empirically due to lack of historical data on innovation. Therefore, two coauthors and I (Akcigit, Grigsby, and Nicholas 2016) went back to the archives and digitized all the historical patent records in the United States since 1836. This effort allowed us to document innovation in the United States over the course of almost two hundred years. In particular, we observe the distribution of innovation across US states and link these innovations to the individual inventors who are behind them.

In this chapter, I review some of the empirical findings from various recent studies on innovation, and the economic and social impacts on the society, to shed some light on the debate about globalization and innovation. First, I will show evidence from US states, with three key facts: more innovation is associated with more growth, social mobility, and happiness. Next I will demonstrate that more trade openness at the state level is associated with more patents. Then I will look at the optimal policies in the context of international trade and innovation. I will argue that if countries wish to compete with others in terms of innovation, impediments to trade could be detrimental, especially in the long run. On the other hand, innovation policies such as the R & D tax credit are helpful in bolstering competitiveness; in fact, they could set off a "race to the top." In addition, I will show that education helps with innovation, especially by producing more inventors. This is again another dimension of international competition that simply generates a race to the top. Finally, I will offer some evidence on the role of immigrants for innovation and how income taxes affect the location choice of superstar immigrants internationally.

SOME RECENT EMPIRICAL FACTS ON INNOVATION

Figure 2.1 provides the first fact from our study (Akcigit, Grigsby, and Nicholas 2016). On the x-axis, we plot the innovation flows over a hundred years, between 1900 and 2000. On the y-axis, we plot the average growth rate of output per capita in different US states over the same period. The figure shows a tight relationship between innovative activity and long-run economic growth at the state level. In addition, we show that there is a causal relationship going from innovation to economic growth. We can summarize the first finding as follows:

Fact 1: More inventive states grew faster on average.

In addition to its impact on economic growth, it is important to understand how innovation affects social mobility. If a child is born to low-skilled parents, what is the likelihood that they are going to have a high-skill job, and how does innovation change this probability? In two parallel studies, using both the historical records cited in our study (Akcigit, Grigsby, and Nicholas 2016) and more recent data provided by Philippe Aghion and coauthors (2019), we addressed this question.

Figure 2.1. Innovation and Long-Run Economic Growth (US States, 1900–2000)

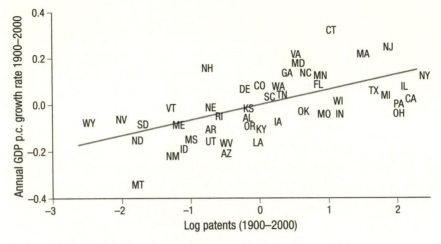

Source: Akcigit, Grisby, and Nicholas 2016.

Figures 2.2 and 2.3 illustrate a strong relationship between social turn-over and innovative activity.[1] The intuition of this result can be seen through the Schumpeterian paradigm, which suggests that innovation allows new entrants to capture markets from old incumbents. This process of creative destruction creates churn in the economy, allowing individuals and firms with limited market shares to grow, and new jobs to open up. As a result, the child of an assembly line worker can end up becoming the next entrepreneur.

Fact 2: Innovation was strongly positively correlated with social mobility.

So far we have seen that innovation is strongly related to economic growth and social mobility. Yet an important question still remains: Do innovation and creative destruction increase happiness? Aghion and coauthors (2016) answer that question.

[1] Figure 2.3 plots the logarithm of the number of patent applications per capita (x-axis) against the logarithm social mobility (y-axis). Social mobility is computed as the probability of belonging to the highest quintile of the income distribution in 2010 (when aged around thirty) when parents belonged to the lowest quintile in 1996 (when aged around sixteen). Observations are computed at the commuting zones level (569 observations). The number of patents is averaged from 2006 to 2010.

Figure 2.2. Innovation and Social Mobility in the Historical United States

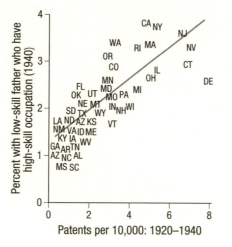

Source: Akcigit, Grisby, and Nicholas 2016.

Figure 2.3. Innovation and Social Mobility in the Modern United States

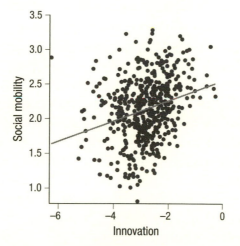

Source: Akcigit, Ates, and Imkpullitti 2018.

Figure 2.4. Innovation and Happiness

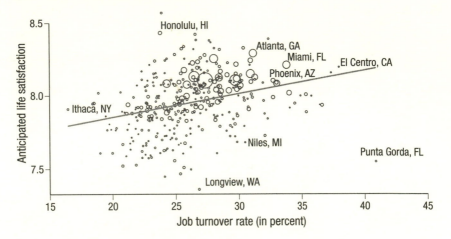

Source: Akcigit, Grisby, and Nicholas 2016.

To measure happiness, we use the Cantril ladder of life from the Gallup-Sharecare Well-Being Index, which asks individuals about both current and future well-being. We follow Steven Davis, John Haltiwanger, and Scott Schuh (1996) when proxying for creative destruction, and use their measure of job turnover, defined as the job creation rate plus the job destruction rate.[2] The data come from the Census Bureau's business dynamics statistics at the metropolitan statistical area level. We find that the effect of creative destruction on well-being is unambiguously positive if we control for unemployment, and less so if we do not, and this effect is stronger in metropolitan statistical areas within states with more generous unemployment insurance policies (see figure 2.4).

Aghion and coauthors' (2016) findings are consistent with the view that innovation creates winners and losers. While innovation leads to growth in earnings (i.e., capitalization effect), it also makes old technologies obsolete and the workers who used to work for the former incumbents become unemployed (i.e., unemployment effect). Recall that the link between innovation and subjective well-being is much stronger in regions where unemployment benefits are higher. From a policy point of view, it is important to not forget those who as a result of innovation become unemployed. This puts a premium on thinking

---

[2] Using firm turnover, namely the sum of the establishment entry and exit rates, as a proxy for creative destruction gives similar results.

Figure 2.5. Interstate Trade and Innovation

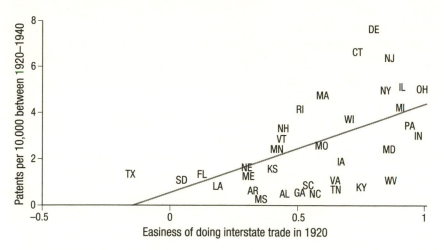

Source: Akcigit, Grisby, and Nicholas 2016.

about retraining programs to facilitate the transition of newly unemployed workers to new technologies.

Fact 3: The effect of innovation and creative destruction on individual well-being is positive.

So far I have presented three reasons why innovation is important for society: economic growth, social mobility, and happiness. The next big question is, How can we foster innovation and technological progress, especially in a world that is getting more and more globalized?

I will separate the rest of the discussion into two parts, focusing first on firms, and then on the individuals and in particular on inventors driving innovation.

FIRMS

Globalization is connecting different parts of the world together. Are connected regions more innovative? My coauthors and I (Akcigit, Grigsby, and Nicholas 2016) look at the relationship between transportation costs and the innovativeness of different regions. One striking historical fact about the more innovative US regions is that they were more connected to the outside world. They were more connected in the sense that the shipment costs were lower and there was more labor mobility into those regions (see figure 2.5).

This result seems to be encouraging for the impact of globalization on innovation. But would this cross-state result generalize to the cross-country setting? When we go to an international scale, we have a global economy with policies carried out at the national level. Within nations, there are strong incentives to push for nationalistic policies since the national identity of the winners and losers becomes an important policy object.

Recently there have been a lot of arguments in favor protectionist policies, especially going in the direction of raising tariffs and trade barriers, and moving away from globalization. Instead of moving away from globalization by trying to close borders or hike tariffs, a more promising approach could be to embrace it, and try to navigate through globalization with the right industrial or innovation policies. In a recent paper (Akcigit, Ates, and Impullitti 2018), my coauthors and I study the role of trade and innovation policies on economic welfare in a globalized world.

Debates on public policy and economic growth should not ignore the fact that innovations do not fall from the sky. They are created by firms and inventors who respond to economic incentives; and crucially, incentives are shaped by public policy. In the United States, the 1970s was a period of productivity slowdown that raised concerns about the country's declining international competitiveness. At the time, John McTague of the Reagan White House said, "Foreign competition in the technology intensive industries poses a more serious threat to our country's position in the international marketplace than ever before in our history" (cited in Hallacher 2005, 2). There are possible policies to deal with this "problem"—the most discussed one being import tariffs. These debates, however, resulted in the introduction of the federal R & D tax credit for the first time in 1981 (which has been in effect ever since).

Figure 2.6 shows the introduction of the federal-level R & D tax credit in 1981 (vertical gray bar centered on 1981). In addition, starting from 1982 with Minnesota, many different states introduced R & D tax credit at the state level. In figure 2.6, the height of the vertical bars to the right of 1981 illustrates the number of states that introduced the R & D tax credit in that year. What has been the outcome of these policies? Figure 2.6 also shows the R & D intensity of the US companies, defined as the R & D spending relative to sales. While the average

Figure 2.6. Federal and State-Level R & D Tax Credit, R & D Spending, and Innovation

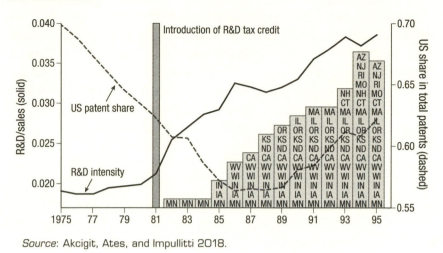

Source: Akcigit, Ates, and Impullitti 2018.

R & D intensity was relatively flat prior to 1981, it started to rise sharply after the introduction of the R & D tax credit. The same figure also depicts the patent share of US firms in the global economy. With an expected delay, the annual share of patents registered by US residents in the total patent applications increased as well, as denoted by the dotted line in the same figure. Specifically, while there was a sharp decline in patent shares between 1975 and 1985, from 70 to 55 percent, we observe a massive reversal, and in many of those technological fields, thanks to the aggressive innovation policies introduced, the United States managed to restore its leadership.

My coauthors and I (Akcigit, Ates, and Impullitti 2018) assess the effects of import tariffs and R & D subsidies as possible policy responses to foreign technological competition in a dynamic general equilibrium growth model. Our quantitative investigation illustrates that in static terms, globalization (defined as reduced trade barriers) has an ambiguous effect on welfare, while in dynamic terms (i.e., when we allow for an accumulation of such effects over time), intensified globalization boosts domestic innovation through induced international competition. Accounting for transitional dynamics, we compute optimal policies over different time horizons. The model suggests that the introduction of the R & D tax credit in 1981 was an effective policy response to foreign competition, generating substantial welfare gains in the long run. A counterfactual exercise shows that increasing trade barriers as an alternative policy response produces gains only in the short run, and only when introduced unilaterally, while leading to large losses in the medium and long run. Protectionist measures generate large dynamic losses from trade; less competition diminishes innovation incentives and productivity growth. Finally, we demonstrate that less government intervention is needed in a globalized world, thanks to intensified international competition as a result of lower trade barriers.

INDIVIDUALS

Innovations are a human activity and major source of economic growth. It is therefore crucial to understand the process through which individuals become inventors and start with the following question: Who becomes an inventor? Inequality in opportunities to get proper education could prevent citizens as well as society from realizing their full innovative potential. The strong complementarity between innovation and education is documented in studies looking at the United States (Akcigit, Grigsby, and Nicholas 2017) and Finland (Aghion et al. 2017).

In figure 2.7, we (Akcigit, Grigsby, and Nicholas 2016) document the relationship between education and the probability of becoming an inventor. On the x-axis, we plot different education groups. On the y-axis, we calculate the probability of becoming an inventor within each group. While the leftmost group has no education, the rightmost one has at least a college degree. What is evident in this figure is that there is a massive rise in the likelihood of becoming an inventor as the education level increases. What about parental background? Figure 2.8 answers that question. This time on the x-axis, we plot the percentile of the parental income. While the leftmost group has the poorest parents, the rightmost group has the richest parents. What is striking about this figure is that for the most part up to the ninety-fifth percentile, the link between parental income and children's probability of inventing is not related.

For the group in the top 5 percent, we see an extremely strong relationship, which indicates that innovation is indeed concentrated among rich families. An important result (Akcigit, Grigsby, and Nicholas 2016) is that the strong positive impact of parental income vanishes

Figure 2.7. Own Education

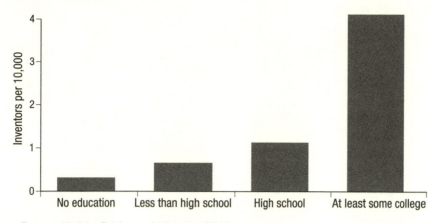

Source: Akcigit, Grisby, and Nicholas 2016.

Figure 2.8. Parental Income

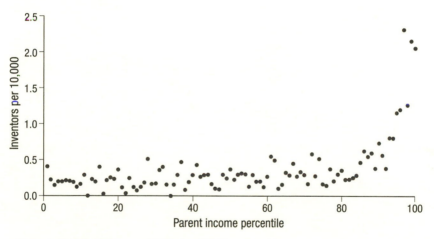

Source: Akcigit, Grisby, and Nicholas 2016.

once children's education is controlled for. This result, together with these two figures, suggests that parental resources are a critical determinant of children's innovation, mainly due to their influence on children's education. An important policy conclusion from this finding would be that providing equal opportunity to children for education could be a powerful innovation policy.

From the founding of the United States up to the recent presidential election, the impact of immigrants has been a focal point of debate.

Figure 2.9. The Geography of the United States' Immigrant Inventors, 1880–1940

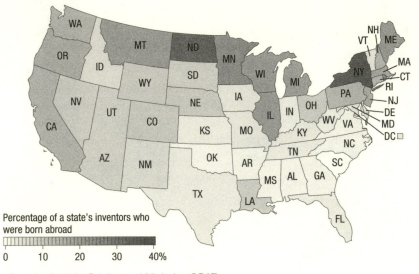

Percentage of a state's inventors who were born abroad

0   10   20   30   40%

Source: Akcigit, Grisby, and Nicholas 2017.

The relationship between immigration and innovation is especially contentious and relevant. What is the contribution of immigrants to US innovation? Given the global scarcity of talents, understanding the role of immigrant inventors for US economic growth is crucial. In one study (Akcigit, Grigsby, and Nicholas 2017), using patent records and federal census data, my coauthors and I provide broad evidence of the impact of immigrants on US innovation and document labor market outcomes for migrant inventors (see figure 2.9). We construct a measure of foreign-born expertise, and show that technology areas where immigrant inventors were more prevalent between 1880 and 1940 experienced faster growth between 1940 and 2000. We also demonstrate that immigrant inventors were more productive during their life cycle than native-born inventors, although they received significantly lower wage levels than their native-born counterparts. Overall, our results suggest the contribution of foreign-born inventors to US innovation was substantial, but we also find evidence of assimilation frictions in the labor market.

What kind of policies are attracting or discouraging inventors? When it comes to policy debates, it is important to also take into account the

Figure 2.10. US Tax Reform Act of 1986 and Inventor Migration

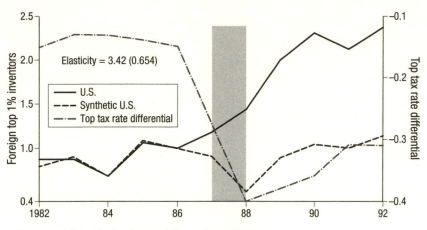

Source: Akcigit, Baslandze, and Stantcheva 2016.

Figure 2.11. Denmark's 1992 Preferential Tax Reform

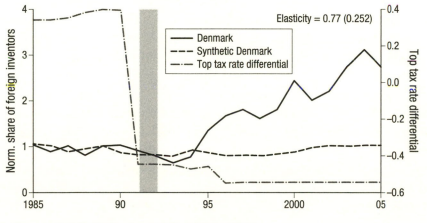

Source: Akcigit, Baslandze, and Stantcheva 2016.

disincentive effect of taxes on individuals and inventors in particular. Many of the prolific inventors around the world are international migrants, and their location choice is affected by country-specific policies. In a recent work (Akcigit, Baslandze, and Stantcheva 2016), my coauthors and I analyze the impact of top marginal income tax rates on the international mobility of inventors. Among many other things, we study the changes in tax codes in various countries, as illustrated in figures 2.10 and 2.11.

Figure 2.10 shows the 1986 policy reform that reduced the top marginal tax rate in the United States. The effect has been a rise in the number of foreign superstar (highest-quality) inventors who migrate to the United States. Similarly, figure 2.11 depicts the policy change in Denmark in 1992 that lowered the top tax rate for high-income foreign researchers. The result of this change is again a significant rise in the number foreign inventors in the country. Lower taxes induce inventors to immigrate.

The analysis in two studies (Akcigit, Ates, and Impullitti 2018; Akcigit, Baslandze, and Stantcheva 2016) show the (dis)incentive effects of policies. These findings suggest that wrong policies could impose significant costs on society through their adverse effects on innovation incentives and economic growth.

CONCLUDING REMARKS

Innovation is good for society for at least three reasons: it leads to economic growth, social mobility, and happiness. On the firm side, globalization could encourage more innovation, if we guide our innovation policy in an informed way, especially thinking about how competition will have differential effects in different industries. When it comes to individuals, a strong education policy could be an influential innovation policy. Similarly, immigration policy could be an influential innovation policy in itself. And I want to end by acknowledging the fact that the papers described above were written with coauthors who are originally from eight different countries and currently reside in five different countries. This is a great example that shows the way globalization makes us more productive in knowledge creation.

REFERENCES

Aghion, Philippe, Ufuk Akcigit, Antonin Bergeaud, Richard Blundell, and David Hémous. 2019. "Innovation and Top Income Inequality." *Review of Economic Studies* 86, no. 1 (January): 1–45.

Aghion, Philippe, Ufuk Akcigit, Angus Deaton, and Alexandra Roulet, 2016. "Creative Destruction and Subjective Well-Being." *American Economic Review* 106, no. 12 (December): 3869–97.

Aghion, Philippe, Ufuk Akcigit, Ari Hyytinen, and Otto Toivanen. 2017. "Social Origins and IQ of Inventors." NBER Working Paper 24110. Cambridge, MA: National Bureau of Economic Research.

Akcigit, Ufuk, Sina T. Ates, and Giammario Impullitti. 2018. "Innovation and Trade Policy in a Globalized World." NBER Working Paper 24543. Cambridge, MA: National Bureau of Economic Research.

Akcigit, Ufuk, Salomé Baslandze, and Stefanie Stantcheva. 2016. "Taxation and the International Mobility of Inventors." *American Economic Review* 106, no. 10 (October): 2930–81.

Akcigit, Ufuk, John Grigsby, and Tom Nicholas. 2016. "The Rise of American Ingenuity: Innovation and Inventors of the Golden Age." NBER Working Paper 23047. Cambridge, MA: National Bureau of Economic Research.

———. 2017. "Immigration and the Rise of American Ingenuity." *American Economic Review, Papers and Proceedings* 107, no. 5 (May): 327–31.

Davis, Steven J., John Haltiwanger, and Scott Schuh. 1996. "Small Business and Job Creation: Dissecting the Myth and Reassessing the Facts." *Small Business Economics* 8, no. 4 (August): 297–315.

Hallacher, Paul M. 2005. *Why Policy Issue Networks Matter: The Advanced Technology Program and the Manufacturing Extension Partnership.* Lanham, MD: Rowman and Littlefield.

IMF (International Monetary Fund). 2018. *World Economic Outlook.* Washington, DC: International Monetary Fund.

Krugman, Paul. 1994. *The Age of Diminishing Expectations: US Economic Policy in the 1990s.* Cambridge, MA: MIT Press.

PART II

GLOBALIZATION, DEVELOPMENT, AND INEQUALITY

3

Trade Strategy, Development, and the Future of the Global Trade Regime

DANI RODRIK

There is little doubt these days that trade has played an important role in those countries that managed to get their act together and grow rapidly. But there is more debate on exactly what it means to "get your act together" when it comes to taking advantage of trade. Certainly, the most successful countries—those in East Asia—have not simply liberalized their imports and capital flows, and then simply waited for the magic to work. Vietnam and China, and before them South Korea and Taiwan, are all examples of countries that pushed for exports while significantly delaying their liberalization on the import side. These countries also made effective use of a wide range of industrial policies to fundamentally alter their patterns of comparative advantage and stimulate new industries.

Perhaps paradoxically, the countries that fit the traditional textbook liberalization mold better produced meager results—even though they globalized too—in the sense of increasing trade volumes and attracting foreign investment. Many of the Latin American countries, I think, are particularly disappointing in that way. That's certainly not because they didn't try. In fact, they opened to the world economy in a much more significant and determined way. They liberalized unilaterally and signed on to trade agreements. Yet they did not get the same kind of benefits out of trade. The aggregate productivity performance of countries like Mexico and Brazil, for instance, has been poor.

So what this diverse experience tells us is that trade is a facilitator, but you must sequence your import liberalization carefully and do other things that would ensure you take advantage of it.

WHAT MAKES FOR SUCCESS IN TRADE?

Two things, in particular, stand out as I look at this diverse experience. One is that it was critical to maintain employment in the transition, especially in industries that would be hit hard by openness. That is one of the things that Asian countries did well: they promoted exports and participation in world markets, while shielding employment in some of the sectors that would have been adversely affected.

To see the importance of this more clearly, think of the economy essentially being made up of three kinds of jobs: the high-productivity jobs, the so-so jobs, and the low-productivity jobs. East Asian countries opened by making sure that the middle tier of employment did not quite disappear during the process. In South Korea and Taiwan, this objective was achieved by delaying import liberalization. In China and Vietnam, it was done by deliberately protecting the state enterprises where much of that mid-productivity employment was.

In other countries—typically in Latin America—where they liberalized quickly on the import side, they lost that sort of middle tier of jobs quickly. We see that in the sharp drop of manufacturing employment or dip in employment in parastatals in Africa. The trouble is that workers displaced in this fashion generally didn't end up moving into the most productive parts of the economy. Instead, they ended up going to the less productive part: informal sectors, and in some cases, even back in traditional agriculture.

We will learn in Rafael Dix-Carneiro's contribution to this volume (chapter 9) about what happened during Brazil's import liberalization. It's a story that's fairly common across Latin America. Countries open their economies on the import side and subject their manufacturing firms to global competition. And they lose, essentially, all the less productive formal manufacturing sector. This does wonders for the productivity of the remaining manufacturing activities because they're all the highest-productivity firms. But the workers who are displaced basically end up in even less productive areas of the economy. So liberalization has exacerbated the dualism in these economies. And in Mexico, we famously have the problem of "two Mexicos." One part is productive and highly connected to North America, while the other part is badly lagging. The trouble is that the latter sector expands and absorbs employment. The consequence is one of the worst economy-wide productivity growth rates in the region.

In these countries, we therefore have the paradox that overall productivity lags even though the most modern parts of the economy appear to do extremely well—essentially by absorbing the most advanced technologies, but not absorbing much labor at all. At the level of the economy as a whole, there is massive misallocation.

Now let me open a parenthesis here for the more technically minded. From an economist's standpoint, it is not at all evident what it means to say that "you should open up by encouraging exports rather than liberalizing imports." In general equilibrium, these two strategies are one and the same. I remember having these arguments with the late Alice Amsden, who used to make the distinction in explaining Korea's success. I contended to the contrary that the Asian sequencing of outward orientation could not have made a difference, due to a proposition in trade theory called Lerner symmetry. Lerner symmetry states that import and export taxes are equivalent, so that it really does not matter which side of the trade balance you work on.

But in practice it clearly did make a difference how you opened. China, of course, is the best example of this difference. Rather than quickly liberalizing on the import side, China liberalized on the export side at the margin through the creation of special economic zones. It did not subject its economy within a relatively short time to an abrupt surge in import competition. It just set aside an enclave within the economy where you could come in and operate under free trade rules, bringing in your intermediate imports duty-free provided you were exporting the final products to the world market. So it was offering incentives at the margin for exports without necessarily reducing incentives for import substitution for a lot of the domestic economy, particularly the state sector.

How do we escape the implication of standard trade theory that it shouldn't matter or that it should all work out the same? This is one area where the micro/macro linkage matters. Go back to the Lerner symmetry theorem. What the theorem assumes is that the macro will take care of itself; the aggregate level of employment and demand will readjust to ensure that all resources are fully employed. In such a world, the micro can be neatly insulated from the macro. Clearly this is something that doesn't happen necessarily in a real-world economy. Thus it does matter whether countries are ensuring that enough jobs are being generated by the export sector before they subject their economy to the full force of import competition. So maybe this is a good time for a mea culpa on my part and belated acknowledgment that Amsden may have been right after all.

If one element in successful cases was to look out for employment in the transition, the other was a concerted investment strategy to stimulate productive diversification and new industries. Hence the export subsidies, directed credit, local content requirements, technology-sharing agreements, and other industrial policies that have characterized economic strategy in East Asia. An exchange rate regime, including capital controls, that maintained a competitive currency and prevented sustained overvaluation was also a common feature. Here again we have a major difference with Latin America and its hasty, ill-fated love affair with financial globalization. When a country relied simply on import liberalization and trade agreements—as Mexico did, to give a notable example—it did not fare all that well.

WHY THE FUTURE WILL NOT LOOK LIKE THE PAST

So much for the past and interpreting it. But what does it all mean for the future?

I think the future will look very different, and we cannot simply extrapolate these past strategies. A major reason is that the kind of export-oriented industrialization that marked all these successful countries is becoming less and less a powerful escalator for growth. I have written extensively about this and documented a process of "premature deindustrialization." That process is driven partly by technology: manufacturing is becoming much more skill and capital intensive. It's driven partly by advanced globalization: countries that have established a head start are harder to dislodge, and import barriers or transport costs provide less protection. And it's driven by demand patterns: as incomes rise, spending shifts from goods to services. Put all this together and countries get the result that it's becoming much harder to get on this escalator of export-oriented industrialization. And even if they get on it, the escalator doesn't take them nearly as high.

In terms of trade, comparative advantage in manufacturing has been moving away from low-income countries because of the increasing skill intensity of manufacturing. If a country can produce shoes more cheaply with 3-D printing, why outsource to low-wage countries?

The bottom line is that it's going to be hard for African or low-income Latin American countries to replicate the Asian experience. This fact doesn't make trade less important, but it does suggest that countries will have to put a lot more emphasis on some alternative strategies as well.

ALTERNATIVE STRATEGIES?

There are low-income countries that still have some industrialization ahead of them, and obviously it makes sense for these countries to create an environment that's going to be conducive to industrialization. I would put much of nonresource-rich sub-Saharan Africa and possibly India in this category. But I think some scaling down of expectations is in order. India and many African countries are putting a lot of emphasis right now on the possibilities that they might industrialize in an export-oriented fashion, thereby creating a lot of jobs in that way. Significant caution may be called for instead.

I think even countries like Vietnam, which are to some extent emulating the East Asian model, will not eventually industrialize to the extent that South Korea or Taiwan did, or that Singapore did in earlier decades. I think industrialization is going to run out of steam much sooner because of the factors that I mentioned earlier.

That means that we are going to have to put much more stress on domestic demand. It will require developing a large middle class that can sustain demand for a broad range of services. It will mean going back to the traditional, conditional convergence story, based on investing in good governance and human capital. So growth and convergence remain possible, but it is unlikely we can get miracle growth rates out of this recipe in the absence of rapid industrialization.

Middle-income countries such as those in Latin America may have greater opportunities because they already have many extremely productive firms in their advanced sectors. I think the key there will be to come up with industrial policies, or productive development policies as they are called in the region, which increase the linkages of these frontier firms with the rest of the economy—using more domestic suppliers, increasing investment upstream, and better training workers. It's going to be as important to decrease the productive heterogeneity and dualism within those countries as it is going to be to ensure that you can go further with trade and globalization.

This picture leads to a somewhat-different spin on how we think about industrial policy, which is also increasingly going to be not about manufacturing per se. It's going to be a lot more about services, many of which may not be tradable. This goes back to thinking in terms of economy-wide efforts rather than simply export-oriented manufacturing.

HOW BIG IS THE PROTECTIONIST THREAT?

Looming ahead there is now perhaps a bigger threat: that the Trump administration will bring the entire postwar trade regime to ruin. We need to consider seriously the possibility of a return to trade wars and knee-jerk protectionism.

For the most part, we have seen more smoke than fire so far when it comes to actual protectionism. If you want to feel alarmed, you can go to a site called Global Trade Alert and click on a chart that shows protectionist measures in red all over the global map. But there is not a discernible rising trend in recent years—except for in the United States—and there is certainly plenty of liberalization as well (which you can see in green on the same site).

Trump himself has done his bit in terms of raising tariffs, such as on solar cells, washing machines, steel, and aluminum. It may sound like a lot, but it is not really all that new—leaving aside Trump's antics. We had a protectionist outburst in the 1980s too, when so-called voluntary export restraints proliferated. At least tariffs are better than voluntary export restraints. The NAFTA renegotiation has not produced a dramatic change. I was never a fan of the TPP and am not unhappy to see the United States walk out of it. The only people who really like the TPP seem to be the geopolitical types who see it as part of some grand American strategy in the region. But as a trade agreement, it was a mixed bag economically and had high political costs. Similarly, in NAFTA it is not bad that the investor-state dispute settlement mechanism has been weakened, though the strengthening of intellectual property provisions is certainly a move in the wrong direction. Trade negotiations with China are ongoing, but my guess is that Trump will eventually settle.

I was somewhat in a minority regarding the likely damage to world trade when Trump took over. I said that I really didn't anticipate Trump would bring fundamental changes in US trade policy. I still believe that is true. If we look at how our existing trade agreements privilege specific corporate and financial interests, we realize that the regime is a lot more mercantilist than economists think. Trump's approach just makes this a little bit more obvious.

As I see it, US trade policies are driven by a fundamental change in the underlying political economy of trade agreements that was cemented in the 1990s. We used to worry that trade policy was made by protectionists on the import side and that trade volumes would be depressed by a protectionist bias. This is a completely inaccurate description of today's political economy. Export-oriented interests and protrade forces have significantly more power these days. Ultimately, I still think that these business interests will prevail on Trump and we will not see a dramatic reversal into protectionism.

The same is true in the developing world. The dramatic liberalization there is sustained not through external pressure, or WTO disciplines or dispute settlement. It's maintained thanks to the political power of domestic interests that see themselves as beneficiaries of existing policies.

With regard to the global trade regime, my feeling is that we should have declared victory in the Doha Round and walked away quite a few years ago. I really don't see the kind of global deal we had in the Uruguay Round coming out of the current round at all. Plurilateral agreements in which like-minded countries agree on further disciplines without all countries having to sign up may make more sense in the future (as argued by Michael Trebilcock in chapter 14).

One of the most worrying aspects of present-day trade agreements is the strengthening of Trade-Related Aspects of Intellectual Property Rights (TRIPS). This is highly undesirable, because TRIPS are not particularly development friendly. We think of trade deals as agreements that countries sign for mutual benefit. But stronger intellectual property rights protections are essentially a transfer of rent from low-income countries to high-income ones. And I would add that even in the high-income countries, there's a lot of evidence now that suggests that strong patent protections are not especially conducive to innovation in the new industries in which we want to promote innovation.

The shortcomings of existing trade agreements offer good examples of how global and regional trade negotiations are captured by particular special interests. We used to think that those special interests are the protectionists on the import-competing side. But as in the case of TRIPS, the lobbies that get their way most often actually are groups interested in expanding trade and foreign investment. The problem is that this is no longer necessarily particularly advantageous for many developing countries.

Something we really should understand about the global trade regime is that it's more open than it has ever been. I would stick my neck out at this point to say that I cannot think of a single country whose growth and development prospects are currently being hampered significantly because of excessive protectionism in its export markets. Perhaps this will change. But I see little evidence for panic so far.

4

China's Steroids Model of Growth

KEYU JIN

We are just past the fortieth anniversary of China's momentous opening up and reform program, launched by Deng Xiaoping in 1978. During this forty-year period, China has transformed itself from a once economic backwater into the world economy's most connected component. GDP per capita rose over fiftyfold, almost a billion people have been lifted out of poverty, and China is fast rising to be the world's leader in cutting-edge technology.

Entering into the fifth decade of China's economic reforms, it is an opportune moment to reflect on the successes and failures of China's development path. What is distinctive and different about China's path to prosperity is that it has been accompanied by significant state involvement. State leadership and industrial policies have been the norm rather than the exception. On the surface, "mobilization economics" seemed to have produced stellar results: in all but a few decades, China became the world's largest exporter and a manufacturing powerhouse.

But observing the Chinese economy today, it is not without serious macroeconomic challenges: China's debt to GDP ratio is one of the highest in the world, its growth rate has significantly slowed down, total factor productivity growth has fallen to nil in the last decade, and financial risk is mounting. Some of these problems have manifested themselves in the global arena: large trade surpluses, interventions in the exchange rates, and excess capacity in steel, gas, and mining. These have given pretexts for trade frictions and currency wars, and a general excuse for politicians to cast aspersions on China. It has come to be accepted that China has displaced workers in industrial countries and induced greater inequality. Whether this reflects unfair practices or simply China's success continues to be a subject of intense debate.

Historical experience has seen a number of instances of big industrial pushes, such as those in the Soviet Union as well as in Singapore, Japan, and Korea. The industrialized world is also not unfamiliar with strong state involvements and active government policies when things needed to be done. Indeed, governments did not leave it to the devices of the market to bring about rapid production.

Few would deny that the Chinese government has also been instrumental in driving rapid growth in the 1978–2008 period. Is there something to take away from the Chinese experience for developing countries? Is such a growth model one of emulation? In this chapter, I argue that there could be long-term ramifications of industrial policies if they linger around for too long without adaptation. Like "steroids," they feel good in the short run, but almost always toxic in the long run. The drawback of such a model is that it puts off the need to unleash an economy's productivity, and over time, more artificial boosters are needed to keep the cycle going. Moreover, the consequences are not only confined to domestic issues but can have spillovers that would affect the global economy at large too.

Until the last decade, China's industrial push helped accelerate aggregate productivity growth. A large volume of resources flowed from low-productivity agriculture sectors to high-productivity manufacturing sectors (Brandt, Hsieh, and Zhu 2007). The rapid mobilization of resources including the vast and speedy construction of infrastructure helped the Chinese economy take advantage of scale economies. Explicit and implicit subsidies for the export sector further helped the Chinese economy take off. If domestic demand was too weak, China could produce for the world.

Still, the subsidies needed to come from somewhere. At the surface level, the state was behind the big push. But ultimately the resources came from Chinese households. A financial system dominated by state banks controlled most households' savings, and the cap on the deposit rate kept the cost of capital at bay. With a large amount of resources at hand, the state directed its lending to strategic industries and firms, in addition to offering a variety of preferential treatments. Over time, though, continued state allocation of resources became less and less efficient, exacerbating the misallocation of resources and reducing productivity growth. Under soft budget constraints, the state was able to continue supporting ailing firms—a practice that led to both excess capacity as well as the rise of zombie firms in many sectors. To keep the economy going and maintain a steady pace of growth, further distortive policies must be put in place. The cycle propels and perpetuates itself.

Thus, despite common perception, the policies pursued over the past forty years and the economic challenges in the Chinese economy today are not disparate issues. They are interlinked and interrelated—driven by common roots. The phenomena of slow growth, rising debt, and excess capacity, not to mention environmental depredation, are arguably driven to some extent by industrial policies that have lingered for too long. For a long period of time, the state mentality was that industrialization was tantamount to modernization. The wildly optimistic dream of Mao Tse-tung to surpass the United States and United Kingdom through increasing steel production occasioned the practice of people voluntarily melting kitchen pots and scrapping metal in their backyards.

There is little disagreement that industrial policies carry with them some benefits. Knowledge externality, agglomeration effects, and increasing returns, for instance, can warrant some degree of state intervention in the beginning. The difficulty is weaning the economy off drugs before they become the economy's lifeline.

A main contribution of this chapter is to use China's experience as a case study to examine the potential long-term consequences of industrial policies. It first provides a broad overview of the type of industrial policies introduced starting from the 1990s. It then illustrates how they have come to cause a diverse set of macroeconomic malaises from which the Chinese economy suffers today. Finally, the chapter discusses two sets of thorny policy issues regarding the sustainability of the Chinese development model. One is the cost, timing, and controversy over how to phase out the distortionary state interventions, which the chapter documents. The first set of issues is relevant for a number of countries. The second pertains to the international spillovers that this model brings about. Particularly relevant is the case of China because the success of an export-led model pursued by a country that carries significant global weight will invariably generate large imbalances in the international trading system. I conclude that a successful phasing out of these distortions can benefit not only global economic stability but also mitigate its own domestic risks and challenges to sustainability.

ECONOMY-WIDE INDUSTRIAL POLICIES

Industrial policies that are targeted toward certain sectors and firms are distinct from those of a more general nature. Those adopted at the economy-wide level in China include suppression of wages, financial repression, subsidized credit for particular firms or sectors, and devaluation of the real exchange rate. Many of these policies were widely adopted by other developing countries. Dani Rodrik (2008) provides a systematic study of the effects. Oleg Itskhoki and Benjamin Moll (2019) collate much of the evidence on such policies practiced in Japan, Korea, Taiwan, Malaysia, Singapore, Thailand, and China.

WAGE SUPPRESSION

Wage suppression can occur when workers have weak bargaining power, there are bans or restrictions on unions and other forms of organized labor, or there are explicit upper bounds on nominal and/or real wage growth. There is evidence that many of these patterns featured prominently in East Asian economies. In the case of China, one piece of evidence reflecting wage suppression is that manufacturing wages have lagged behind manufacturing labor productivity, leading to a continuous decline in labor costs.[1] Another notable trend is the rapid decline in the wage share—from 67 percent of the gross national product in the mid-1980s to 56 percent by 2007. Over this period, net exports as a share of GDP rose by about 10 percentage points.

In a study of the structure of wages in China, Suqin Ge and Dennis Tao Yang (2014) note that wage growth depends on the wage growth of basic labor and the wage premium in the state sector. Prior to 1994, minimum wage laws didn't even exist.[2] It was not until 2004, when the

[1] For a study that shows that labor productivity outstripped wage growth, see Du and Qu 2009.

[2] For background on and the history of minimum wage regulations in China, see Fang and Lin 2015.

government raised concerns over disadvantaged workers, that new laws were promulgated to raise minimum wages every two years. Many local governments were still able to bypass these rules.[3] In addition, there has been extensive suppression of labor rights (Scott 2008).

FINANCIAL REPRESSION AND GENERAL SUBSIDIZATION OF CREDIT

Between 1990 and 2015, the real rates of return on Chinese demand deposits, one-year deposits, and five-year deposits were –3.2, 1.1, and 1.6 percent, respectively.[4] The majority of Chinese household savings are held in the form of bank deposits. In contrast, the real rate of return on capital reached an average of 22 percent between 1990 and 2014.[5] The significant gap between the return on household wealth and the rate of return in the economy at large is one of the hallmarks of the Chinese financial landscape.

The types of financial repression policies implemented in China include interest rate controls on bank deposits, controls and regulations on credit allocations, barriers to financial sector entry, state ownership in the banking sector, and capital account restrictions (see Johansson 2012; Lardy 2008). The People's Bank of China controls deposit and lending rates, although the latter was recently liberalized. As inflation rose in recent decades, the degree of financial repression naturally intensified. Nicholas Lardy (2008) estimates that financial repression imposed an implicit tax on households, amounting to US$36 billion in 2008, or 4.1 percent of GDP. Corporates are major beneficiaries, as they have enjoyed a low cost of capital owing to cheap deposits. Between 2002 and 2008, the interest rate on one-year loans was a full 8.1 percent lower in real terms than in 2002.

Still, the greatest beneficiary of financial repression has been the government. Importantly, by keeping domestic interest rates (and hence the opportunity cost of money) low, financial repression has lowered the cost of the government's sterilized intervention, deployed extensively

[3] According to Mark Melnicoe (2017), only six provinces raised minimum wages in 2017.
[4] Data come from the China Economic and Industry Database (CEIC) and the National Bureau of Statistics of China (NBS).
[5] Updated calculations based on Bai, Hsieh, and Qian 2006.

Figure 4.1. Household Disposable Income in China (Percent of GDP)

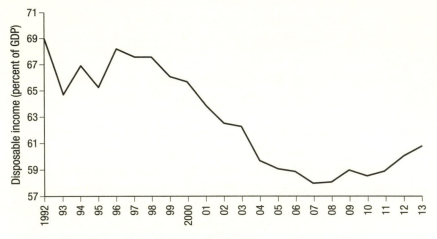

Source: China Economic and Industry Database.

to maintain a depreciated, and hence more competitive, exchange rate. As official foreign exchange rate reserves rose steeply in the last few years, the cost of sterilization in order to maintain price stability (and thereby help slow *real* currency appreciation) also increased. By holding down interest rates to reduce the costs of the necessary domestic bond issuance, the government was able to avoid having to appreciate the renminbi to counter the pressure of the external current account surplus.

In sum, through financial repression, households were in part subsidizing corporate borrowing and in part subsidizing an undervalued real exchange rate. According to Lardy's (2008) calculations, the government captured more than half of the implicit net tax imposed on households through financial repression.

Observing the share of Chinese households' disposable income in national income, one can note a striking result: a prolonged decline from the 1990s to just before the Great Recession in 2008. Whereas household income shares tend to be fairly stable at a higher level in other economies, particularly in advanced ones, that share fell from nearly 70 percent of GDP to below 60 percent (see figure 4.1). It is also worth noting that household income categories of all types declined (as a share of GDP)—including investment income and government transfers (Aziz and Cui 2007).

TARGETED SUBSIDIES

The other type of industrial policy comprises those that specifically aim at propping up certain industries and firms. These can be tax subsidies, preferential loans, land subsidies, government grants, favorable input prices, or asset transfers to favored firms at prices that are below market value. Since the 1990s, the Chinese government has tried to steer the industrial structure in favour of "heavyweight" industries, such as machinery, automobiles, iron, and steel.

To take one example, the steel industry received about US$27.11 billion worth of energy subsidies between 2000 and 2007.[6] Directly measurable subsidies to China's paper industry reached at least US$33.1 billion between 2002 and 2009. In 2009, China overtook the United States to become the biggest car market in the world. This achievement is due in no small part to the large subsidies given to the auto parts industry—where discernible subsidies between 2001 and 2011 reached at least US$27.5 billion. The Chinese government has committed an additional US$10.5 billion in subsidies for 2012–20.

Similarly, there is a wide range of policies that favor exporting firms. Firms exporting the majority of their production enjoy various preferential policies, such as fiscal advantages, softer loans, and priority access to infrastructure and land. These "pure exporter subsidies" resulted in more than a third of manufacturing firms selling 90 percent or more output abroad between 2000 and 2006 (compared with only 0.7 percent in the United States and 1.9 percent in France during the same period) (see Defever and Riaño 2016).

UNINTENDED MACROECONOMIC CONSEQUENCES

How can development policies of the type described above fit with the trends observed in China in the last few decades? And how does a vicious cycle of misallocation propel itself?

---

[6] Energy subsidies for thermal coal, coking coal, electricity, pulp, and recycled paper over this period reached about US$3.05 billion, US$12.65 million, US$777.78 million, US$25 billion, and US$1.69 billion, respectively. These figures are taken from Haley and Haley 2013, which conducts an in-depth study of subsidies in Chinese industrial sectors.

Figure 4.2. GDP Composition in China

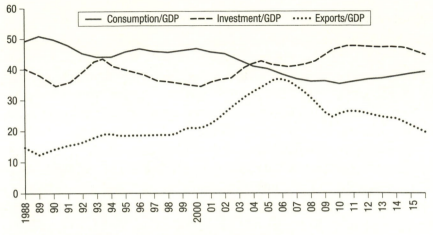

Source: World Bank, World Development Indicators.

China has seen an unusually low consumption to GDP ratio. Right before the Great Recession in 2008, the consumption share of GDP was only 35 percent, having declined by 10 percentage points since the 1990s (see figure 4.2). The low consumption share contrasts not only with the much higher share observed in advanced countries such as the United States (71 percent) but also with other high-saving Asian economies such as Japan (55 percent) and Korea (53 percent) as well as the similarly poorer and large economy of India (57 percent). The flip side was a dramatic increase in the aggregate savings rate. Though all components of national savings—corporate and government—helped, household savings contributed the most, as it rose from 15 percent of household income in 1990 to 30 percent by 2008.

High household savings (or weak household consumption) can result from a falling share of household income in GDP and/or an actual rise in the household savings rate. We have seen in figure 4.1 that the household income share has declined precipitously since the mid- to late 1990s. Thus, by holding down household income via the dual strategy of financial repression and wage suppression, China's industrial policies have given rise to overall weaker consumption dynamics.

A key aspect of financial repression is that a substantial share of household savings falls under the control of the government. By controlling these resources, the government is afforded substantial leeway in funneling lending toward favored sectors and well-connected firms.

Where does this lending go? A substantial portion of the loans was apportioned to industrial goods and manufacturing as well as infrastructure.[7] Lending also flowed into large and usually inefficient state-owned enterprises rather than productive, private firms.[8] Worthy of note is that the divergence in the productivity levels of state and nonstate firms over the course of this period was momentous. In 1978, the total factor productivity levels of state and nonstate firms in manufacturing industries were about the same, but by 2004, private firms' total factor productivity level was 80 percent higher (Brandt, Hsieh, and Zhu 2007, 2015). The upshot is that severe credit misallocation crowds out resources for private firms, and in turn, lowers aggregate returns and productivity.[9] In fact, both the average rate of return to capital and total factor productivity (TFP) growth have fallen sharply in recent decades (figures 4.3 and 4.4).

---

[7] Prior to 2009, bank loans to finance investment in the heavy industry sectors accounted for 7.1 percent of GDP, compared with 1.3 percent for the light sectors (e.g., education, health care, and scientific research). Even more important is the asymmetry of credit allocation in the immediate stimulus response to the global financial crisis: the increase in heavy loans as a percent of GDP (from 7.1 percent in the fourth quarter of 2008 to 9.4 percent in the fourth quarter of 2009) was three times as large as that of light loans (from 1.3 to 2.1 percent over the same period). A majority of the increase in heavy loans was channeled into real estate, as the ratio of real estate loans to GDP during 2009–10 rose to 4.2 percent, which was close to half the ratio of total heavy loans to GDP.

[8] Franklin Allen, Jun Qian, and Meijun Qian (2005) show that most private businesses have been excluded from the formal credit channels, and private investment was primarily financed by firms' own savings. Diego Anzoategui, Mali Chivakul, and Wojciech Maliszewski (2015) also document that a number of firms enjoy privileged access to credit when creditors presume that they are implicitly supported by the government. There is evidence that state-owned enterprises have enjoyed better access to finance than their private counterparts, even after controlling for industry and individual firm characteristics. Yan Bai, Dan Lu, and Xu Tian (2018) provide evidence that relatively smaller firms have lower leverage, face higher interest rates, and operate with higher marginal products of capital

[9] In addition, Yi Huang, Marco Pagano, and Ugo Panizza (2016) provide evidence of "local crowding-out." When local debt as a share of GDP quadrupled between 2006 and 2013, banks curtailed funding to private domestic firms in order to underwrite the debt issued by the local governments. This effectively forced a reduction in private investment.

Figure 4.3. The Aggregate Return to Capital in China

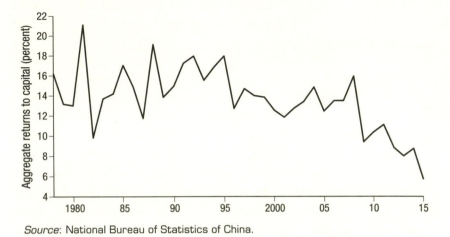

Source: National Bureau of Statistics of China.

In addition, various forms of "soft budget constraints" for state-owned enterprises further worsen the misallocation problem and reduce credit efficiency. State banks keep afloat many ailing state-owned enterprises and unprofitable projects that have already suffered enormous capital losses (see Allen et al. 2012; Walter and Howie 2012). Part of the reason is that creditors expect the state-owned enterprises to be bailed out regardless of their financial status, and thus are willing to continue extending them credit at costs substantially lower than what private firms with similar or better prospects can obtain. The incentive of these privileged firms is therefore to build up financial leverage. Another motivation behind soft budget constraints is that once sunk costs have been incurred, there is a familiar temptation to "evergreen" and pour in even more resources in the hope of turning around unprofitable and untenable projects.

It is thus not difficult to understand how the process of financial extraction determining the supply side of financial resource allocation, coupled with soft budget constraints that feed the demand side of financial resource allocation, can jointly increase distortions, and how such distortions reduce investment efficiency in China. The lower the return to capital—and those returns have indeed come down substantially in recent years (see figure 4.3)—the more the government needs to continue to pump money into the system. The economy's momentum is effectively sustained on steroids.

Figure 4.4. Total Factor Productivity (TFP) Growth in China

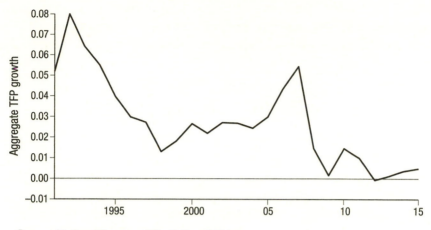

Source: National Bureau of Statistics of China.

Hence, it is also easy to grasp how the rise of zombie companies and problem of overcapacity can come about. Lorenzo Caliendo, Fernando Parro, and Aleh Tsyvinski (2016) show that the sectors in which the distortions described above have increased the most are exactly the ones that suffer from excess capacity. Among zombie firms—firms that stay in operation because of subsidies in the form of continual bank loans and/or overpriced projects bankrolled by the state—the highest proportion in 2007 appeared in the industrial and manufacturing sectors (see Tan, Huang, and Woo 2016).[10] Industrial policies at both the macro and micro levels thus have contributed in no small part to today's low productivity as well as the malaises of many industrial and state-owned firms.

Identifying the deeper roots underneath such a range of interrelated economic and financial developments goes far beyond mere theoretical interest. This identification ultimately shapes policy design and response. For example, what could the Chinese government choose to do to deal with zombie companies? It could continue to roll over the debt of insolvent borrowers—evergreening as practiced in Japan in the 1990s—or give these companies preferential treatment, such as awarding them large-scale projects, disbursing long-term loans, or lowering the inter-

[10] For example, 15 percent of firms in water, gas, petroleum, chemical fibers, and mining sectors qualified as zombie firms.

est rates they pay.[11] By tackling directly the *symptoms* rather than addressing underlying deeper distortions, however, the problems can be exacerbated. Importantly, one must see these issues not as wholly separate events driven by independent causes but instead as parts of a systemic whole.

A VICIOUS CYCLE: HOW TO ESCAPE?

The unified framework proposed in this chapter to explain China's economic challenges highlights the potential long-term consequences of industrial policies that stick around for too long. Clearly, the above discussion puts at center stage one particular privilege of the Chinese government: the unparalleled ability of the state to steer the financial system to serve intended policies. Whether it is the ability to extract resources, control interest rates, or direct lending, the Chinese government's power is unique. This is precisely why these industrial policies have been deeper, longer, and had more far-reaching effects than in other nations. The flip side is that the policies' damage can be more dramatic.

The "blessing" of central control of the economy's commanding heights turns into a curse when the economy is cast into a vicious economic circle. Lackluster consumption coming from a suppressed household sector means that the government needs to rely on investment to keep up the pace of growth. Over time, the return on projects falls and productivity slows down. Compelled by the need to deliver growth, the government has to devise ever more distortionary policies—as recently manifested by the continuous injection of liquidity into the economy along with the temptation to inflate the housing sector and foster activities through shadow banking.[12] Not surprisingly, debt levels and M2/GDP ratios in China are among the highest in the world today.

---

[11] For examples, see Tan, Huang, and Woo 2016. This article uses firm-level data for the period of 2004–7 to show that government investment tended to favor zombie companies, and in turn, the performance of nonzombie firms was inhibited.

[12] Shadow banking usually refers to credit intermediation that happens in an environment where prudential regulatory standards are applied to a significantly lower degree than for regular banks engaged in similar activities. In China, the size of wealth management products (best understood as an asset-backed term deposit and narrow measure of the size of shadow banking activities) grew from about 1 to 2 percent of GDP in 2006 and 2007, to 25 percent by 2014. A broader measure of shadow bank-

Of course, one must acknowledge that a strong state capable of encouraging savings even if it doesn't always allocate them productively is still better than one that discourages savings accumulation. One can imagine a far worse scenario of an economy wherein resources are diverted for conspicuous consumption of the elites, typically leaked out as luxury goods are imported from abroad, and where insufficient domestic savings hinders domestic investment and increases reliance on less stable varieties of foreign capital inflows. This scenario—typical of many lower-income countries—can undermine growth and increase financial instability.

That said, in the case of China, a natural question arises: How does one break out of the vicious circle? How does one get off steroids before toxicity wreaks havoc, perhaps with permanent damage? And how does one come off artificial performance enhancers in a way that avoids huge disruptions and pain? Perhaps the reason why the Chinese government has found it so difficult to "rebalance" the economy—with recent efforts making some problems arguably worse—is that its interpretation of the root causes of the imbalances is somewhat misconceived.[13] Is the imbalance in the economy really one of underconsumption and over-investment? Or is the imbalance merely a manifested symptom of some deeper distortions that reflect an imbalance between households and governments as well as the private sector and the state?

Of course, weeding out the distortions is the most direct way to steer the country toward a more efficient, innovation-driven, service-oriented economy. But removing distortions or unwinding habitual policies may be difficult, either because that task most likely requires a short-term slowdown in growth that is inadmissible for the government or because various interest groups may block certain reforms that would harm their interests.

Under these circumstances, there is a case to be made for raising household consumption. The reason is that higher household consumption can naturally push the economy toward a more efficient equilibrium. First, raising household consumption means a reduction in the

---

ing is the growth in trust and entrusted loans. These products grew from 5 percent of GDP in 2007 to 25 percent of GDP in 2014.

[13] Since the RMB 4 trillion stimulus package implemented in 2009, the allocation of resources has deteriorated and productivity growth has slowed down even further (see Song and Xiong 2017).

financial resources that can be extracted by the government. Second, rising consumption means greater demand for private firms' goods and services. Thus, higher consumption can drive resources toward the more productive private firms—particularly when the financial system cannot do the job. The recent rapid rise in productivity growth in the service sectors along with the emergence of some of the most technologically advanced and innovative companies—fueled by consumption growth—is testimony to its importance above and beyond its direct impact on growth.

Of course, another advantage of higher consumption is that it would likely raise imports, especially from advanced economies, thereby helping to diffuse current trade tensions. Allowing higher household consumption would benefit consumers most if accompanied by import liberalization that expanded the array of products available to buy.

One may then wonder whether policy changes can actually stimulate consumption in a meaningful way. Recent evidence suggests that they can, and that China's high savings rate is not just a reflection of immutable consumption habits or culture. The high savings rate is likely a consequence of the financial system's inadequacies and inefficiencies, enforcement of the one-child policy (Choukmhane, Coeurdacier, and Jin 2017), and rise in housing prices.

All these developments are linked to policy. One obvious policy innovation would be to raise transfers to households, reducing the imbalance between households, corporates, and the government. These policies, however, may be politically infeasible. Another way, ironically, is to prop up housing prices and make people feel richer (the wealth effect). But higher home prices raise issues of financial stability.

Perhaps a more plausible action for the Chinese government to undertake in the current juncture is to roll back household credit constraints. Chinese households are severely credit constrained compared to either their East Asian or US counterparts (see Coeurdacier, Guibaud, and Jin 2015).[14] Allowing the young in particular to borrow—whether it is to buy large durables, invest in education, or purchase housing—will boost consumption and reduce savings. The recent emergence of large

---

[14] For example, the mortgage debt for a typical US household was around 87 percent of GDP in 2008, compared to the 11 percent in China (data from BIS and China National Bureau of Statistics). Also, as of 2011, around 62 percent of Americans (over fifteen years old) had credit cards, in contrast to 11 percent in China.

numbers of peer-to-peer lending platforms and the race by banks to rapidly expand their credit card business in the face of rising competition both point to the implicit, unmet demand for household borrowing. In support of this idea, Nicolas, Coeurdacier, Stéphane Guibaud, and I (2015) used micro data to show that tight household credit constraints are an important factor behind the high household savings rate in China.

China's case demonstrates the fact that a large economy in pursuit of its own domestic industrial policies can have large spillovers onto the global economy. While it is true that Chinese manufacturing production has displaced some workers in the advanced economies (Autor, Dorn, and Hansen 2013), it is also true that Chinese consumers have been subsidizing US and European consumers with cheap exports, somewhat to the Chinese consumers' own detriment. The model has also created large external imbalances, though they have started to come down in the last decade. Nonetheless, trade frictions and international tensions are only rising, particularly when the global economic growth is still tepid. In the past forty years, we have seen an influx of toys, furniture, and apparel to European and US shores. The same might be true for electric cars in the next ten years. This would only work if on top of demanding Chinese goods, Chinese consumers are increasing their imports from abroad.

The remarkable achievements of the Chinese growth story may have come at a cost—one only beginning to be exposed over time. While there is little dispute that industrial policies may deliver desirable benefits, how these industrial policies are enacted and when to phase them out are topics that deserve more serious contemplation. Indeed, the question of whether the Chinese growth model is a successful one that is worthy of emulation by other developing countries remains open. Maybe this question will only be put to rest when and if China successfully manages a structural transition. A "miracle" has yet to be established.

REFERENCES

Autor, David H., David Dorn, and Gordon H. Hanson. 2013. "The China Syndrome: Local Labor Market Effects of Import Competition in the United States." *American Economic Review* 103, no. 6 (October): 2121–68.

Allen, Franklin, Jun Qian, and Meijun Qian. 2005. "Law, Finance, and Economic Growth in China." *Journal of Financial Economics* 77, no. 1 (July): 57–116.

Allen, Franklin, Jun Qian, Chenying Zhang, and Mengxin Zhao. 2012. "China's Financial System: Opportunities and Challenges." In *Capitalizing China*, edited by Joseph P. H. Fan and Randall Morck, 63–148. Chicago: University of Chicago Press.

Anzoategui, Diego, Mali Chivakul, and Wojciech S. Maliszewski. 2015. "Financial Distortions in China: A General Equilibrium Approach." IMF Working Paper 15/274. Washington, DC: International Monetary Fund.

Aziz, Jahangir, and Li Cui. 2007. "Explaining China's Low Consumption: The Neglected Role of Household Income." IMF Working Paper 97/181. Washington, DC: International Monetary Fund.

Bai, Chong-En, Chang-Tai Hsieh, and Yingyi Qian. 2006. "The Return to Capital in China." *Brookings Papers on Economic Activity*, 37: 61–102. Washington, DC: Brookings Institution.

Bai, Yan, Dan Lu, and Xu Tian. 2018. "Do Financial Frictions Explain Chinese Firms' Saving and Misallocation?" NBER Working Paper 24436. Cambridge, MA: National Bureau of Economic Research.

Brandt, Loren, Chang-tai Hsieh, and Xiaodong Zhu. 2007. "Policy Perspectives from the Bottom Up: What Do Firm-Level Data Tell Us China Needs to Do?" In *Policy Challenges in a Diverging Global Economy*, edited by Reuven Glick and Mark M. Spiegel, 281–301. San Francisco: Federal Reserve Bank of San Francisco.

———. 2015. "Growth and Structural Transformation in China." In *China's Great Economic Transformation*, edited by Loren Brandt and Thomas G. Rawski, 683–728. New York: Cambridge University Press.

Caliendo, Lorenzo, Fernando Parro, and Aleh Tsyvinski. 2016. "Misallocation in the Global Economy." Mimeo, Yale University.

Choukhmane, Taha, Nicolas Coeurdacier, and Keyu Jin. 2017. "The One-Child Policy and Household Saving." Mimeo.

Coeurdacier, Nicolas, Stéphane Guibaud, and Keyu Jin. 2015. "Credit Constraints and Growth in a Global Economy." *American Economic Review* 105, no. 9 (September): 2838–81.

Defever, Fabrice, and Alejandro Riaño. 2016. "Protectionism through Exporting: Subsidies with Export Share Requirements in China." CESifo Working Paper 5914. Munich: CESifo Group.

Du, Yang, and Yue Qu. 2009. "Labor Compensation, Labor Productivity, and Labor Cost Advantage." *China Economist* (September–October): 25–35.

Fang, Tony, and Carl Lin. 2015. "Minimum Wages and Employment in China." *IZA Journal of Labor Policy* 4, no. 22 (December): 1–30.

Ge, Suqin, and Dennis Tao Yang. 2014. "Changes in China's Wage Structure." *Journal of the European Economic Association* 12, no. 2 (January): 300–336.

Haley, Usha C. V., and George T. Haley. 2013. *Subsidies to Chinese Industry: State Capitalism, Business Strategy, and Trade Policy.* Oxford: Oxford University Press.

Hsieh, Chang-Tai, and Peter J. Klenow. 2009. "Misallocation and Manufacturing TFP in China and India." *Quarterly Journal of Economics* 124, no. 4 (November): 1403–48.

Huang, Yi, Marco Pagano, and Ugo Panizza. 2016. "Public Debt and Private Firm Funding: Evidence from Chinese Cities." IHEID Working Paper 10-2016. Geneva, Switzerland: Graduate Institute of International and Development Studies.

Itskhoki, Oleg, and Benjamin Moll. 2019. "Optimal Development Policies with Financial Frictions." *Econometrica* 87, no. 1 (January): 139–73.

Johansson, Anders C. 2012. "Financial Repression and China's Economic Imbalances." In *Rebalancing and Sustaining Growth in China,* edited by Huw McKay and Ligang Song, 45–65. Canberra: Australian University Press.

Lardy, Nicholas R. 2008. "Financial Repression in China." Working Paper PB08-8. Washington, DC: Peterson Institute for International Economics.

Melnicoe, Mark. 2017. "China: Wage Increases Level Off with Economy." Bloomberg BNA, May 5.

Rodrik, Dani. 2008. "The Real Exchange Rate and Economic Growth." *Brookings Papers on Economic Activity*, Fall, 365–412. Washington, DC: Brookings Institution.

Scott, Robert E. 2008. "The China Trade Toll." Briefing Paper 219. Washington, DC: Economic Policy Institute .Song, Zheng, and Wei Xiong. 2017. "Risk in China's Financial System." Mimeo, Chinese University of Hong Kong.

Tan, Yuyan, Yiping Huang, and Wing Thye Woo. 2016. "Zombie Firms and the Crowding-Out of Private Investment in China." *Asian Economic Papers* 15, no. 3 (October): 32–55.

Walter, Carl E., and Fraser J. T. Howie. 2012. *Red Capitalism: The Fragile Financial Foundation of China's Extraordinary Rise.* Singapore: John Wiley and Sons.

5

Inequality, Globalization, and Technical Change in Advanced Countries: A Brief Synopsis

FRANÇOIS BOURGUIGNON

In his 1997 presidential address to the Royal Economic Society titled "Bringing Income Distribution in from the Cold," the late British economist Tony Atkinson (1997) contended that the time was ripe to bring the study of economic inequality back into mainstream economic analysis. He has been proven right—with a vengeance. In the two decades that followed Atkinson's prescient lecture, income inequality has become a prominent topic in the public policy debate as well as a mainstay of new research in economics, sociology, and political science. Recent events including the 2016 US election, Brexit, and a variety of nationalistic and populist movements in continental Europe and elsewhere owe much to concerns about rising inequality and other social dislocations. While these developments are often blamed on globalization, understanding the full range of forces at play clearly requires a deeper grasp of the underlying determinants of income distribution.

Given this background, three important questions arise. First, is it really the case that income inequality is on an increasing trend in most countries, fed by the surge in trade and reallocation of production activity in the global economy, or could it simply be that the public *perception* of inequality is evolving? For example, the media's massive publicizing of the stellar earnings of top football players, rock stars, and big companies' CEOs, or the astronomical wealth of a few billionaires, may exacerbate public perceptions that overall inequality is rising beyond what the data actually show.

Second, could such a decoupling between facts and perceptions have been exacerbated by the stagnation of real per capita incomes in many countries as well as greater "austerity" in fiscal policies, which may be seen as threatening the future of the welfare state's economic safety net?

Finally, does the public perception of income inequality also derive from other attributes of social discontent, including with employment precariousness, the quality of new jobs, and the lack of economic prospects as well as shrinking of opportunities for the young generation to climb the social ladder?

This chapter reviews the evidence available about the evolution of inequality in advanced countries and major emerging economies over the past thirty years. The aim is to give a snapshot of actual trends based on some of the best available data, and in doing so, try to rationalize the public perception of rising inequality noted above along with the possible causal roles of trade, technology, and public policies.

A main takeaway is that the available data show substantial diversity across countries. While it is true that income inequality today is higher in several countries than it was in the mid-1980s, it remained unchanged and even declined in some others. Most important, however, wherever and whenever inequality rose, the time profile itself is diverse. In fact, only a few countries exhibit a conspicuous upward trend in inequality over the entire thirty-year period. Another key takeaway is that the forces that shape the evolution of inequality within countries are complex. In particular, it is hard to discern the effect of common external factors like trade and technology in a broad cross-country panel. Indeed, I will argue below that country-specific policy reforms are responsible for the most noticeable changes in inequality. Even though it could also be argued that such policy reforms may themselves reflect globalization and technology pressures, the effects of the latter are at best indirect. Overall, it would thus be difficult to conclude today that inequality is rising everywhere under the direct pressure of globalization or technical change. But this begs the question of why data-based evidence seems at odds with public perceptions of rising inequality and the role of globalization pressures therein.

The remainder of this chapter is organized into two parts. The first part is devoted to a quick tour d'horizon of the evolution of income inequality around the world. The second part reflects on the factors explaining that evolution and the potential role of globalization. The conclusion envisages ways in which the measurement of inequality could be broadened to fit better the public perception of actual trends.

A TOUR D'HORIZON OF THE EVOLUTION OF INCOME INEQUALITY OVER THE LAST THIRTY YEARS

A thorough review of inequality data does not fully fit the often-heard opinion that "inequality is rising everywhere," according to which such an evolution is a main characteristic of the early twenty-first century. A widely used measure of inequality is the distribution of "equivalized household disposable income"—that is, the distribution of national income across citizens generated by imputing to every citizen in the population the income of the household they belong to divided by the number of consuming units in that household. Equivalized disposable income may be considered as an approximation of the concept of individual economic welfare, explaining why this definition of income coupled with the so-called Gini coefficient is widely used in describing economic inequality.[1] Using this measure, what emerges from the comparison across countries is that only a few countries exhibit a uniformly increasing inequality trend over the last three decades. Things are different when focusing on the inequality of gross or market incomes— incomes before taxes and transfers—as evaluated using tax data. With this alternative definition and data source, inequality had been increasing in a majority of countries until the early 2000s. Since then, however, inequality seems to have stabilized.

Figures 5.1a through 5.1d below show the evolution of the Gini coefficient of equivalized household disposable income in several countries, including major advanced economies (OECD data) and big emerging economies (World Bank data). The first three figures refer to developed countries, which have been sorted according to patterns in the

---

[1] The Gini coefficient measures the inequality among values in the *frequency distribution* of income. When it is zero, it denotes perfect equality—that is, all individuals in a country have the same income. A Gini coefficient of one denotes maximal inequality, as in this case a single person has all the income and all others have none.

Figure 5.1 Inequality of Equivalized Household Income, 1985–2015

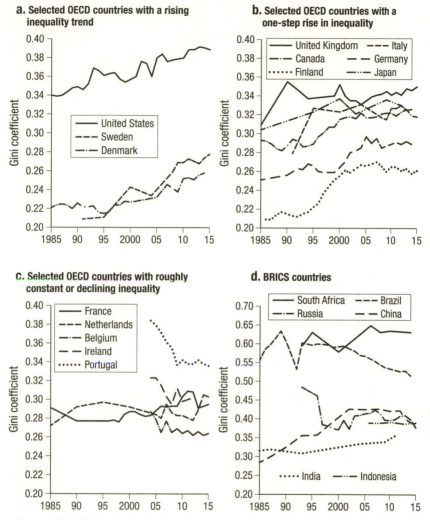

a. Selected OECD countries with a rising inequality trend

b. Selected OECD countries with a one-step rise in inequality

c. Selected OECD countries with roughly constant or declining inequality

d. BRICS countries

Source: (a)-(c) Organization for Economic cooperation and Development. (d) Povcalnet, World Bank.

evolution of inequality. Figure 5.1a illustrates a few countries where inequality is undoubtedly on an increasing trend. Few countries exhibit such a time pattern, such as the United States, on the one hand, and two Nordic countries, on the other. Figure 5.1b shows countries where inequality increased over some period and then stabilized. This pattern is observed in several countries, including major European countries—

Germany, Italy, and the United Kingdom—but also Finland and Canada. For all countries in figures 5.1a and 5.1b, it is the case that inequality today is higher than it was in the mid- or late 1980s—a point repeatedly stressed by the OECD (2011).[2] Yet it is only for a few countries that it can be said that inequality has been continuously increasing. In most countries, the increase of inequality seems to have been more of the one-off type. But of course this has no implication whatsoever for the future.

Figure 5.1c confirms the diversity of inequality patterns by showing countries where inequality barely changed over the last decades or even decreased. The Netherlands and France are in the first category, although the time behavior of the Gini coefficient has been somewhat unstable in recent years. Considering that a change in the Gini coefficient below 1.5 percentage point is barely significant, however, the long-run profile of inequality may be considered as flat for both countries.[3] Data are available for much shorter periods for other countries appearing in figure 5.1c. Yet it is interesting that the three additional countries shown there—Belgium, Ireland, and Portugal—exhibit a downward trend in inequality entering into the new millenium.

Although I will focus henceforth on advanced countries, it is noteworthy that the same diversity in the time profile of inequality holds among Brazil, Russia, India, Indonesia, China, and South Africa—the so-called BRIICS countries—as depicted in figure 5.1d. We can see constancy, at one of the highest levels of inequality in the world, for South Africa, a sharp decline in Brazil after the turn of the millennium, and increasing inequality in the three emerging Asian economies with stabilization in China over the last decade, and a little later in Indonesia.

In short, the overall picture of the evolution of the inequality of equivalized disposable income over the last thirty years in major advanced and emerging countries is not that of a continuous and uniform rise in inequality. Inequality is certainly higher today than what it was

----

[2] This report is in part responsible for the widespread view that inequality "keeps rising" in most OECD countries, partly under the pressures of globalization and technical change.

[3] A change of 1.5 percent is roughly twice the standard deviation of the statistical estimation of the Gini coefficient for the whole population. Note also that the overall inequality changes in figures 5.1a and 5.1b are above that threshold.

twenty or thirty years ago in several countries, but it has stabilized in many of them. There also are countries where the change in inequality has been minor, and even countries where inequality has declined in the recent period—sometimes drastically, as in Brazil.

The picture is somewhat different when considering the evolution of *market* incomes based on tax records rather than the disposable or after-tax incomes that household surveys report. It is well known that the latter tend to undersample or underestimate top incomes, which are much better captured by tax data—even though probably still underestimated due to tax evasion. In a better effort to capture this top income dimension of inequality, much work has been devoted to building databases on "top income" inequality—that is, the share of top income groups in the total income accruing to physical persons. The data that I use next are drawn from the World Inequality Database (http://wid.world). They refer to the top 1 percent income share, and cover the G7 and several other advanced countries, selected for the pattern of the evolution of top income shares.[4]

In figures 5.2a and 5.2b, countries have been split into two groups, as before: countries where the top 1 percent income share has increased substantially over the last three decades (figure 5.2a), and countries where the top share has remained more or less constant, except for transitory shocks, over the same period (figure 5.2b). Although figure 5.2a gives a sense that inequality is on an increasing trend in many countries, the same observation as in the earlier samples of equalized disposable incomes applies. In several countries, the rise of the top 1 percent income share took place mostly in the late 1980s and 1990s, but stabilized in the 2000s. This is true of Canada, France, Italy, and both Finland and Sweden. It is more difficult to guess what is happening in the United States and United Kingdom because of strong fluctuations after the 2008 financial crisis. In both countries, however, it cannot be ruled out that a plateau has been reached since. Because recent data are missing, it is difficult to say whether Germany and Japan would follow the same pattern. In any case, the general pattern of a strong increase in inequality in the late 1980s and 1990s, and then a slowing down and, in some cases, stabilization, is readily

---

[4] Data are available for a few emerging countries in the World Inequality Database, but their time coverage is limited, and data are often missing for the recent period.

apparent in figure 5.2a. Diversity in the evolution of top income inequality is illustrated by the countries in figure 5.2b—Denmark and the Netherlands in particular, where the profile of inequality is especially flat.

Again, it is important to bear in mind that income data based on tax records can differ substantially from equivalized disposable income data based on surveys. The former data refer to market income, cover non-taxpayers only in an aggregate way, generally don't take into account the composition of households—either because they are based on tabulated data, or when micro records are accessible, because they refer to tax units or single individuals rather than households—and most important, don't take into account redistribution through taxes and transfers. But of course they cover all the population, in particular top incomes undersampled and underreported in household surveys.[5] Thus, it should not be a surprise if the two data sources give different results. Comparing figures 5.1 and 5.2, several such contradictions are apparent: inequality increases in the United Kingdom throughout the 1990s based on the top 1 percent income share, whereas it is more or less constant based on the Gini; it increases in Germany from 2005 on, whereas it is flat based on the Gini; it stabilizes in the late 2000s in Sweden, while the inequality of equivalized disposable income rises, and the reverse is true in Denmark. Yet there also are cases where the two inequality measures have parallel time profiles, as in Canada, Finland, and the Netherlands.

Although related, both measures of inequality describe different aspects of it. It thus makes sense to rely on both sources when evaluating the evolution of inequality, as they spotlight different aspects of the distribution. Doing so for the countries appearing in figures 5.1 and 5.2 leads to the conclusion that up to the early or mid-2000s, the increase in inequality was sometimes underestimated in the surveys used to evaluate the Gini coefficient of equivalized incomes. This would be the case for countries like the United Kingdom, Germany, Japan, and France. On the contrary, over the more recent period—ten to fifteen years, depending on the country—both data sources converge in suggesting that inequality has been rather stable.

[5] Note that in the case of Denmark and Sweden, register data covering the entire population rather than surveys are used to evaluate inequality in equivalized household disposable incomes.

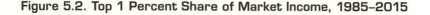

Figure 5.2. Top 1 Percent Share of Market Income, 1985–2015

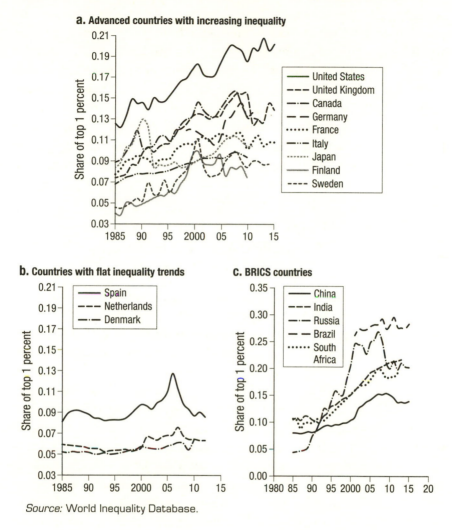

a. Advanced countries with increasing inequality

b. Countries with flat inequality trends

C. BRICS countries

Source: World Inequality Database.

Figure 5.2c for emerging countries shows similarity in the evolution of inequality for China and Russia (increase and stabilization) and India (continuous since the mid-1990s). Unlike with the survey Gini, however, it illustrates a continuous increase for South Africa—although it is not clear that data are fully homogeneous over time—and constancy for Brazil, instead of the sharp drop depicted in figure 5.1d.[6]

[6] A working paper by Marc Morgan (2017) tries to piece together the two sources—a difficult task for the reasons expressed above. Morgan finds that merging top incomes

Another dimension of inequality not considered here for lack of space is individual labor earnings. There too, scrutiny of the available data points to some diversity across countries.[7] Earnings inequality as measured by the ratio of the ninetieth percentile to the median increased substantially and continuously in the United States, and until the early 2000s in the United Kingdom. This ratio, however, remained rather stable in other countries, including the other G7 countries. At the bottom of the earnings distribution, on the other hand, the ratio of the median to the tenth percentile was uniformly stable among almost all advanced countries, except in the case of Germany, where it increased noticeably in the first half of the 2000s.

CAUSES FOR CHANGES IN INEQUALITY: GLOBALIZATION AND TECHNOLOGY CHANGE OR POLICIES?

Heavy emphasis has fallen lately on the role of globalization in exacerbating inequality in advanced countries as well as the impact of technical change around the world. Basic intuition and simple economic theory indeed suggest that Asia's upsurge in global trade, combined with skill-biased technical change, led to substitution of Asian low-wage workers, machines, and algorithms for low- and, more recently, medium-skill labor elsewhere, thus hurting those in the lower part of the earnings and income distribution in other regions. Also, because globalization has been associated with extensive geographic reallocation of economic activity across national borders aimed at reducing labor costs, it tends to benefit the shareholders and managers of global companies at the forefront of the globalization process. Likewise, technical change must have benefited the owners of the hard or soft equipment that substituted labor.

Much has been written on these channels through which globalization and technical change could have directly affected the degree of

---

and survey data leads to no change in the Gini coefficient. Yet the survey-tax data merging methodology is far from mastered, so this result must be taken with a grain of salt. Following the heuristic approach underlined above, the best that can be said is that the drop in inequality has been less pronounced than indicated by the survey data.

[7] The available numbers are essentially OECD and International Labor Organization data for full-time employees.

inequality. Yet empirical evidence of such effects has been more difficult to amass. The search for such evidence has largely focused on the United States, in part because of the early and pronounced increase in inequality observed there. In the 1990s, work based on a simple Heckscher-Ohlin trade model with skilled and unskilled labor as the two factors of production found a minor role for the increase in manufacturing imports from developing countries. The bulk of the increase in inequality was thus attributed to technical change, as a kind of unexplained residual of the analysis. More recently, David Autor, David Dorn, and Gordon Hanson (2013) found a more substantial effect by looking at employment and wages in local markets that were more exposed to Chinese competition. But some even more recent work seems to be challenging this finding (see Lu and Hufbauer 2017). Perhaps globalization has had a larger impact on inequality by raising the share of capital income (see IMF 2017b), but it would be difficult to disentangle that role from technical progress or other pressures on wages, like de-unionization or the slow progress of real minimum wages.

Overall, my reading of the evidence on the role of trade growth in increasing economy-wide inequality in the United States is that trade's effects have been limited (see also chapters by Anne Krueger and Laura Tyson as well as the more nuanced view in Paul Krugman's chapter in this volume distinguishing between trade developments before and after the turn of the millennium). A leading role for trade is no more plausible for other advanced countries, in the first place because inequality has not increased as much and as continuously as in the United States. To the extent that many countries have been exposed to the same competition from the emerging world, simple reasoning would suggest that the absence of a clear unequalizing trend in most of them might be evidence that globalization indeed played a minor role in the rise of inequality in the United States, or that other countries were able to voluntarily or involuntarily neutralize its effects. I would argue that the same may be true regarding the distributional effect of technical change (see Tyson's chapter in this volume and references therein).

Evidence on increasing skill premiums due to skill-biased technical change in the United States has been largely documented. Evidence on European countries since 1995 seems to be in the opposite direction, except in the United Kingdom (see Crivellaro 2014). This is consistent with the evidence mentioned above about labor earnings inequality, and may reflect a different evolution of the relative supply and demand of skills in the various countries as well as possibly more wage rigidity in continental Europe.

One may also wonder whether the relative constancy of earnings inequality in Europe is consistent with the job polarization that is thought to be induced by technological change. Maarten Goos and Alan Manning (2007) and Autor and Dorn (2013) have shown how the relative demand for labor was diminishing for intermediate occupations in the middle-wage range respectively in the United Kingdom and United States. Goos, Manning, and Anna Salomons (2014) demonstrated that this was the case for most continental European countries. Here too, however, the impact on earnings inequality is ambiguous. It depends on the way that wages will react to changes in both the supply and demand side of the labor market, or are institutionally constrained. It should be also noted that the standard ninetieth/fiftieth and fiftieth/tenth percentile ratios used to describe the inequality of earnings may not be well adapted to grasp the effect of polarization, as much depends on how the median changes. A finer analysis of the earnings distribution is needed.

What stands out as far more apparent in shaping the evolution of inequality of equivalized incomes in those countries where it has significantly increased over the last thirty years is that as mentioned earlier, the increase is limited in time; and more important, its main causes are readily apparent, consisting most often of reforms in the government redistribution system. This can be more readily seen by focusing on the cases of the European countries included in figures 5.1 and 5.2, which I discuss next.[8]

In the case of the United Kingdom, most of the increase in inequality over the last thirty years took place during the 1980s, clearly as the result of the Thatcherian reforms of the tax and benefits systems as well as the assaults on the unions. Reforms comprised many measures, from cutting the income tax—and compensating the revenue loss by indirect taxation—to reducing unemployment compensation and other welfare payments, to fighting union power (see Glennester 2004). The rise in

---

[8] The analysis would be similar in the case of Canada. See Green, Riddell, and St-Hilaire 2016.

the German Gini coefficient of equivalized income was concentrated in the early 2000s, and can be associated in part with the Hartz reforms of the labor market and unemployment compensation system. There indeed seems to be an agreement that this reform meant to make the labor market more flexible and strengthen labor incentives ended up making those who remained unemployed worse off, and increased the number of "working poor" through so-called micro jobs (see Burda and Seele 2016).[9] In Italy, the rise in inequality was concentrated in the early 1990s, and associated with the abolition of wage indexation and centralized wage bargaining (Fiorio 2011). In Finland, inequality rose mostly in the second half of the 1990s, after the economy was liberalized following a deep crisis in the early 1990s. This process included a reform of the tax system that lowered the marginal tax rate on capital income from 63 to 25 percent, plus cuts in the welfare system (Riihelä, Sullström, and Tuomala 2002).

Regarding the two European countries with a rising trend in figure 5.1a, Denmark and Sweden, reforms in the redistribution system have played an important role in generating more inequality, even though in both countries, inequality remains in the bottom range of the international distribution among developed countries. In Sweden, reforms followed the severe economic crisis that hit the country in 1992–93. They comprised a long sequence of measures to strengthen economic incentives at the cost of more inequality. These included tax reforms leading to lower marginal tax rates on income, the introduction of a dual taxation system for labor and capital income, the abolition of the wealth and inheritance taxes, a lowering of illness insurance compensation, the decentralization of wage bargaining, and less generous unemployment insurance.[10] Unlike in the Swedish case, detail is unfortunately not available to explain the rise in inequality in Denmark, though it seems clear that tax reforms and changes in the social insurance system have certainly played a role. In fact, the main evidence about the role of redistribution comes from comparing the degree of inequality of market incomes with that of disposable incomes (Neamtu and Westergaard-Nielsen 2012, 7). The former

[9] Other explanations have also been suggested. See IMF 2017a.

[10] For a general account of these reforms, see Freeman, Swedenborg, and Topel 2010.

increased somewhat in the late 1990s and has remained flat ever since then (figure 5.2b), whereas the latter increased slowly and continuously from the mid-1990s on (figure 5.2a). This difference is clearly attributable to the redistribution system. Indeed both series are based on the same data, and the main difference between them is the definition of income.

In summary, when inequality rose in European countries, it did so most often during a limited time, and was associated with specific reforms of the redistribution system and labor market. This seems true even of the two countries where inequality was subject to a rising trend. This finding does not necessarily imply, however, that other factors affecting inequality were not also present. In every country, researchers have shown that various "structural" factors were at play too, such as aging and the increase in the proportion of pensioners, increasing female labor force participation, changes in the return to schooling, assortative mating, and so on. Does this mean that the common international forces for more inequality invoked to explain the rising inequality in the United States were not present on the European side? Probably not. Market income inequality as represented by the top 1 percent income share has been increasing rapidly in a majority of countries at least until the turn of the millennium, sometimes irrespective of policy reforms. Also, some researchers have found in the evolution of the inequality of earnings in Europe mechanisms quite similar to those observed in the United States.[11]

In the United States too, there have been various tax reforms during the period under analysis, most notably the 1986 reform as well as later changes in cash transfers and the earned income tax credit. Deunionization may have also played a role. Yet analysts seem to agree that the impact of these factors on inequality has been limited and can certainly not explain all the increase in equivalized income inequality (see, for example, Blank 2011, 158–63). The available data on equivalized incomes do not permit precise measurement of inequality before and after taxes and transfers, so it is hard to evaluate exactly the aggregate impact of changes in government redistribution. There seems, however, to be a consensus on imputing a large part of the increase in

[11] As, for instance, in Germany (see Burda and Seele 2016; Dustmann, Ludsteck, and Uta Schönberg 2009; Card, Heining, and Kline 2013) or Sweden (see Freeman, Swedenborg, and Topel 2010).

inequality to technical change and, as seen above, to a much lesser extent globalization. In any case, the difference between the evolution in the United States and Europe remains striking, as European countries, and probably emerging ones, were subject to the same globalization and technological shocks as the United States.

Two possible explanations of the US-Europe difference seem plausible. First, more than in the United States, labor market and redistribution institutions in Europe have been able to compensate for the global factors driving inequality. This compensation may have been mediated through labor market regulations—especially binding minimum wages in several countries—more active labor market policies, better unemployment compensation, or higher tax rates on high incomes. Other country-specific structural changes may also have contributed to that result, even though they would have to be clearly identified. Second, changes in redistribution or labor market regulation that have been found to be responsible for the observed increase in inequality may have been coincident with changes linked to technical change or globalization, making it difficult to disentangle one effect from the other.

What is clearly missing to more precisely discern the roles of globalization and technical change in the evolution of inequality is a thorough decomposition analysis of those changes—one that would account for all observed causes of changes in inequality. Existing work in that direction is extremely partial and concentrates only on specific aspects of inequality.

Finally, as far as the distributional impact of globalization is concerned, one qualification must be made to the foregoing discussion emphasizing the role of policy reforms. It is possible, and indeed likely, that some of the reforms undertaken in European countries to strengthen incentives, despite their impact on inequality, were themselves caused by globalization as well as the need to lower production costs and boost the international competitiveness of domestic firms. If so, the impact of globalization would thus be indirect, working through the policy channel. Many reforms have certainly been justified by this kind of argument. But in some cases, attributing to globalization the need for reforms without which a country's public finances and levels of unemployment would become economically and socially unsustainable may just be another expression of political rhetoric.

CONCLUSION

Two main points can be drawn from the evidence reviewed above on changes in income inequality in advanced countries and their possible causes.

First, it is simply not true that inequality is on a three-decade rising trend everywhere. Evidence based on equivalized disposable income, as observed in household surveys, shows this is true only for a few countries. In other countries, inequality has often increased over the past thirty years, but only during limited spans of time. Evidence based on the top 1 percent income shares, estimated from income tax data, show a more uniform increase in market income inequality with fewer exceptions. The increase, however, seems most frequently concentrated in the late 1980s and 1990s.

Second, evidence that the main cause of increased inequality is globalization and technical change is not compelling. Even though it is difficult to make the distinction between the two factors, the evidence seems stronger when considering the rising inequality trend in the United States. It is much weaker in other countries, where inequality changes seem to be explained by policy reforms. Is it the case that household survey data miss top incomes, which were the main beneficiaries of globalization and technical change? Then the rather-widespread global increase in the top 1 percent income share could provide evidence of common forces affecting inequality across countries. But in that case, why are there exceptions, and why would the rising trend disappear in the 2000s?

If it is difficult to find rigorous empirical evidence of the unequalizing roles of globalization and technical change, why is it so obvious in the public opinion of some countries that these factors are responsible for mounting inequality everywhere? Is this opinion based on the relative gain of top incomes over the long run, the feeling of increasing international constraints on national policies, growing skill gaps and job polarization, or the slowdown in the long-run pace of growth—all of which exacerbate the perception of inequality? Or is it the case that income inequality, which is the focus of the economic analysis of inequality, is only one of the various dimensions of inequality that the public opinion takes into account? Inequality in job tenure prospects, medium-run opportunities, and uncertainty about one's children's future also are among voters' major concerns. Most of these dimensions of inequality are difficult to measure, but they may be the source of the frustration recently expressed through the political system in several countries. This is an important area for future research in the economics of inequality.

REFERENCES

Atkinson, Anthony B. 1997. "Bringing Income Distribution in from the Cold." *Economic Journal, Royal Economic Society* 107, no. 441 (March): 297–321.

Autor, David H., and David Dorn. 2013. "The Growth of Low-Skill Service Jobs and the Polarization of the US Labor Market." *American Economic Review* 103, no. 5 (August): 1553–97.

Autor, David H., David Dorn, and Gordon H. Hanson. 2013. "The China Syndrome: Local Labor Market Effects of Import Competition in the United States." *American Economic Review* 103, no. 6 (October): 2121–68.

Blank, Rebecca M. 2011. *Changing Inequality.* Berkeley: University of California Press.

Burda, Michael, and Stefanie Seele. 2016. "No Role for the Hartz Reforms? Demand and Supply Factors in the German Labor Market, 1993–2014." SFB 649 Discussion Paper 2016-10. Berlin: Humboldt-Universität zu Berlin.

Card, David, Jörg Heining, and Patrick Kline. 2013. "Workplace Heterogeneity and the Rise of West German Wage Inequality." *Quarterly Journal of Economics* 128, no. 3 (August): 967–1015.

Crivellaro, Elena. 2014. "College Wage Premium over Time: Trends in Europe in the Last 15 Years." Department of Economics Working Paper 03/WP/2014. Venice: Ca' Foscari University of Venice.

Dustmann, Christian, Johannes Ludsteck, and Uta Schönberg. 2009. "Revisiting the German Wage Structure." *Quarterly Journal of Economics* 124, no. 2 (May): 843–81.

Fiorio, Carlo V. 2011. "Understanding Italian Inequality Trends: A Simulation-Based Decomposition."*Oxford Bulletin of Economics and Statistics* 73, no. 2 (April): 255–75.

Freeman, Richard B., Birgitta Swedenborg, and Robert H. Topel. 2010. "Introduction." In *Reforming the Welfare State: Recovery and Beyond in Sweden,* edited by Richard B. Freeman, Birgitta Swedenborg, and Robert H. Topel, 1–24. Chicago: University of Chicago Press.

Glennester, Howard. 2004. "Mrs Thatcher's Legacy: Getting It in Perspective." *Social Policy Review* 16: 231–50.

Goos, Maarten, and Alan Manning. 2007. "Lousy and Lovely Jobs: The Rising Polarization of Work in Britain." *Review of Economics and Statistics* 89, no. 1 (February): 118–33.

Goos, Maarten, Alan Manning, and Anna Salomons. 2014. "Explaining Job Polarization: Routine-Biased Technological Change and Offshoring." *American Economic Review* 104, no. 8 (August): 2509–26.

Green, David, W. Craig Riddell, and France St-Hilaire. 2016. "Income Inequality in Canada: Driving Forces, Outcomes and Policy." In *Income Inequality: The Cana-*

dian Story, edited by David Green, W. Craig Riddell, and France St-Hilaire, 1–73. Montreal: Institute for Research on Public Policy.

International Monetary Fund (IMF). 2017a. "Germany: Selected Issues." IMF Country Report 17/193. Washington, DC: International Monetary Fund.

———. 2017b. "Understanding the Downward Trend in Labour Income Shares." In *World Economic Outlook*, chapter 3. Washington, DC: International Monetary Fund.

Lu, Zhiyao, and Gary Clyde Hufbauer. 2017. "Has Global Trade Fueled US Wage Inequality? A Survey of Experts." Policy brief. Washington, DC: Peterson Institute for International Economics.

Morgan, Marc. 2017. "Extreme and Persistent Inequality: New Evidence for Brazil Combining National Accounts, Surveys and Fiscal Data, 2001–2015." WID.world Working Paper 2017/12. Paris: World Inequality Lab.

Neamtu, Ioana, and Niels Westergaard-Nielsen. 2012. "How Are Firms Affected by the Crisis and How Do They React?" Economics Working Paper 2012-11. Aarhus, Denmark: Aarhus University, Department of Economics and Business Economics.

OECD (Organization of Economic Cooperation and Development). 2011. *Divided We Stand: Why Inequality Keeps Rising*. Paris: Organization for Economic Cooperation and Development.

Riihelä, Marja, Risto Sullström, and Matti Tuomala. 2001. "What Lies Behind the Unprecedented Increase in Income Inequality in Finland during the 1990s." Working Paper 0102. Tampere: University of Tampere, School of Management.

PART III

GLOBALIZATION, DEINDUSTRIALIZATION, AND LABOR MARKET ADJUSTMENT

6

Globalization: What Did We Miss?

PAUL KRUGMAN

Concerns about possible adverse effects from globalization aren't new. In particular, as US income inequality began rising in the 1980s, many commentators were quick to link this new phenomenon to another new phenomenon: the rise of manufactured exports from a group of newly industrializing economies.

Economists—trade economists, anyway—took these concerns seriously. After all, standard models of international trade do say that trade can have large effects on income distribution: the famous 1941 Stolper-Samuelson analysis of a two-good, two-factor economy showed how trading with a labor-abundant economy can reduce real wages, even if national income grows. There was every reason to believe that the same principle applied to the emergence of trade with low-wage economies exporting not raw materials but rather manufactured goods.

And so during the 1990s, a number of economists, myself included (Krugman 1995), tried to assess the role of Stolper-Samuelson-type effects in rising inequality. Inevitably given the standard framework, such analyses did in fact find some depressing effects of the growing trade on the wages of less educated workers in advanced countries. As a quantitative matter, however, they generally suggested that the effect was relatively modest and not the central factor in the widening income gap.

Meanwhile, the political salience of globalization seemed to decline as other issues came to the fore. So academic interest in the possible adverse effects of trade, while it never went away, waned.

In the past few years, however, worries about globalization have shot back to the top of the agenda, partly due to new research, and partly due to the political shocks of Brexit and Trump. And as one of the people who helped shape the 1990s' consensus—that the income distribution effects of rising trade were real but modest—it seems appropriate to ask now what we missed. What aspects of rising trade did we fail to either see at the time or anticipate?

THE 1990S' CONSENSUS

This is a short chapter, not a literature review, so I don't want to go through all the various 1990s' analyses that tried to assess the distributional effects of trade. Instead, let me summarize the methodological and quantitative conclusions that became fairly orthodox by the mid-1990s.

In terms of methodology, there was, for a time, some confusion (and a bit of heated debate) over how to use data on trade to assess wage impacts. Most studies focused on the volume and particularly the factor content of trade—the labor and other resources embodied in exports, and the labor and other resources that would have been required to produce imports. Some economists vehemently objected to this approach, since Stolper-Samuelson is strictly speaking about prices rather than quantities—that is, it's about the relationship between goods prices and factor prices. Yet goods prices are endogenous; when trying to assess the impact of globalization, it made no sense to treat prices as a causal variable.

What eventually emerged from this debate was a "but for" approach: asking how different wages would have been *but for* the rise of manufactured exports from developing countries—increases that were minimal in 1970, but significantly higher by the mid-1990s. It turned out that this approach was also consistent with a factor content calculation: the effect of North-South manufactures trade on advanced economies was, in simple models, equivalent to what would have happened if the OECD had been a closed economy experiencing immigration of less educated workers and emigration of more educated ones corresponding to the factors embodied in the goods being traded.

And the basic fact in the mid-1990s was that imports of manufactured goods from developing countries, while much larger than in the past, were still small relative to the size of advanced economies—around 2 percent of GDP. Given reasonable estimates of factor intensities and elasticities of substitution, this wasn't enough to cause more than a few percent change in relative wages. This number wasn't trivial, but it wasn't big enough to be a central economic story either.

This was a moderately comforting result for free trade advocates. But what did the 1990s' consensus miss?

HYPERGLOBALIZATION

It is, I'd argue, quite possible, and even likely, that assessments of the impact of trade made circa 1995, inevitably relying on data from a couple years earlier, were right in finding modest effects. In retrospect, however, trade flows in the early 1990s were just the start of something much bigger, or what Arvind Subramanian and Martin Kessler (2013) have dubbed "hyperglobalization."

Until the 1980s, it was arguable that the growth of world trade since World War II had mainly reflected a dismantling of the trade barriers erected during the interwar period; world trade as a share of world GDP was only slightly higher than it had been in 1913. Over the next two decades, however, both the volume and nature of trade moved into uncharted territory.

Figure 6.1 shows one indicator of this change: manufactured exports from developing countries, measured as a share of world GDP. As you can see, what seemed in the early 1990s like a major disturbance in the trade force was just the beginning.

What caused this huge surge in what was, in the 1990s, still a fairly novel form of trade? The answer probably includes a combination of technology and policy. Freight containerization was not exactly a new technology, but it took time for businesses to realize how the reduction in transshipping costs made it possible to break up value chains, moving labor-intensive parts of the production process overseas. Meanwhile, there was a broad move away from import-substituting industrialization toward outward-looking policies, and of course China made a dramatic shift from central planning to a market economy focused on exports.

Since manufactured exports from developing countries, measured as a share of the world economy, are now triple what they were in the

Figure 6.1. Developing Country Exports of Manufactured Goods as Percent of World GDP

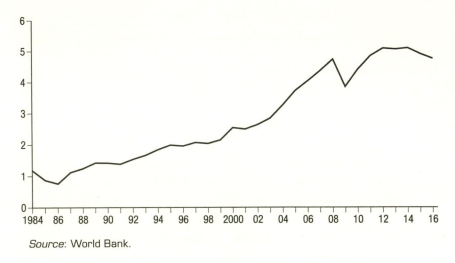

Source: World Bank.

mid-1990s, should we conclude that the effect on income distribution has also tripled? Probably not, for at least two reasons.

First, a significant part of the increase in developing country exports reflects the rapid growth of South-South trade, which is an important story, but not relevant to the impacts on advanced country workers. Even more important, though, the nature of this trade growth—involving a breaking up of the value chain—means that the factor content of North-South trade hasn't risen nearly as fast as the volume.

Consider two cases: imports of apparel from Bangladesh and imports of iPhones from China. In the first instance, we are in effect importing the services of less educated workers, putting downward pressure on the demand for such workers in the United States. In the second case, most of the value of the iPhone reflects inputs from high-wage, high-education countries like Japan; we are in effect importing skilled as well as unskilled labor, so the impact on income distribution should be much smaller.

Despite these qualifications, it's clear that the impact of developing country exports grew much more between 1995 and 2010 than the 1990s' consensus imagined possible, which may be one reason concerns about globalization made a comeback.

Figure 6.2. U.S. Nonoil Trade Balance and Manufacturing Employment

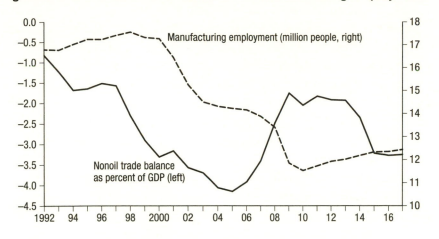

Sources: US Bureau of Economic Analysis; US Bureau of Labor Statistics.

TRADE IMBALANCES

One major contrast between most economic analyses of globalization's impact and those of the broader public—including, of course, Trump—is the focus, or lack thereof, on trade imbalances. The public tends to see trade surpluses or deficits as determining winners and losers; the general equilibrium trade models that underlay the 1990s' consensus gave no role to trade imbalances at all.

The economists' approach is almost certainly right for the long run, both because countries must pay their way eventually, and because trade imbalances mainly affect the relative shares of traded and non-traded sectors in employment, with no clear effect on the overall demand for labor. Yet in the long run we are all dead, and rapid changes in trade balances can cause serious problems of adjustment—a broader theme that I'll return to shortly.

Consider, in particular, the developments shown in figure 6.2, which compares the US nonoil trade balance (which is overwhelmingly manufactured goods) with US manufacturing employment.

Until the late 1990s, employment in manufacturing, although steadily falling as a share of the total employment, had remained more or less flat in absolute terms. But manufacturing employment fell off a cliff after 2000, and this decline corresponded to a sharp increase in the nonoil deficit of around 2.5 percent of GDP.

Does the surge in the trade deficit explain the fall in employment? Yes, to a significant extent. A trade deficit doesn't produce a one-for-one decline in manufacturing value added, since a significant share of both exports and imports of goods includes embodied services. But a reasonable estimate is that the deficit surge reduced the share of manufacturing in GDP by around 1.5 percentage points, or more than 10 percent, which means that it explains more than half of the roughly 20 percent decline in manufacturing employment between 1997 and 2005.

Again, this is over a relatively short time period and focuses on absolute employment, not the employment share. Trade deficits explain only a small part of the long-term shift toward a service economy. But soaring imports did impose a significant shock on some US workers, which may have helped cause the globalization backlash.

And surging trade deficits due to such things as the Asian financial crisis and its aftermath are, as I said, part of a broader story of adjustment issues.

RAPID GLOBALIZATION AND DISRUPTION

When trade theorists talk about the distributional effects of trade, they tend to use one of two models (or classes of models). Heckscher-Ohlin models treat factors of production as fungible across industries, so that possible adverse effects involve broad classes of workers, such as workers without college. Specific-factor models, by contrast, treat factors—definitely capital, but perhaps labor as well—as being stuck in particular industries.

It's possible, and probably even correct, to think of specific factors as representing the short run while Heckscher-Ohlin represents the long run. How long is the long run? Good question.

The 1990s' consensus, however, focused almost entirely on Heckscher-Ohlin-type analysis, asking how the growth of trade had affected the incomes of broad labor classes, as opposed to workers in particular industries and communities. This was, I now believe, a major mistake—one in which I shared a hand.

The thing is, anyone who worked on the political economy of trade policy knew that fights over tariffs look very much as if they come out of a specific-factors world: labor and capital within a given industry are generally on the same side in trade policy disputes, not on opposite sides as they would be if they were thinking about the broad factoral distribution of income. It should have been obvious that the general politics of globalization would reflect that same reality.

That is, never mind the question of how trade affects the blue-collar/white-collar wage gap or aggregate Gini coefficient; the politics of globalization were likely to be much more influenced by the experience of individual sectors that gained or lost from shifting trade flows.

This is where the now-famous analysis of the "China shock" by David Autor, David Dorn, and Gordon Hanson (2013) comes in (see also Hanson's chapter in this volume). What they mainly did was to shift focus from broad questions of income distribution to the effects of rapid import growth on local labor markets, showing that these effects were large and persistent. This represented a new and important insight.

To make partial excuses for those of us who failed to consider these issues twenty-five years ago, at the time we had no way of knowing that either the hyperglobalization shown in figure 6.1 or the trade deficit surge shown in figure 6.2 were going to happen. And without the combination of these developments, the China shock would have been much smaller. Still, we missed a crucial part of the story.

A CASE FOR PROTECTIONISM?

What did the 1990s' consensus that the adverse effects of globalization were modest miss? A lot. Developing country exports of manufactures grew far beyond their level at the time that consensus emerged. The combination of this rapid growth and surging trade imbalances meant that globalization produced far more disruption and cost for some workers than the consensus had envisaged.

So does this mean that—not to put too fine a point on it—Trump is right and a trade war would be in the interests of workers hurt by globalization?

The answer is, as you might guess, no. This answer is based not so much on some rigid commitment to free trade at all costs as on the nature of the losses that globalization imposed. Basically, the big problem with surging globalization wasn't so much changing demand for broadly defined factors of production, as the disruption was caused by rapid change. And that rapid change appears to be largely behind us: many indicators suggest that hyperglobalization was a onetime event, and trade has more or less stabilized relative to world GDP. You can even see that leveling off in figure 6.1.

As a result, major disruptions now would be more likely to come from an attempt to reverse globalization than from leaving the current trade regime in place. At this point, millions of decisions about where to put plants, and where to move and take jobs, have been made on the assumption that the open world trading system will continue. Making that assumption false, by raising tariffs and forcing a contraction of world trade, would force a whole new wave of disruption along with a whole new set of winners and losers.

So while the 1990s' consensus on the effects of globalization hasn't stood the test of time very well, one can acknowledge that fact without accepting the case for protectionism now. We might have done things differently if we had known what was coming, but that's not a good reason to try turning back the clock.

REFERENCES

Autor, David H., David Dorn, and Gordon H. Hanson. 2013. "The China Syndrome: Local Labor Market Effects of Import Competition in the United States." *American Economic Review* 103, no. 6 (October): 2121–68.

Krugman, Paul. 1995. "Growing World Trade: Causes and Consequences." *Brookings Papers on Economic Activity*, 1: 327–62. Washington, DC: Brookings Institution.

Subramanian, Arvind, and Martin Kessler. 2013. "The Hyperglobalization of Trade and Its Future." Working Paper 13-6. Washington, DC: Peterson Institute for International Economics.

Economic and Political Consequences of Trade-Induced Manufacturing Decline

GORDON H. HANSON

This chapter presents an overview of recent research on the impact of international trade on the US labor market. It draws on a series of papers by David Autor that I coauthored (Autor, Dorn, and Hanson 2013, 2016; Autor et al. 2014), where we examine the labor market and sociopolitical effects of the dramatic increase in global trade with China, following the latter's transition from a centrally planned economy to a market economy. We identify such effects by exploiting the sharp variation in US regional exposure to what we call the "China trade shock" resulting from the long-standing regional differences in industrial specialization in the United States.

Our empirical approach is by no means the first to use regional economies as laboratories in which to analyze the wider labor market consequences of exposure to international trade.

George Borjas and Valerie Ramey (1995) pioneered this approach in examining the consequences of expanded US trade with Japan, while Petia Topalova (2010) and Brian Kovak (2013) consider regional exposure to trade liberalization in India and Brazil, respectively. What makes the China trade shock distinct is the scale of China's economy, magnitude of its export boom, and overwhelming comparative advantage in labor-intensive manufacturing products, many of which were made in the United States.

The motivation for understanding the labor market impacts of trade shocks—and the China shock in particular—has been intensified by the election of a US president who is not only skeptical about the benefits of international trade and several landmark US trade agreements but also prepared to threaten a broad range of trading partners with tariffs, risking widespread disruption to the world trading system. Whatever one's politics, it is important to comprehend how we arrived at a moment in which the long-standing US embrace of openness to trade has come into question.

To understand how we got here, think back twenty-five years to a time when there was greater optimism about the potential for globalization to deliver a shared prosperity. That optimism led policy makers to tout trade liberalization—in the United States, via signing NAFTA, endorsing the Uruguay Round of global trade talks, and approving China's membership in the WTO—as a means to raise national living standards. Today, the discussion is much less about how China has improved material well-being in the United States and much more about how China has hollowed out the US manufacturing sector. Our collective surprise in arriving at this juncture has raised questions about the traditional US stance toward trade.

How did we get to this point? Consider the standard textbook characterization of the Stolper-Samuelson theorem, which indicates how an event like the China shock would affect US labor markets through the lens of standard trade theory. In response to trade liberalization in a less skilled yet labor-abundant country (China), a skill-abundant economy (the United States) would experience an increase in the wage of more skilled workers relative to the wage of less skilled ones. Yet this is not really the outcome that we've observed. As we progressed through the 1990s, there was a strong sense that globalization hadn't mattered much for the US wage structure (Katz and Autor 1999; Krugman's chapter in this volume). There was a further belief that in response to trade shocks, workers would easily reallocate across sectors and regions, such that the impacts of a trade shock would be distributed widely across low-skilled workers in the US economy. Our work (Autor, Dorn, and Hanson 2103, 2016), along with that of many other scholars, has helped overturn this conventional wisdom.

Today, we have come to appreciate that trade has contributed to the decline in US manufacturing employment (Acemoglu et al. 2016; Pierce and Schott 2016). The impact of trade on labor markets comes less from its economy-wide impacts than from its disruptive effects on particular regions. If we examine US regions that have been maximally exposed to the China trade shock—including communities in the Midwest and Southeast—we see substantial declines in manufacturing employment. Such impacts may not be surprising in light of China's strong comparative advantage in labor-intensive manufacturing. What is surprising is how little these regions have adjusted to job loss. If manufacturing jobs are lost in, say, Middletown, Ohio, we would expect workers to leave the region to find work elsewhere or firms to be attracted to the region to hire the newly available labor. What we have seen instead is that workers have not moved away from Middletown, nor have new firms arrived. Some displaced workers have ended up among the long-run unemployed, while others have exited the labor force entirely. Few workers have succeeded in moving into nontraded activities. In fact, employment in nontraded activities in these locations fell modestly, although the trade impact on nontraded employment is not precisely estimated. Job loss was especially acute for less educated workers, where the magnitudes of employment decline in manufacturing were nearly matched by the magnitude of employment decline in nonmanufacturing activities. The China trade shock thus was similar to a negative local aggregate demand shock, the local impacts of which were magnified as the shock was transmitted to nontraded goods and services.

To gain further perspective on the labor impacts of the China trade shock we shift the focus from comparing outcomes across regions to comparing outcomes across workers (Autor et al. 2014). Suppose we go back to 1991 and consider two workers who are identical in every observable respect—age, gender, current earnings, recent earnings growth, size and average pay of their employer, and years of tenure at their employer—except one, which is their industry of employment. Let's compare groups of similar workers where some work in industries that are hit by the China trade shock and others work in industries that are not directly affected by the shock. For purposes of illustration, we will define a trade-exposed worker to be one whose industry is in the seventy-fifth percentile in terms of the increase in import penetration by China and a nontrade-exposed worker to be one whose industry is in the twenty-fifth percentile in the increase in import penetration by China.

Considering outcomes for these two types of workers over the sixteen years following 1991, we see that more trade-exposed workers have cumulative income that is approximately 16 percent lower than that of less trade-exposed workers. These more exposed workers are more likely to separate from their initial employer (i.e., their employer in 1991), and then suffer a drop in earnings at their initial employer and lower earnings at subsequent employers in later years. Across the board, the more exposed workers see inferior labor market outcomes.

These differential outcomes for more and less trade-exposed workers are not uniform across the distribution of earnings. Among more and less trade-exposed workers who have high initial earnings (workers in the top tercile of wage earnings in their birth cohort), there are few differences in cumulative earnings after 1991. Among high-wage earners, those more exposed to trade are more likely to leave their initial employer and undergo churning across employers. Yet while they lose some earnings up front, they tend to recoup them in later jobs that they take up among employers who are less exposed to foreign trade. The adverse consequences of trade on earnings are thus overwhelmingly concentrated among low-wage workers (those in the bottom tercile of earners in their birth cohort in 1991).

Why are the impacts of trade on earnings so concentrated by industry and skill level? To answer this question, consider the regional dimension of the China trade shock. Because manufacturing regions tend to be rather narrowly specialized, an adverse trade shock has impacts that are equivalent to a regional recession. Research by Steven Davis and Till von Wachter (2011) shows that the impacts of job loss, which since the work of Louis Jacobson, Robert LaLonde, and Daniel Sullivan (1993) we have known leads to large short-run and smaller long-run reductions in earnings, are much worse when job loss occurs during recessions. Because the impact of the China shock is like a regional recession, the consequences of trade-induced job loss for earnings are particularly acute.

If job loss from the China shock has such deleterious effects on exposed workers, why are its economy-wide impacts on earnings not larger? The reason is that manufacturing accounts for a small share of US employment—less that 14 percent even at the beginning of the China shock. Recent work on the general equilibrium consequences of US trade with China uses quantitative trade models, calibrated based on empirical work (Caliendo, Dvorkin, and Parro 2015; Galle, Rodríguez-Clare, and Yi 2015). This literature shows that on net, trade with China has positive effects on US national welfare, although these effects are small, consistent with the overall small gains from trade for the US economy (Arkolakis, Costinot, and Rodríguez-Clare 2012). Whereas we have not learned much new from the China shock in terms of the aggregate impacts of trade, we have learned that trade-induced manufacturing decline has concentrated disruptive effects on specific types of workers, particularly those with lower wages residing in regions specialized in labor-intensive manufacturing.

Another important lesson from the China trade shock concerns the role of government programs in mitigating the impacts of job loss (Autor, Dorn, and Hanson 2013). Overall, these programs offset no more than 10 percent of trade-induced declines in income. Perhaps surprisingly, few of these benefits come through the Trade Adjustment Assistance (TAA) program, the primary US government program designed to help workers who have lost their jobs because of import competition. Of the sixty dollars in extra per capita benefits that a more trade-impacted region (one in the seventy-fifth percentile of trade exposure) receives relative to a less trade-impacted region (one in the twenty-fifth percentile of trade exposure), only three cents came from TAA. Stunningly, the increase in uptake of Social Security Disability Insurance resulting from the trade shock was three hundred times larger than that from TAA. Because workers who take up Social Security Disability Insurance tend to stay on the program for the rest of their working lives, the policy mechanisms that have helped workers adjust to the China shock appear to be ones that effectively induce workers to stay out of the labor market. To a first approximation, the primary policies that workers are using to adjust to trade shocks may be hindering their ability to reenter the labor force.

I turn now to the question with which I began this discussion, which is the political consequences of trade-induced manufacturing decline. In recent work, my coauthors and I have exploited regional variation in exposure to the China shock to examine whether trade-induced declines in manufacturing employment have had a role in the increase in political polarization that has occurred in the United States over the past several decades (Autor et al. 2017). Because the process of polarization began in the 1970s, we know that trade with China cannot be its primary cause. We examine a narrower time window, from the year 2000 forward, during which polarization has progressed and right-wing groups affiliated with the Tea Party movement have risen in prominence.

When we compare regions that are more versus less exposed to trade with China, we see that more exposed regions are more likely to elect right-wing congressional legislators. These results hold for the period 2002–10, and are unaffected by adding controls for initial regional demographic, economic, and political conditions. One might ask whether this rightward shift is part of a secular conservative trend such that any shock that contributes to turnover among legislators would induce a net movement to the right in terms of elected representatives. To address this concern over secular shifts, we separate regions according to potential sources of heterogeneity in political responses to economic shocks. Following the political science literature, we separate congressional districts by whether they were initially in Republican or Democratic hands. And following the political economy literature, which emphasizes the role of ethnic and racial fractionalization in political conflict, we separate regions by whether whites accounted for an initial majority or minority of residents. Either separation reveals a polarized response to trade shocks in terms of the type of legislators they put in office. In majority-white regions, an adverse trade shock induces a shift toward more conservative congressional representatives, including those associated with the Tea Party. In majority-nonwhite areas, an adverse trade shock induces a shift toward more left-wing elected legislators. These findings suggest our results on trade shocks contributing to political polarization are not the result of a secular shift toward conservative candidates. Rather, they indicate that voters at different ends of the political spectrum respond to economic shocks by moving toward the political extreme to which they are most proximate.

As a further exercise, we examine whether the political response to the China trade shock helps in understanding the rise of right-wing populism—a phenomenon present in both Europe and the United States. To do so, we break apart the change in regional trade exposure due to increased exports by China into components associated with industries initially more intensive in the employment of white males and those initially more intensive in the employment of other types of workers (females and nonwhite males). This separation of workers follows from abundant evidence that support for populist politicians is stronger among less educated white men. We find that the trade-induced rightward shift in the types of legislators who were elected is due entirely to shocks to industries that are relatively intensive in the employment of white men. Adverse trade shocks to industries that are relatively intensive in the employment of nonwhite men have no impact on the type of legislators who are elected.

To close, I will mention why job loss in manufacturing has such magnified economic, political, and social impacts. What makes manufacturing special is that it provides less educated men an opportunity to earn relatively high incomes—an opportunity that becomes much more elusive outside that sector. When manufacturing jobs disappear, affected communities therefore can be severely disrupted, with consequences that may tend to unravel the social fabric. Contrary to our expectations a quarter century ago, trade has severely disrupted US communities in which manufacturing employment was concentrated. While it can be argued that the bulk of the employment effects of the China trade shock are now past, their political consequences have proved to be longer lasting. For the reasons discussed above and elsewhere in this volume (see the chapters by Edward Alden and Jeffry Frieden), such consequences may remain with us for many years to come.

REFERENCES

Acemoglu, Daron, David H. Autor, David Dorn, Gordon H. Hanson, and Brendan Price. 2016. "Import Competition and the Great U.S. Employment Sag of the 2000s." *Journal of Labor Economics* 34 (S1): S141–98.

Arkolakis, Costas, Arnaud Costinot, and Andrés Rodríguez-Clare. 2012. "New Trade Models, Same Old Gains?" *American Economic Review* 102, no. 1 (February): 94–130.

Autor, David H., David Dorn, and Gordon H. Hanson. 2013. "The China Syndrome: Local Labor Market Effects of Import Competition in the United States." *American Economic Review*, 103, no. 6 (October): 2121–2168.

———. 2016. "The China Shock: Learning from Labor Market Adjustment to Large Changes in Trade." *Annual Review of Economics* 8, no. 1 (October): 205–40.

Autor, David H., David Dorn, Gordon H. Hanson, and Kaveh Majlesi. 2017. "Importing Political Polarization? The Electoral Consequences of Rising Trade Exposure." Mimeo, University of California at San Diego.

Autor, David H., David Dorn, Gordon H. Hanson, and Jae Song. 2014. "Trade Adjustment: Worker Level Evidence." *Quarterly Journal of Economics* 129, no. 4 (September): 1799–860.

Borjas, George J., and Valerie A. Ramey. 1995. "Foreign Competition, Market Power, and Wage Inequality." *Quarterly Journal of Economics* 110, no. 4 (September): 1075–110.

Caliendo, Lorenzo, Maximilano Dvorkin, and Fernando Parro. 2015. "The Impact of Trade on Labor Market Dynamics." NBER Working Paper 21149. Cambridge, MA: National Bureau of Economic Research.

Galle, Simon, Andrés Rodríguez-Clare, and Moises Yi. 2015. "Slicing the Pie: Quantifying the Aggregate and Distributional Effects of Trade." Mimeo, University of California at Berkeley.

Jacobson, Louis S., Robert LaLonde, and Daniel G. Sullivan. 1993. "Earnings Losses of Displaced Workers." *American Economic Review* 83, no. 4 (September): 685–709.

Katz, Lawrence F., and David Autor H. 1999. "Changes in the Wage Structure and Earnings Inequality." In *Handbook of Labor Economics*, edited by Orley Ashenfelter and David Card, 3A: 1463–555. Amsterdam: Elsevier Science.

Kovak, Brian K. 2013. "Regional Effects of Trade Reform: What Is the Correct Measure of Liberalization?" *American Economic Review* 103, no. 5 (August): 1960–76.

Pierce, Justin R., and Peter K. Schott. 2016. "The Surprisingly Swift Decline of U.S. Manufacturing Employment." *American Economic Review* 106, no. 7 (July): 1632–62.

Topalova, Petia. 2010. "Factor Immobility and Regional Impacts of Trade Liberalization: Evidence on Poverty from India." *American Economic Journal: Applied Economics* 2, no. 4 (October): 1–41.

8

International Trade an Inequality in Developing Economies: Assessing Recent Evidence

NINA PAVCNIK

Economists often emphasize that international trade raises a nation's aggregate welfare while protectionism detracts from it. This mainstream view resonates well with that emanating from global public opinion surveys, according to which trade and business ties with other countries is regarded as a "good thing" by most respondents in all countries surveyed using a common methodology (figure 8.1).[1] Yet both the profession's mainstream view of aggregate trade benefits as well as that of the average citizen have been sitting uncomfortably with the greater prominence of antitrade politics in recent years, especially in the United States and some other advanced countries (see chapters in this volume by Jeffry Frieden, Edward Alden, and Michael Trebilock). This dissonance suggests that the roots of the antitrade backlash lie not so much in misconceptions about *aggregate* gains from international commerce but rather in its distributional consequences. If so, understanding the antitrade backlash requires a closer look at trade's impact on inequality.

---

[1] Figure 8.1 shows the results of a 2014 survey by the Pew Global Attitudes Project, in which individuals across forty-four countries with GDP per capita ranging from $2,000 to $50,000 were asked a simple question: Are global trade and business ties good for their own country?

Figure 8.1. Percentage of Respondents Saying Trade and Business Ties Are Good for Own Country

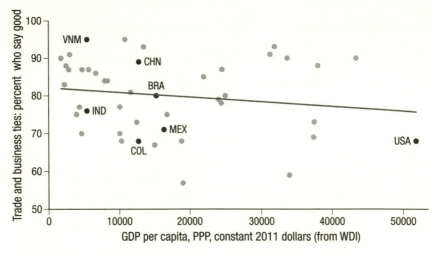

Source: Pavcnik 2017.

Chapter 5 (by François Bourguignon) examined trends in income inequality mostly in advanced countries and potential links with foreign trade exposure. This chapter focuses on emerging markets and developing economies (EMDEs). Drawing on existing surveys (Goldberg and Pavcnik 2007; Goldberg and Pavcnik 2016; Pavcnik 2017), I summarize the key findings of empirical research on trade and inequality in EMDEs, and reviews the evidence on the effectiveness of measures aimed at compensating those left behind by international trade.

Thanks to better data and more extensive research, the past twenty-five years have witnessed significant progress in our understanding of trade's impact on inequality in EMDEs. An overarching finding is that international trade is not, on balance, the main culprit for increased inequality in those countries (Goldberg and Pavcnik 2007; Helpman 2016; Pavcnik 2017). Yet the adverse effects of trade on income equality are much more nuanced than those predicted by traditional trade theory, which in turn had been guiding trade policy prescriptions for EMDEs in the 1980s and 1990s. As I will argue below, the fact that such adverse economic effects are more nuanced does not justify overlooking them because they are nevertheless dramatic and long lasting among the affected populations. Moreover, they can spill over to the educational opportunities and outcomes of the next generation as well as the provision of public goods in the adversely affected communities. Although direct evidence on the effectiveness of compensating those left behind by international trade is scarce, the existing evidence suggests that current redistributive policies have failed to adequately compensate those who lose out.

WHY FOCUS ON POORER COUNTRIES?

Why should one concentrate on trade's effects on inequality in EMDEs? After all, figure 8.1 indicates that if anything, the average EMDE citizen holds an even more favorable view of foreign trade than their advanced country peer. Moreover, recent public discussions and research have mainly focused on trade's contribution to lifting millions out of poverty and raising overall living standards in EMDEs (see IMF/WB/WTO 2017; Anne Krueger's chapter in this volume; Angus Deaton's chapter in this volume)—in turn rationalizing why protectionist calls are mostly visible in high-income countries.

Yet the distributional consequences of trade in EMDEs may simply be less salient currently, in part because these economies have recently experienced faster aggregate growth rates than high-income countries, with absolute living standards rising even for those with relatively low incomes. These differential growth trends will likely continue into the near future, so the backlash may take longer to materialize.[2] Nonetheless, distributional consequences should not be ignored; trade inevitably generates winners and losers, and those hurt by trade will have the incentive to call for greater protection. This effect is likely to become all the more important once economic growth in EMDEs slows down as convergence with high-income countries proceeds. The current backlash against trade in a handful of poorer countries, recently including Argentina, illustrates that a similar temptation to use international trade as a scapegoat and succumb to protectionism could emerge more widely, especially during economic downturns. Indeed, developing countries can revert to protectionism more easily because they face higher tariff bounds within the WTO.

[2] For instance, the IMF (2018) projects current annual growth at approximately 5 percent among emerging economies, or more than double the roughly 2 percent forecast for advanced economies.

WHAT HAVE WE LEARNED ABOUT TRADE AND INEQUALITY IN DEVELOPING COUNTRIES?

As noted above, economists have long known that international trade generates winners and losers, within developing and developed countries alike. Even basic theoretical models that don't consider any frictions in credit or labor markets, such as the Heckscher-Ohlin model, suggest that trade will change the distribution of income. In a simple version of the workhorse Heckscher-Ohlin model, trade is predicted to reduce the real earnings of more educated workers and increase the real earnings of less educated workers in poorer countries, which tend to be relatively more abundantly endowed with less educated workers. This pattern implies that trade is expected to not only generate aggregate gains but also simultaneously reduce inequality and poverty in poorer countries.

These predictions were fundamental to the policy prescriptions about trade liberalization in the 1980s and 1990s. Krueger (2004), the first deputy managing director of the IMF during the early 2000s and a contributor to this volume, stated that one of the key missions of the institution has been to "consistently urge governments to liberalize unilaterally in their own self-interest"—the rationale being that "the benefits of unilateral liberalization overwhelmingly accrue to the country doing the liberalizing." Following the recommendations from institutions such as the IMF and World Bank, many EMDEs implemented policies to lower trade barriers.

The collective evidence from over twenty-five years of studies suggests that increased international trade is not the primary cause of higher wage inequality in developing countries. An extensive literature review reveals a consensus that trade can explain only a fraction of aggregate increases in inequality in EMDEs. This conclusion is reached by surveys focusing on quantitative models of trade (Helpman 2016) as well as empirical studies that have examined the inequality consequences of a broad range of trade liberalization episodes (Goldberg and Pavcnik 2007; Pavcnik 2017).

At the same time, the literature indicates that trade's effects on inequality are context specific and substantially more nuanced than traditional trade theory predictions, which guided trade policy prescriptions in the 1980s and 1990s. More specifically, inequality effects depend on the specifics of the trade policy or trade patterns, transmission mechanisms involved, and degree of mobility of labor and capital across firms, industries, and regions. Trade's effects on inequality therefore do not simply depend on worker education or industry affiliation; an individual's firm affiliation and geographic location also play roles. The lack of mobility is now better known to hinder the process of adjustment to international trade and that barriers to mobility are context specific, meaning that they depend, for instance, on the economic conditions and social norms of the country in question (Pavcnik 2017). Last but not least, the impact on inequality of trade depends not just on the educational attainment of affected individuals but also on their position in the national income distribution. These are the key takeaways from the evidence about trade's impact on inequality in EMDEs that I will discuss and summarize in greater detail now.

UNEQUAL EFFECTS OF TRADE ON WORKERS DEPEND ON WORKERS' FIRM AFFILIATION

Although traditional trade theory emphasized worker education and industry affiliation as shaping trade's impact on inequality, workers' firm affiliation also matters for inequality. Within narrowly defined industries, firms differ in terms of their performance, whether measured by productivity or product quality, and trade can widen the gap between workers employed by better- and worse-performing firms. Why is this the case? To begin with, in the face of increased international trade, better-performing firms are better able to withstand and adjust to import competition. For example, evidence from Naércio Aquino Menezes-Filho and Marc-Andreas Muendler's (2011) study of Brazil indicates that job losses from import competition are mostly concentrated in less productive firms. Besides possessing heightened resilience to import competition, well-performing firms are better positioned to take advantage of exporting opportunities. This adaptability can increase their revenues and translate to pay raises for their workers. Because better-performing firms tend to pay higher wages to begin with, this widens the gap in wage inequality between their workers and observationally equivalent workers in nonexporting firms.

Alongside this increase in interfirm inequality, trade can widen the intrafirm wage gap between more and less educated workers in EMDEs.

For example, exporting opportunities place a premium on skill, which is highly related to worker education. In order to export to consumers in advanced countries—consumers who tend to demand goods of higher quality than those typically produced in poorer countries—exporting firms require high-skilled workers. They are needed, as Eric Verhoogen (2008) and Irene Brambilla, Daniel Lederman, and Guido Porto (2012) explain, not only to produce these goods but also to market and distribute them more efficiently to foreign destinations. Increased export opportunities, especially to high-income country destinations, therefore bring about an increase in labor demand toward high-skilled workers, which is reflected in a corresponding rise in the relative wage of skilled, educated workers.

From the perspective of workers, these firm-specific responses to trade have implications that extend beyond wage inequality. The differences in job characteristics across firms suggest that the workers who might be losing jobs due to import competition may not have the skills that meet the needs of firms in the same industry benefiting from export opportunities. Such a skill mismatch may increase the adjustment costs of trade even within an industry, especially for less educated workers.

THE IMPORTANCE OF THE INFORMAL SECTOR IN EMDEs

While difficult to measure and often neglected in the international trade literature, the informal sector plays an important role in the economies of many EMDEs, employing up to 70 or 80 percent of a country's workforce (La Porta and Shleifer 2014). For example, at the onset of their respective trade liberalization episodes, the informal sector accounted for 80 percent of all manufacturing employment in India, 68 percent in Vietnam, and 30 percent in Brazil. Calculated across all industries, 85 percent of workers in Vietnam and 58 percent in Brazil were employed by informal firms. Individuals employed in the informal sector tend to earn lower income than observationally equivalent individuals in the formal sectors. Consequently, an understanding of how trade affects inequality would not be complete without examining how international trade affects the informal sector. Indeed, the two examples below illustrate how the informal sector plays an important role in the responses of labor markets to trade.

In low-income countries, new exporting opportunities can have significant positive effects on individuals employed in the informal sector through general equilibrium labor market effects. For instance, new exporting opportunities can promote the reallocation of workers away from the informal sector and into the formal one, where firms are more productive. This was the case in Vietnam after the 2001 US-Vietnam Bilateral Trade Agreement lowered US tariffs on Vietnamese goods. The lower exporting cost disproportionately raised the profitability of the more productive formal firms, thereby shifting the composition of employment from informal microenterprises to more productive formal sector employers (McCaig and Pavcnik 2018). Obtaining a formal sector job changes the way workers are attached to the labor force as well: workers get paid more for the same skills, work more stable hours, are less likely to hold multiple jobs, and gain access to benefits.

The informal sector also provides an important margin of adjustment of workers to import competition. For example, following Brazil's import liberalization in the 1990s, the informal sector absorbed workers who were displaced from formal sectors into unemployment by increased import competition (see Rafael Dix-Carneiro's chapter in this volume and references therein). In the five- to ten-year aftermath of this episode, the regions more exposed to import competition experienced increased growth in nonemployment and informal employment relative to less affected regions. Over the long run, the informal sector slowly absorbed displaced workers, so that the total employment growth twenty years after the trade reform was similar across regions. The overall regional earnings (formal and informal), however, continued to be lower in hard-hit regions even twenty years after the onset of reforms. These adjustment mechanisms would be overlooked had one's attention been confined to the formal sector.

UNEQUAL EFFECTS OF TRADE ARE ALSO GEOGRAPHICALLY CONCENTRATED AND PERSISTENT IN EMDEs

The effects of international trade on earnings and employment are geographically concentrated and unequal within a country. Because different regions within a country face different levels of exposure to import and export shocks, the effects of trade on earnings in each region can vary. Individuals in regions with a high concentration of industries benefiting from lower export costs fare better than individuals in less exposed regions. By the same logic, individuals in regions with a high concentration of industries subject to import competition fare worse than individuals in less exposed regions. All in all, the effects of trade on inequality take on a spatial dimension. This channel is supported by evidence from several developing countries, including India, Brazil, China, Vietnam, and Mexico. It is also consistent with evidence for the United States.

These effects might at first appear puzzling. While conventional economic models would predict that wage inequalities across regions will be arbitraged away, this is not the case in EMDEs because of imperfect worker mobility—a friction also prevalent in advanced economies (see the chapter by Gordon Hanson in this volume), but sometimes far stronger in EMDEs. True, in EMDEs some individuals do migrate toward economic opportunities, as evidence from Vietnam and China illustrates (McCaig 2011; Erten and Leight 2017). But highly imperfect mobility out of adversely affected regions remains puzzling. Even five to nine years after large adverse trade shocks, inequality persists due to minimal outward migration, as documented in Petia Topalova's (2007, 2010) studies of India's 1991 import liberalization. Since then, further studies have emerged to substantiate Topalova's findings in several other EMDEs, including Brazil and Mexico.

One example of geographically concentrated gains from trade can be found in Vietnam's 2001 export liberalization—a result of the Bilateral Trade Agreement with the United States. According to Brian McCaig (2011), as exporters faced lower tariffs in the United States, individuals in regions with a higher concentration of exporting industries received disproportionate benefits from increased international trade. Such regions saw larger increases in wages (especially for less educated workers) and larger declines in poverty. Better-off regions also observed the in-migration of workers. The reallocation of workers across sectors and regions of Vietnam might have been easier in that country than in other settings. At the time of the reform, Vietnam had latent comparative advantage in unskilled labor-intensive manufacturing as well as a comparatively young and relatively well-educated population, which according to Dix-Carneiro (2014), tends to face lower adjustment costs.

We can juxtapose Vietnam's situation with that of India's 1991 import liberalization, which substantially lowered import tariffs. While aggregate poverty in India declined following this liberalization episode, Topalova (2007, 2010) has pointed out that not every district had the same response to international trade. Specifically, families living in harder-hit districts (i.e., districts with a relatively higher concentration of import-competing industries) were made worse off by trade relative to less affected districts. These harder-hit districts saw relative declines in both industrial and agricultural wages, translating into a widespread rise in poverty. The resultant inequalities across districts persisted due to low interdistrict worker mobility, especially for the poor. People simply did not migrate away from hard-hit regions; less than 5 percent of urban individuals moved within ten years, and less than 1 percent of rural individuals did. According to Kaivan Munshi and Mark Rosenzweig (2016), this might be because Indian workers tend to rely on informal social networks within their castes and therefore face a disincentive to relocate.

The two case studies illustrate how international trade—through both exporting and importing—can generate geographically concentrated benefits and losses within a country. While people do migrate toward economic opportunity, emigration from adversely affected regions is limited. Indeed, these adverse effects can persist (and actually worsen) for as long as twenty years following import liberalizations (Dix-Carneiro and Kovak 2017). The two examples also highlight that barriers to mobility are context specific; they depend, for instance, on the economic and demographic conditions and social norms of the country in question.

NEGATIVE SPILLOVERS ON CHILDREN'S EDUCATIONAL OUTCOMES AND PROVISION OF PUBLIC GOODS

A final issue to consider is that the effects of trade are not only spatial but also temporal in the sense that trade can have lasting intergenerational consequences by influencing children's schooling decisions. Two coauthors and I (Edmonds, Topalova, and Pavcnik 2009; Edmonds, Pavcnik, and Topalova 2010) demonstrate how this persistence plays out in the context of the abovementioned Indian trade liberalization. Import competition resulted in an adverse income shock, which led many families in exposed districts to pull their children out of school. As a result, children, and especially girls, living in these districts experienced relative declines in school attendance, school completion, and literacy rates. This lower educational attainment among school-age children can then translate to lower lifelong income, well after the liberalization episode. In the case of India, families living near subsistence did not send their children to school to save on schooling costs. Indeed, policy interventions that reduced the cost of attending school (such as provision of midday meals in school) helped mitigate some of the decline in school attendance.

Educational outcomes can be further affected if geographically concentrated adverse effects of trade spill over to the provision of public goods in the adversely affected communities. For example, in the context of the United States, Leo Feler and Mine Senses (2017) showed how the quality of education, public safety, and public welfare all suffered in US regions that experienced a larger decline in the local tax base due to Chinese import competition. If communities dedicate fewer resources to education, this can further reduce the opportunities of children residing in these communities.

WHAT CAN BE DONE TO COMPENSATE THOSE LEFT BEHIND BY TRADE?

The above discussion illustrates that increased import competition makes some individuals worse off (at least in relative terms), especially those who are relatively less educated, initially working in poorly performing firms or import-competing industries, and residing in areas with a higher concentration of import-competing industries. These adverse effects tend to be highly concentrated and long lasting, and spill over to children's educational opportunities and the provision of public goods in affected communities. Although direct evidence on the effectiveness of compensating those left behind by international trade is scarce, the little there is suggests that current redistributive policies have failed adequately to compensate those left behind.

Returning to protectionism in response is clearly undesirable, as it would reduce the aggregate benefits from international trade, which are estimated to be particularly sizable in EMDEs, as noted above. But how can we ensure equality of opportunity and broader sharing of the gains from trade? This question will become more salient in EMDEs as growth eventually slows down. In China, for instance, there is rising concern about the welfare of the rural elderly, who can no longer rely economically on either state pensions or support from younger family members, many of whom have migrated to urban areas to pursue better-paid opportunities in export-oriented industries (Cai and Cheng 2014; Giles, Wang, and Zhao 2010).

Governments might be poorly equipped when it comes to mitigating the adverse shocks and uncertainty associated with globalization, especially in periods of slower growth. In the case of EMDEs, this incapacity is amplified as many governments struggle to recover lost tariff revenue through alternative forms of taxation (Bown and Crowley 2016). To the extent that redistribution programs exist, they are often ineffective. As discussed in the chapters by Hanson and Lori Kletzer in this volume, trade adjustment assistance even in a high-income country such as the United States contributed less to the transfer payments of affected individuals than long-term Social Security disability assistance—which is known to discourage employment and be an inefficient form of social transfer. David Autor, David Dorn, and Gordon Hanson (2013) calculate that overall, including Social Security disability, transfer payments offset only about 10 percent of the income loss for US individuals affected by import competition from China.

Active labor market policies have been touted in recent years, both in academic and policy circles, as the way to promote new employment opportunities. Some examples include vocational training, wage subsidies, and programs that reduce search and match frictions between employers and employees. The evidence from randomized controlled trials, however, does not warrant an encouraging outlook for what has been tried so far. A recent survey by David McKenzie (2017) that evaluates twenty-four programs in ten EMDEs offers some striking results. Only one of the twenty-four studies actually achieved statistically significant results, and only 2 to 3 percent of the participants actually gained employment because of the programs. Interestingly, the average policy maker, when interviewed, predicted that 24 percent of the participants would get a job. This contrast reveals a sizable disconnect between expectation and reality: policy makers as well as participants are overly hopeful about programs that so far have been both expensive and ineffectual.

This is not to suggest that all active labor market policies are ineffective. On the contrary, taken as a whole, these studies and further experimentation may be able to give us clues as to where to direct our attention. The one successful program in McKenzie's survey was a job recruitment campaign in India. As Robert Jensen (2012) explains, the centerpiece of this program was providing young women in villages with information about job opportunities in business call centers in urban areas. Essentially, the program aimed to tackle frictions, such as limited information about job opportunities, which limit labor movement in response to spatial mismatches in labor supply and demand. The success of the India campaign seems to suggest that going forward, it might be worth exploring the effectiveness of programs that offer individuals information (and transportation/reallocation support) about employment opportunities elsewhere.

Geographically concentrated losses of trade can often affect entire communities through declining local resources and the provision of local public goods. This situation is more likely to arise in countries where local governments are responsible for the provision of public goods and rely on local sources of taxation. Of these public services affected, education stands out as particularly important. Better-educated individuals can adjust more easily to globalization; if families and communities dedicate fewer resources to education as a result of these adverse shocks, they may be initiating a long-lasting poverty cycle. Targeted policy interventions that reduce the cost of attending school and encourage education might help counteract these trends.

CLOSING REMARKS

All things considered, it is imperative for policy makers in EMDEs not to ignore international trade's distributional consequences as well as the unequal access to the gains from aggregate growth, whether growth stems from international trade or technological progress more broadly. Even though backlash against globalization has generally been restrained in EMDEs compared with the advanced economies, there is a risk of increasing antitrade sentiment as growth is buffeted by the global business cycle and converges down toward advanced economy levels.

The solutions available right now to address the growing inequality problem are, admittedly, far from adequate. But as informed policy experimentation narrows down what works and what does not, there is hope that small successes on the local level might eventually translate into more broadly applicable remedies.

REFERENCES

Autor, David H., David Dorn, and George H. Hanson. 2013. "The China Syndrome: Local Labor Market Effects of Import Competition in the United States." *American Economic Review* 103, no. 6 (October): 2121–68.

Bown, Chad P., and Meredith A. Crowley. 2016. "The Empirical Landscape of Trade Policy." In *The Handbook of Commercial Policy*, edited by Kyle Bagwell and Robert W. Staiger, 3–108. Amsterdam: Elsevier.

Brambilla, Irene, Daniel Lederman, and Guido Porto. 2012. "Exports, Export Destinations, and Skills." *American Economic Review* 102, no. 7 (December): 3406–38.

Cai, Yong, and Yuan Cheng. 2014. "Pension Reform in China: Challenges and Opportunities." *Journal of Economic Surveys* 28, no. 4 (July): 636–51.

Dix-Carneiro, Rafael. 2014. "Trade Liberalization and Labor Market Dynamics." *Econometrica* 82 (3): 825–85.

Dix-Carneiro, Rafael, and Brian K. Kovak. 2017. "Trade Liberalization and Regional Dynamics." *American Economic Review* 107, no. 10 (October): 2908–46.

Edmonds, Eric V., Nina Pavcnik, and Petia Topalova. 2010. "Trade Adjustment and Human Capital Investment: Evidence from Indian Tariff Reforms." *American Economic Journal: Applied Economics* 2, no. 4 (October): 42–75.

Edmonds, Eric V., Petia Topalova, and Nina Pavcnik. 2009. "Child Labor and Schooling in a Globalizing Economy: Some Evidence from Urban India." *Journal of European Economic Association* 7, no. 2–3 (April–May): 498–507.

Erten, Bilge, and Jessica Leight. 2017. "Exporting out of Agriculture: The Impact of WTO Accession on Structural Transformation in China." Mimeo.

Feler, Leo, and Mine Z. Senses. 2017. "Trade Shocks and the Provision of Local Public Goods." *American Economic Journal: Economic Policy* 9, no. 4 (November): 101–43.

Giles, John, Dewen Wang, and Changbao Zhao. 2010. "Can China's Rural Elderly Count on Support from Adult Children? Implications of Rural-to-Urban Migration." *Journal of Population Ageing* 3, no. 3 (December): 183–204.

Goldberg, Pinelopi K., and Pavcnik, Nina. 2007. "Distributional Effects of Globalization in Developing Countries." *Journal of Economic Literature* 45, no. 1 (March): 39–82.

———. 2016. "The Effects of Trade Policy." In *The Handbook of Commercial Policy*, edited by Kyle Bagwell and Robert W. Staiger, 161–206. Amsterdam: Elsevier.

Helpman, Elhanan. 2016. "Globalization and Wage Inequality." NBER Working Paper 22944. Cambridge, MA: National Bureau of Economic Research.

IMF (International Monetary Fund). 2018. *World Economic Outlook*. Washington, DC: International Monetary Fund.

IMF/WB/WTO (International Monetary Fund, World Bank, and World Trade Organization). 2017. "Making Trade the Engine of Growth for All: The Case for Trade and for Policies to Facilitate Adjustment." Washington, DC: International Monetary Fund.

Jensen, Robert. 2012. "Do Labor Market Opportunities Affect Young Women's Work and Family Decisions? Experimental Evidence from India." *Quarterly Journal of Economics* 127, no. 2 (May): 753–92.

Krueger, Anne. 2004. "Willful Ignorance: The Struggle to Convince the Free Trade Skeptics." Address to the Graduate Institute of International Studies, Geneva, May 18.

La Porta, Rafael, and Andrei Shleifer. 2014. "Informality and Development." *Journal of Economic Perspectives* 28, no. 3 (Summer): 109–26.

McCaig, Brian. 2011. "Exporting out of Poverty: Provincial Poverty in Vietnam and U.S. Market Access." *Journal of International Economics* 85, no. 1: 102–13.

McCaig, Brian, and Nina Pavcnik. 2018. "Export Markets and Labor Reallocation in a Low-Income Country." *American Economic Review* 85, no 1 (July): 1899–1941.

McKenzie, David. 2017. "How Effective Are Active Labor Market Policies in Developing Countries? A Critical Review of Recent Evidence." Policy Research Working Paper 8011. Washington, DC: World Bank.

Menezes-Filho, Naércio Aquino, and Marc-Andreas Muendler. 2011. "Labor Reallocation in Response to Trade Reform." NBER Working Paper 17372. Cambridge, MA: National Bureau of Economic Research.

Munshi, Kaivan, and Mark Rosenzweig. 2016. "Networks and Misallocation: Insurance, Migration, and the Rural-Urban Wage Gap." *American Economic Review* 106, no. 1 (January): 46–98.

Pavcnik, Nina. 2017. "The Impact of Trade on Inequality in Developing Countries." NBER Working Paper 23878. Cambridge, MA: National Bureau of Economic Research.

Topalova, Petia. 2007. "Trade Liberalization, Poverty, and Inequality: Evidence from Indian Districts." In *Globalization and Poverty*, edited by Ann Harrison, 291–336. Chicago: University of Chicago Press.

———. 2010. "Factor Immobility and Regional Impacts of Trade Liberalization: Evidence on Poverty from India." *American Economic Journal: Applied Economics* 2, no. 4 (October): 1–41.

Verhoogen, Eric A. 2008. "Trade, Quality Upgrading, and Wage Inequality in the Mexican Manufacturing Sector." *Quarterly Journal of Economics* 123, no. 2 (May): 489–530.

9

Trade and Labor Market Adjustment: Recent Research on Brazil

RAFAEL DIX-CARNEIRO

This chapter examines recent research on how the Brazilian labor market adjusted to the trade liberalization episode of the early 1990s. The results I discuss are important for at least three reasons in the context of the chapters on trade and labor market adjustment featured in this volume.

First, the Brazilian trade liberalization is a valuable episode we can learn from regarding labor market adjustment to trade. This episode consisted of large, unilateral, import tariff reductions between 1990 and 1995. Average tariffs fell from 31 to 13 percent, and there was ample variation in the magnitude of tariff cuts across sectors. More important, trade liberalization in Brazil can be viewed as a once-and-for-all event. While import tariffs were gradually reduced between 1990 and 1995, these remained relatively constant thereafter. This allows us to trace the evolution of liberalization's effects over time.

Second, Brazil has excellent data sources on the labor market, covering a period including the trade liberalization episode. Among these data sources is the *Relação Anual de Informações Sociais*, an administrative data set starting in 1986 that provides high-quality information on all formal sector workers and firms in the country. In particular, it is possible to track workers over time as well as across firms, sectors, and regions. The research discussed here also employs multiple rounds of the decennial demographic census covering the period ranging from 1970 to 2010 to obtain information on the Brazilian informal sector or the labor market as a whole.[3] Together, these data enable us to carry out a comprehensive and detailed analysis on how the Brazilian labor markets adjusted to trade.

Third, this research complements the evidence that Gordon Hanson and Lori Kletzer explore in this volume; that evidence focuses on how labor markets in a developed country, such as the United States, responded to increasing import competition, especially from China. Given Brazil's status as an important middle-income country and its quite-different labor market structure compared to the United States, it is interesting to contrast these two countries' experiences in adjusting to globalization. In addition, although the rise of China was probably the single most important development in the global economy in the past thirty years, it is usually agreed by economists that the emergence of China is a "done deal" and it is unlikely that we will witness another comparable episode in our lifetime. In contrast, although Brazil went through a major trade liberalization episode in the 1990s, it remains a relatively protected economy, with import tariffs across sectors averaging 10.4 percent.[4] Therefore, understanding how Brazil's labor markets adjusted to trade liberalization is useful to inform policy makers planning another wave of trade liberalization.

TRADE LIBERALIZATION IN BRAZIL

Details about trade liberalization in Brazil can be found in my work (Dix-Carneiro and Kovak 2017), but figure 9.1 illustrates that trade liberalization led to large import tariff reductions, and there was ample variation in how different sectors were affected. For instance, sectors such as agriculture and mining were virtually unaffected by changes in trade policy, whereas sectors such as apparel, rubber, pharmaceuticals, and the auto industry faced large declines in protection.

[3] The informal sector accounts for approximately half of overall employment in Brazil. A worker is considered informal if they are informally employed by a firm (off the books and invisible to the government) or self-employed. In each case, the worker does not receive the benefits or regulatory protections offered in the formal labor market.

[4] Author's calculations using 2010 UNCTAD TRAINS data and a similar level of aggregation as shown in figure 9.1. The twenty-fifth percentile of the distribution of 2010 import tariffs is 5.3 percent, and the seventy-fifth percentile is 13.9 percent, with sectors being protected with over 30 percent tariffs (clothing and footwear).

Figure 9.1. Import Tariff Changes between 1990 and 1995

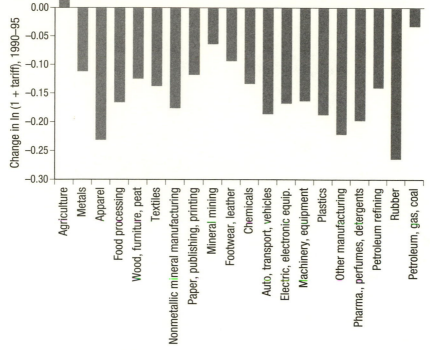

Note: Industries sorted based on 1991 national employment (largest on the left, and smallest on the right).
Source: Dix-Carneiro and Kovak 2019.

A recent but prominent literature has exploited the fact that sector-specific shocks, such as those depicted in figure 9.1, can have substantially different effects on labor market outcomes across regions within a country (Topalova 2010; Autor, Dorn, and Hanson 2013; Kovak 2013; Hakobyan and McLaren 2016). To understand why, suppose that workers face large barriers in moving across regions within a country. In that case, we would expect labor demand in an "apparel town" to fall relative to labor demand in an "agriculture town," as tariff cuts were much steeper in apparel compared to agriculture. This intuitive idea was formalized and rationalized by Brian Kovak (2013), who showed how sector-specific tariff changes can be translated into region-specific labor demand shocks, depending on differences in industry composition across locations. In short, Kovak demonstrates that the regional labor demand shock induced by trade liberalization is given by a weighted average of

Figure 9.2. Local Labor Demand Shocks Induced by Liberalization: Regional Tariff Reductions

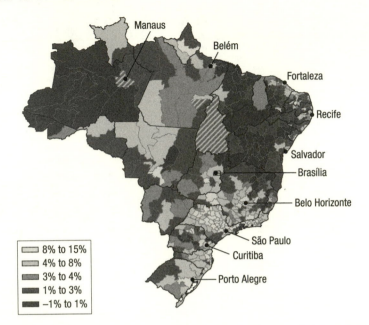

Notes: Lighter regions faced larger tariff reductions, whereas darker regions faced smaller tariff reductions. Labor demand in lighter regions was negatively affected relative to darker regions.
Source: Dix-Carneiro and Kovak 2019.

sector-specific tariff declines, where weights are given by sector-specific employment shares in that region. These shocks are called "regional tariff reductions." Figure 9.2 shows how labor demand was affected across local labor markets in Brazil in response to trade liberalization by plotting the distribution of these regional tariff reductions. Darker regions are mostly specialized in sectors facing small tariff declines, such as agriculture. In contrast, lighter regions are mostly specialized in sectors facing larger tariff declines, such as apparel and the auto industry. It is important to notice that there is ample variation in how regions were affected by trade liberalization.

FORMAL LABOR MARKET OUTCOMES

My coauthor and I (Dix-Carneiro and Kovak 2017) investigate how region-specific labor market outcomes have responded to these local

Figure 9.3. Effects of Liberalization on Formal Sector Regional Employment

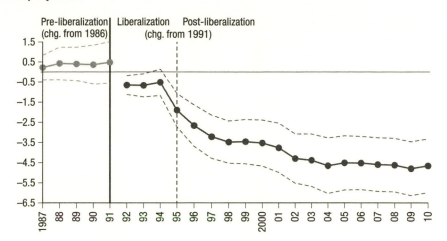

Notes: The markers illustrate the effects of trade-induced local labor demand shocks (from 1990 to 1995) on the change in regional (log) formal employment from 1991 to the year listed on the x-axis. Negative estimates imply larger employment declines in regions facing larger tariff reductions (relative to less affected regions). Dashed lines represent 95 percent confidence intervals. Preliberalization trends are measured relative to 1986.
Source: Dix-Carneiro and Kovak 2017.

shocks induced by the tariff cuts, tracking the evolution of these effects over time. Figure 9.3 shows that regions facing larger (negative) shocks induced by liberalization experienced declines in formal sector employment *relative* to regions facing smaller shocks.[5] These effects gradually increased following the beginning of liberalization and only stabilized fifteen years afterward. In particular, these results demonstrate that formal sector employment adjustment in response to trade liberalization was large but slow.

Before I discuss how regional wages responded to these local labor demand shocks induced by liberalization, it is instructive to comment on how wages were expected to evolve. A model that is often employed by economists assumes that workers are generally not mobile across regions in response to local economic shocks in the short run, but are increasingly so as time unfolds. This view is consistent with the dy-

[5] The effects reviewed in this chapter can only reveal the relative effects of Brazil's trade liberalization on local labor markets. This is a well-known limitation of reduced-form estimates in the presence of important general equilibrium effects—a common feature of all the trade and local labor markets literature.

Figure 9.4. Effects of Liberalization on Formal Sector Regional Earnings

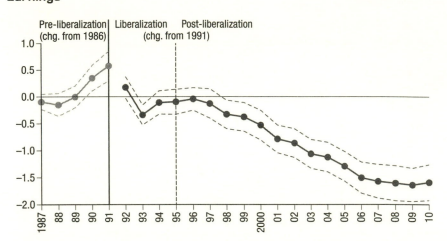

Notes: The markers illustrate the estimated effects of trade-induced local labor demand shocks (from 1990 to 1995) on the change in regional (log) formal earnings from 1991 to the year listed on the x-axis. Negative estimates imply larger employment declines in regions facing larger tariff reductions (relative to less affected regions). Dashed lines represent 95 percent confidence intervals. Preliberalization trends are measured relative to 1986.
Source: Dix-Carneiro and Kovak 2017.

namic effects illustrated in figure 9.3, which shows formal sector employment gradually responding to the local shocks induced by liberalization. Therefore, following a decline in labor demand in regions facing larger tariff cuts (relative to the national average), we would expect wages to fall on impact because workers are stuck in these regions in the short run. As workers gradually move away from these harder-hit locations, however, equilibrium wages would move up the local labor demand curve to the point where wages are reequalized across regions. This logic suggests that wages in harder-hit locations would decline in the short run relative to the national average, but would then gradually recover, so that the long-run effects on wages across regions should be negligible. Surprisingly, figure 9.4 reveals a quite-different adjustment pattern. My coauthor and I (Dix-Carneiro and Kovak 2017) document that wages in harder-hit locations steadily decline for years and never recover. The long-run decline is three times as large as the short-run one. The effects of liberalization on wages are also slow and persistent. These effects are in sharp contrast to the

Figure 9.5. Effects of Liberalization on Establishment Entry and Exit

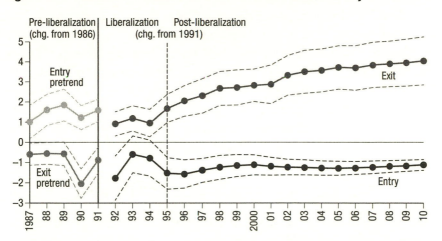

Notes: The markers illustrate the estimated effects of trade-induced local labor demand shocks (from 1990 to 1995) on (log) cumulative regional formal establishment entry
or exit from 1991 to the year listed on the x-axis. Positive exit and negative entry estimates
imply larger rates of exit and smaller rates of entry in regions facing larger tariff reductions (relative to less affected regions). Dashed lines represent 95 percent confidence
intervals. Preliberalization trends are measured relative to 1986.
   Source: Dix-Carneiro and Kovak 2017.

conventional economic logic described in the previous paragraph. What
explains them?

Two ingredients are essential to explain the effects documented in
figure 9.3 and 9.4: slow and incomplete interregional labor mobility,
and dynamics in labor demand. In particular, these dynamics in local
labor demand are driven by the slow adjustment of capital across regions
(because of slow depreciation and new investment being gradually directed toward less affected regions), and slow changes in local productivity driven by agglomeration economies.

Using demographic census data, my coauthor and I (Dix-Carneiro
and Kovak 2017) find that migration does not systematically respond
to trade-induced shocks, corroborating the hypothesis of imperfect
interregional labor mobility in response to shocks. On the other hand,
figure 9.5 illustrates that firm exit increased gradually following liberalization, and investment (measured as firm entry) responded almost
immediately and permanently. As I suggest in one study (Dix-Carneiro
2014), the slow reallocation of capital led to a steady amplification of
the initial local labor demand shock, making workers in harder-hit

regions even less productive over time compared to those in more favorably affected regions. My coauthor and I (Dix-Carneiro and Kovak 2017) also suggest that agglomeration economies amplify the labor market effects of trade liberalization: as firms in harder-hit regions leave the market, the productivity of remaining local firms gradually declines, further reducing local wage and employment growth. Using a simple model of local labor markets, we show that capital reallocation and agglomeration economies together can explain the quantitative scale of the wage and employment effects they document.

THE ROLE OF INFORMAL EMPLOYMENT

The evidence reviewed so far focused on how aggregate formal sector, regional-level labor market outcomes responded to liberalization. To complement this evidence, in another study, my coauthor and I (Dix-Carneiro and Kovak 2019) analyzed how *individual* labor market trajectories of workers responded to the trade-induced labor demand shocks and through what margins they adjusted. Following individual workers over time using the *Relação Anual de Informações Sociais*, figure 9.6 shows that workers initially employed in tradable sectors in harder-hit locations tend to spend less and less time employed in the formal sector relative to workers initially employed elsewhere. Perhaps surprisingly, this effect grew over time. Although figure 9.3 documents that formal employment gradually declined in regions facing steeper tariff cuts relative to the national average, we would expect that individual labor market outcomes would eventually have recovered as workers migrated away from harder-hit regions. The absence of such recovery indicates that individual workers did not systematically migrate away from negatively affected locations—a fact that is corroborated using longitudinal data. Tradable sector workers initially employed in harder-hit locations were more likely to switch to nontradable sectors in response to liberalization. This response, however, did not offset the large losses in employment in tradable sectors. Finally, we (Dix-Carneiro and Kovak 2019) document that the formal employment trajectories of workers initially employed in nontradable sectors were affected almost as much as those of tradable sector workers. This impact illustrates important spillovers from tradable to nontradable sectors locally. These spillovers across sectors raise concerns about policies providing targeted compensation for workers in industries experiencing increased import

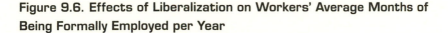

Figure 9.6. Effects of Liberalization on Workers' Average Months of Being Formally Employed per Year

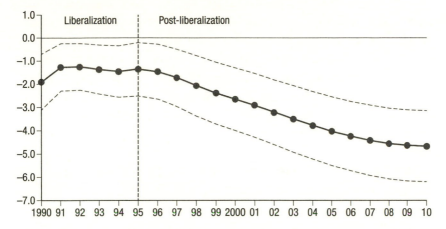

Notes: The markers illustrate the estimated effects of trade-induced local labor demand shocks (from 1990 to 1995) on individual cumulative average number of months formally employed per year from 1991 to the year listed on the x-axis. Negative estimates imply that workers initially in regions facing larger tariff reductions spend a smaller average share of the relevant years formally employed than workers in other regions.

Source: Dix-Carneiro and Kovak 2019.

competition, such as TAA in the United States. When regional labor markets are reasonably integrated across sectors, even workers whose industry did not directly face a trade shock experience the labor market effects of that shock, and policies based on industry targeting will fail to address declining earnings and employment rates for these indirectly affected workers.

Figure 9.6 shows that workers initially employed in harder-hit regions were less and less likely to be found working in the formal sector, but it does not tell us how exactly these workers adjusted. Unfortunately, the Brazilian administrative data do not have information on workers once they leave the formal sector, so it is unclear if workers who leave the formal sector are unemployed, out of the labor force, self-employed, or informally employed. To have a picture of what happens to trade-displaced workers once they leave the formal sector, we (Dix-Carneiro and Kovak 2017) exploit data from the demographic census. The advantage of using such data is that we can identify workers who are formally employed, informally employed, or not employed. The disadvantage of such data is that in contrast to the administrative data, we cannot follow individual workers over time. We (Dix-Carneiro and Kovak 2019) use these data to investigate how the structure of local labor markets responded to the trade-induced local shocks.

In the medium run (1991 to 2000), nonemployment and informal employment increased in harder-hit locations relative to the national average. Yet in the long run (1991 to 2010), nonemployment did not respond to local trade shocks, but informal employment strongly increased in harder-hit regions. Together with the individual worker results, it seems that trade-displaced workers spend time unemployed or out of the labor force, but eventually find reemployment in the informal sector. Therefore, the informal sector seems to partly smooth the labor market outcomes of trade-displaced workers. Without this fallback sector, trade-displaced workers would likely have experienced even longer nonemployment spells.

My coauthor and I (Dix-Carneiro and Kovak 2017, 2019) document that the Brazilian economy adjusted slowly to trade liberalization. It is thus important to understand the implications of such slow adjustment for the gains from trade. I (Dix-Carneiro 2014) address this question in one study, showing that the slow reallocation of workers and capital toward export-oriented industries leads to substantially lower gains from trade compared to traditional frictionless models (which assume that the new equilibrium is reached instantaneously). In that work, I estimate 11 to 26 percent lower gains from trade compared to a situation where reallocation occurs immediately.

In addition, I (Dix-Carneiro 2014) estimate that adjustment costs are heterogeneous across the population. For example, older, less educated, and female workers face substantially higher barriers to mobility across sectors. These workers in import-competing sectors experience substantial losses following liberalization, so governments willing to compensate the losers from trade should pay particular attention to workers with these characteristics.

Lastly, as also discussed in Nina Pavcnik's chapter in this volume, globalization can have important and distinctive effects on welfare far beyond labor market adjustment. In the Brazilian context, for one, two coauthors and I (Dix-Carneiro, Soares, and Ulyssea 2018) show that regions exposed to larger tariff reductions experienced a temporary increase in crime following liberalization. These results highlight an additional dimension of the cost of adjustment to trade shocks. Given that crime generates substantial negative externalities, the adjustment costs triggered by trade shocks can therefore go well beyond the individuals directly affected by them.

CONCLUDING REMARKS

Recent work on the Brazilian experience following the 1990s' trade liberalization episode showed that the adjustment of the labor market was slow and not every region benefited in the same way. As discussed above, the welfare implications of this slow adjustment can be substantial. Moreover, the pattern of adjustment was more complex than conventional theories would predict, highlighting several features absent in existing models of trade and labor markets. First, to understand labor market adjustment in response to globalization, capital and labor markets must be studied simultaneously. Second, the large response of informal employment to trade liberalization (especially in the long run) highlights an additional margin of adjustment that has been understudied in the literature. Finally, globalization can have significant effects beyond the labor market, leading to important externalities within regions.

REFERENCES

Autor, David H., David Dorn, and Gordon H. Hanson. 2013. "The China Syndrome: Local Labor Market Effects of Import Competition in the United States." *American Economic Review* 103, no. 6 (October): 2121–68.

Dix-Carneiro, Rafael. 2014. "Trade Liberalization and Labor Market Dynamics." *Econometrica* 82, no. 3 (May): 825–85.

Dix-Carneiro, Rafael, and Brian K. Kovak. 2017. "Trade Liberalization and Regional Dynamics." *American Economic Review* 107, no. 10 (October): 2908–46.

———. 2019. "Margins of Labor Market Adjustment to Trade." *Journal of International Economics* (March) 117: 125–42.

Dix-Carneiro, Rafael, Rodrigo Soares, and Gabriel Ulyssea. 2018. "Economic Shocks and Crime: Evidence from the Brazilian Trade Liberalization." *American Economic Journal: Applied Economics* 10, no. 4 (May): 158–95.

Hakobyan, Shushanik, and John McLaren. 2016. "Looking for Local Labor Market Effects of NAFTA." *Review of Economics and Statistics* 98, no.4 (October): 728–41.

Kovak, Brian K. 2013. "Regional Effects of Trade Reform: What Is the Correct Measure of Liberalization?" *American Economic Review* 103, no. 5 (August): 1960–76.

Topalova, Petia. 2010. "Factor Immobility and Regional Impacts of Trade Liberalization: Evidence on Poverty from India." 2010. *American Economic Journal: Applied Economics* 2, no.4 (October): 1–41.

PART IV

ADJUSTMENT POLICIES

10

Globalization, Trade, and Growth

ANNE KRUEGER

Globalization affects us in many ways and has many dimensions. The accelerated speed of communications, cross-border migration, and reduced transportation costs for trade, travel, and much more are all dimensions of globalization. Yet I will focus on international trade, which has been an important component, if not the linchpin, of globalization.

The world has been globalizing for more than two centuries. The steamship revolutionized ocean travel, both by reducing time and lowering costs. While globalization had proceeded before that (think of Marco Polo, the East India Company, and other trading ventures), it certainly accelerated after 1800.

The benefits of globalization have been huge. Increasing volumes of trade enabled rising living standards faster and in greater proportions than would otherwise have been possible. Robert Gordon (2016) has documented many of the changes, which had both local and international dimensions, in his recent book. Robert Fogel (2000) has reported economic historians' estimate that in 1800, only about 5 percent of Americans lived above the poverty line of the year 2000! And even they, of course, did not have access to many of the goods and services that comprise today's consumption bundle.

International trade was about 2 percent of world GDP in 1800 and is now over 25 percent. Living standards rose almost continuously in western Europe and North America throughout the nineteenth century and until World War I, when shipping routes, and hence trade, were disrupted. Trade rebounded in the 1920s, but dropped sharply during the Great Depression, due to the Depression itself and the heightened levels of protection that countries mistakenly imposed on imports. Memories of the Smoot-Hawley Tariff Act in the United States are still associated with protection, impediments to economic growth, and the Great Depression.

After the Second World War, almost all the industrial countries resumed growth, with reliance on pent-up demand from the war as well as the opening and liberalization of trade (which was also accelerated by continuing declines in transport and communication costs). Global trade grew nearly twice as fast as GDP, and trade liberalization turned out to be correlated with faster GDP growth (IMF/WB/WTO 2017, 8–9). In the early postwar years, the developing countries at first experienced rapid growth, based in part on the relatively high and growing levels of demand along with high prices for primary commodities. But they did not initially open their economies, and some remained fairly closed to foreign trade well into the 1980s, particularly (but not only) in Latin America. The widespread belief in the first two to three decades after World War II was that growth could best be pursued by "import substitution," to be achieved by erecting high tariff barriers against imports.

But after the 1950s, growth in those countries gradually began to slacken except for the "East Asian tigers," made up of Taiwan, South Korea, Hong Kong, and Singapore—countries that had shifted their growth strategies earlier on away from import substitution and toward an outer orientation. The acceleration of their growth rates was dramatic. Since then, many other countries have learned the lesson and shifted to more open economic policies, and as such, have experienced greatly improved economic performance (which of course was accompanied by other economic policy reforms as well).

For the industrial countries, trade opening was achieved through unilateral trade liberalization as well as the jointly undertaken removal of quantitative restrictions and tariff reductions under the WTO's auspices. The WTO had been established as the GATT after World War II and changed its name in the 1990s. Over the first fifty postwar years, successive rounds of multilateral tariff negotiations reduced the average tariff rate on manufactured goods from about 45 to 5 percent for industrial countries. Despite being free riders who maintained high levels of protection themselves, most of the developing countries at first could sustain their own growth thanks to the rapid growth of trade that ensued with trade liberalization in the industrial countries. But they too began liberalizing unilaterally, and higher growth rates for trade in goods and services—and real GDP—followed.

The global growth that followed these policy moves has been more rapid than ever seen before (except for short periods of recovery after a war or other major disruption). Living standards, life expectancies, and other measures of well-being are all greatly improved for most of the world's population. In industrial countries, growth and rising per capita incomes have continued, although at a rate below that realized in the second half of the last century. Improvements have accelerated, however, in countries such as India that were extremely poor. There, life expectancies at birth in 1950 were twenty-eight for women and thirty-two for men, and are now over sixty and moving toward seventy for both sexes. Living standards have risen, literacy has increased, and real per capita income is now more than three times what it then was. Until the 1990s, Indian economic growth (and the rate of poverty reduction) was fairly slow, as India adopted import substitution and other policies inimical to rapid growth. When major reforms were undertaken in the early 1990s, though, the rate of growth accelerated and poverty rates began falling more sharply. There is no question but that billions of people have been lifted out of abject poverty, and that it could not have happened as much and as fast in the absence of healthy global growth in the international economy.

Recently, some have come to question whether rising living standards and globalization should be an objective of policy. They have argued that while there are gains from growth, some have been left out, and globalization has been responsible. While it is clearly right to be concerned about the losers, there are two considerations that point to the desirability of addressing the plight of those left behind in the context of growth rather than through backtracking on globalization.

The first consideration is that it is always easier to address problems in the context of a growing economy than it is when growth is stagnant or slow. Reversing globalization (and failing to pursue it further) would be throwing the baby out with the bathwater. And it should be noted that over the long run, globalization has enabled improved well-being for virtually everyone, even though there are some losers in the short run.

The second consideration is to question the extent to which globalization is the phenomenon that has led to some being left behind. There is much evidence to the contrary. Economic growth itself brings about changes that require adaptation. In the nineteenth century, agricultural productivity was improving rapidly (due primarily to innovation and capital accumulation, especially with farm equipment), and the prices of agricultural commodities were falling. That enabled the growth of industry and urban areas as food prices fell and the urban labor supply increased with out-migration from agriculture. To a large extent, the process was smooth, and people were in effect "voting with their feet" to seek a better life. Without that dislocation arising from the increased productivity of labor, capital, and land in agriculture, living standards could not have improved to anything like the degree that they did.

While international trade played a role in the transformation from agriculture to industry—it allowed some countries to specialize more in producing manufactures while importing food from abroad—the shift would have happened to a large extent even without trade. But the point here is that increasing agricultural productivity was the product of innovation (the tractor and other farm machinery) and scientific endeavors (the use of fertilizers, pesticides, and so on), and not the result of trade. Growth itself, even when domestic, gives rise to the need for flexible markets and adjustments. Shifting tastes, such as a shift in demand to more meat and vegetables along with fewer grains, also imply the need for shifts in the use of resources. Capital accumulation enables greater investment in machinery and equipment, enabling higher productivity, and therefore higher wages than could otherwise be paid. Yet it also leads to the displacement of some people.

The need for adjustment arises because of shifts in demand (with rising incomes, people spend more of their incomes on nonagricultural goods), technical change (which increases productivity), capital accumulation, and other factors, including international trade. In political discourse, politicians have attributed a high share of dislocation to trade, but that charge is simply not borne out by evidence or analysis. Most serious studies have attributed at most 20 to 25 percent of job dislocation to trade, and that dislocation is gross, as exports also create jobs (see Laura Tyson's chapter in this volume).

To see why other factors are important, consider what happens when a firm goes bankrupt and jobs are lost. It is natural to ask the "cause" of the job loss. It is easiest to make the point by recounting an experience I had in the mid-1970s, when there was also concern about jobs lost "due to trade." An enterprising *New York Times* reporter had written a series of articles after he tracked down many workers who had lost their jobs when a factory in Newark, New Jersey, had closed two years before. According to the reporter, the factory had closed due to a flood of imports. I read the stories with great interest. The reporter investigated the length of time it had taken workers to find other jobs, degree to which their wages were lower in the new jobs, how many had simply retired, and so on.

As it happened, I had just joined a research advisory board for an organization of large businesses that wanted to provide inputs into policy discussions. I went to my first meeting of the board, and it started with a lunch. Sitting next to me was the CEO of the company (which had several plants in various parts of the United States) that had closed its Newark factory. I was of course curious, so started to ask the CEO about it. But when I referenced the closure, he responded, "Oh yes, we moved south, where we could avoid the union." The *New York Times* story, though, had been about the impact of trade. Now it is certainly true that pressures on the industry may have pushed this company to seek ways to cut costs more rapidly than it otherwise would have, but it is also true that the jobs were "lost" to the Newark factory and "gained" in the South. Lower wages in the South were certainly the proximate reason for the adjustment.

In general, when a company shuts down or transfers a line of business, there are multiple things that have gone wrong. These include such problems as poor management, a location that is no longer economic, innovation by competitors (or in goods that compete with the company's product), substitution of machines for labor, and of course imports. Even then, it is often forgotten that payment for imports enables our trade partners to buy more goods in other industries, and as such, offsets part or all of the needed domestic adjustment.

There are two conclusions that follow from this. The first is that you can't identify which jobs are lost through trade; in most instances, there will be multiple causes. The second is that to stop the process and "save jobs" is to stop or hinder the process of economic growth. Saving the "zombie" firms, as they are sometimes called, locks resources into those industries and discourages (or impedes) new entrants into dynamic new industries. I will not comment here on current account or trade deficits; it is recognized by all economists that deficits are frequently the outcome of overly expansionary macroeconomic policies, and can be corrected by appropriate monetary and fiscal measures.

That leads to my central point: it is not clear why those whose livelihood is trade impacted should be treated any differently from the way society provides a social safety net for others in the same situation (albeit affected by innovation or other nontrade developments). Workers are displaced by innovation, shifts in tastes, and other phenomena. It is usually not apparent which reason is the main one in many cases, but even if it is, the appropriate policy should be to target policies based on individuals' situations, not the causes of those circumstances.

Moreover, even when a trade shift occurs, it is not evident that the shift alone will result in layoffs and job losses. Usually, pressures on domestic firms have their greatest impact on those companies with the highest costs. They will typically be the ones with poor management (and the least ability to adapt), poor location, or other difficulties. In only a few cases can one observe the total shutdown of an entire industry, and the survivors are generally the ones with the highest productivity. But from the viewpoint of the worker, or the small town where layoffs occur, the problem is the layoff, not the trade or other factors that precipitated it.

I should note at this point that in the United States, TAA, the program designed to help workers harmed by trade, has been ineffective. Some European countries have been more successful than the United States in dealing with dislocations. Denmark is such a case, in which the Danes basically have redone their labor market policies in such a way that everything is coordinated through local job centers. Employers notify the centers when there are layoffs (and also when there are job openings), regardless of the reason. Workers are required to register with a center. Each center has information on job openings and the skill requirements for different jobs, the worker's skills and job history, and other relevant data. The center coordinates all the policies that affect the worker, including training opportunities that might enhance employability, unemployment compensation, available job openings, and so on. Each worker is assigned a counselor and reports to them weekly. Unemployment compensation is contingent on reporting and following up on counselor suggestions. The duration of unemployment compensation can be extended if the worker is undergoing training and needs longer to complete it. The counselor can even arrange compensation for travel to places offering jobs for which the worker might be suited.

The countries with integrated active labor market policies have been more successful in bringing down the duration of unemployment and the overall unemployment rate than those relying on uncoordinated pillars of training opportunities, job search, and unemployment compensation. The policies are set without regard to whether imports, robots, or other factors led to job loss. Quite aside from the fact that there is no reason why society should differentiate between workers based on the cause of their layoff, the efforts at softening opposition to trade by TAA have in fact had the opposite effect: employers can collude with workers under TAA to claim that job losses were trade related. These claims then lead public opinion to believe trade is the cause of difficulties, even though other factors are at least, if not more, important.

There are reasons to believe that protection has enough unintended consequences that it will contribute to increased, rather than reduced, job losses. As already mentioned, countries exporting more to the United States are enabled to import more. Those exports also generate employment. Further, the ability to outsource parts and components that would be much more expensive if produced in the home market may enable firms to compete more successfully than they could otherwise if disadvantaged by higher costs for some of their inputs. There is often a political outcry against "moving a factory abroad" on the theory that the move causes job losses. It is seldom recognized that the job losses would be greater still if the entire factory in the home country had to shut down (and might be enabled to increase production with lower cost inputs available). In addition, if a country erects high walls of protection against imports and/or creates high hurdles for foreign investment (inward or outward), it is likely that foreign countries will retaliate, with consequent job losses.

A frequently cited example of job losses is the US automobile industry. There can be no doubt that consumer welfare was improved given the competition (and lower prices) provided by the availability of Japanese and European auto imports. But the argument was made that by taking market share away from US producers, the foreign companies had "cost American jobs." It was forgotten that lower car prices enabled many families to own more cars than they otherwise would have, and that the demand for auto services (gas stations, repair facilities, sales outlets, and even roadside restaurants and motels as the cost of auto travel decreased) created jobs. Had Americans owned fewer cars, there would have been fewer jobs in these service industries. The net "job loss" was surely less than the number implied by the increased imports only. Moreover, the Japanese companies had higher profits on their car sales in the United States and used the additional profits to invest in ways that increased their competitive advantage.

There is no doubt that the rhetoric against globalization and pressures for protection have increased. The case must be made convincingly that globalization has generated large benefits, and there are alternative ways of supporting those who are adversely affected by any shift in technology, tastes, capital formation, or trade. Finding an adequate social safety net is crucial. But the odds that job dislocation would be greatly reduced by erecting protectionist barriers are close to zero. And protection itself is a slippery slope: once a company in industry A has received protection, producers in industry B are sure to argue that the protection afforded to A increases their costs and must be mitigated (think autos and steel).

I hope I have said enough to convince you that a new set of policies needs to be developed to address unemployment issues, and the focus should be much more on facilitating adjustment by workers and less on preventing the need for adjustment. More effort and thought needs to go to active labor market policies, not only to deflect pressure from those believing themselves impacted by trade, but also to increase the flexibility of the labor market and reduce the misery of unemployment. Once that happens and protectionist pressures diminish, it is likely that growth could accelerate, at least somewhat, and in turn, further ease needed adjustments.

REFERENCES

Fogel, Robert. 2000. *The Fourth Great Awakening and the Future of Capitalism.* Chicago: University of Chicago Press.

Gordon, Robert. 2016. *The Rise and Fall of American Growth: The U.S. Standard of Living Since the Civil War*. Princeton, NJ: Princeton University Press.

IMF/WB/WTO (International Monetary Fund, World Bank, and World Trade Organization). 2017. "Making Trade an Engine of Growth for All: The Case for Trade and for Policies to Facilitate Adjustment." Washington, DC: International Monetary Fund.

11

Trade and Labor Market Adjustment: The Costs of Trade-Related Job Loss in the United States and Policy Responses

LORI G. KLETZER

Concern about trade-related job loss remains high in the public arena. The concept is well defined in the public mind, even if it continues to be contested by economists. Having written in this area for some time, I use the phrase "trade-related job loss" to convey as clearly as possible the importance of job loss associated with increasing international trade—that is, a focus on job loss and trade.

Losing a job through no fault of one's own is costly. For many workers, earnings losses following trade-related job loss are stubbornly persistent and staggeringly high. In this chapter, I review the evidence on trade-related job losses and discuss how it makes a case for mitigation policies. I also look at policy options that help address the worker and community costs of trade-related job loss, and in so doing, might contribute to making open trade closer to Pareto improving—even if still falling well short of it. In this connection, I highlight the reasons for the disappointing performance of TAA in the United States, and argue that wage insurance policies (see Kletzer and Litan 2001) can go some way toward reducing the earnings losses typically associated with re-employment after trade-related job losses.[1]

---

[1] While trade-related job loss is a source of considerable political and economic anxiety, any kind of job loss through no fault of one's own (such as job displacement) is costly in terms of both reemployment prospects and earnings losses. Why the job

TRADE-RELATED JOB LOSSES ARE REAL

The most contested part of the phrase above is "trade-related," and here research over the past five years has made significant progress, producing sharp estimates of the size and scope of job loss associated with increasing trade. Some of this progress is represented in this volume (see Rafael Dix-Carneiro's and Gordon Hanson's chapters). With better data and more sophisticated econometrics, we know that there is trade-related job loss. And with this improved understanding, there are prospects for a more secure and shared understanding of how the phrase is used. For many years within the economics profession, those paying attention to the cost of trade-related job loss were accused of advocating a reversal of global trade agreements and international integration. Drawing attention to trade-related job loss is not protectionist advocacy, however; it is not about rolling back the clock. It is about doing better for workers and communities. We haven't done well for them and need to do better. Importantly, doing better for workers and communities is a requisite part of moving international integration in a Pareto-improving direction.

In that spirit, this discussion starts with economics bona fides. There are clear net benefits to trade. There are gains to consumers from lower prices, and gains to the overall economy in efficiency and higher aggregate welfare. Theory reveals that trade may redistribute income; and under standard conditions, the gains to the winners are more than sufficient to offset any losses experienced by the workers and producers who suffer adverse consequences from foreign competition. Under the right set of conditions, the winners should therefore be able to compensate the losers.

Theory also establishes that international trade is not generally Pareto improving. In their undergraduate textbook, Paul Krugman and Maurice Obstfeld (2008, 64) observe, "Owners of a country's abundant factors gain from trade, but owners of a country's scarce factors lose. . . . [I]nternational trade tends to make low-skilled workers in the United States worse off—not just temporarily, but on a sustained basis." Open trade is about shifting resources toward their most productive uses,

---

is lost—whether due to increasing trade, technological change, or shifts in consumer demand—may be secondary in determining the size and scope of the earnings losses.

and these shifts can be costly. To put a finer point on it, discussion of Pareto improvements requires that we contemplate compensation of losers by winners.

I (Kletzer 2001) was part of a line of research from the Peterson Institute for International Economics (then the Institute for International Economics) called the Globalization Balance Sheet. The project title intentionally evokes the benefits and costs, and winners and losers, from increasing global economic integration, and brought a counterview or nuance to the *conventional wisdom*. David Autor, David Dorn, and Gordon Hanson (2016, 207–8) summarize the conventional wisdom circa 2000 as follows:

- Trade had not in recent decades been a major contributor to declining manufacturing employment or rising wage inequality in developed countries.
- Workers employed in import-competing sectors could readily reallocate to other sectors if displaced by trade.
- Due to the "law of one price" for skill, any labor market impacts of trade would be felt by low-skill workers generally, not by trade-exposed workers specifically.

The China Shock research agenda and findings, as summarized by Hanson in chapter 7, brought down this conventional wisdom, using the impact of China's recent export growth (the China shock).

There was a *less conventional wisdom* prior to the China Shock. I (Kletzer 2001) offered less conventional wisdom, using US data from the 1970s through the 1990s along with research from the early 2000s:

- The consequences of trade-related job loss for the domestic labor market is a key political economy issue for the future of US international economic policy.
- Trade liberalization is often a focal point for anxiety about job insecurity.
- That focus can be misplaced; trade ranks behind technological change and immigration as a source of job loss and declining real wages for less educated workers.
- Losing a job is costly—for workers, families, and communities—in the short and long term.
- What matters is the kind of job lost and kind of job regained, and much less so why the job was lost.

Research on the China shock has reaffirmed much of this less conventional wisdom. Importantly, this new research has shown that while aggregate losses from trade were small at the macro level, they were large for the workers in the regions that were most affected. Even for workers not in manufacturing, local losses of manufacturing jobs were costly. Particularly for less skilled or less educated workers, for whom a job in manufacturing was the main or only path to the middle class, the loss of these jobs was costly.

In data from the United States in the 1990s, the Displaced Worker Surveys revealed that import-competing manufacturing workers faced a higher risk of job loss and lower probabilities of reemployment. Their lower reemployment probabilities were tied in some degree to the industries where they had worked. It was also tied to their demographic and labor market characteristics. They were generally less educated and had longer job tenures. A lasting cost of job loss was lower pay on the new job. From the late 1970s to the late 1990s, more than 40 percent of displaced manufacturing workers, no matter what industry they came from, experienced earnings losses, with about 25 percent experiencing earnings losses of 30 percent or more. The sector of reemployment really mattered for these earnings losses. For a less skilled worker, reemployment in manufacturing could mitigate earnings losses. This type of reemployment, however, also exposed workers to future risk of job loss.

There is a broader perspective that comes from continuing to look at the less conventional wisdom of the past. Louis Jacobson, Robert LaLonde, and Daniel Sullivan (1993), using administrative data for a sample of Pennsylvania workers, found large (approximately 25 percent) earnings losses, even five or six years after a job loss. Using Canadian administrative data, Philip Oreopoulos, Marianne Page, and Ann Stevens (2008) looked at the intergenerational cost of job loss. They found that sons whose fathers had been displaced have annual earnings that are lower than the earnings of sons of fathers who did not experience job loss. This result is driven by the experience of children with family incomes at the bottom of the income distribution. The authors were not able to determine causes for this finding. In the time since, however, research has shown that sons of working-class families are in fact far less likely to finish high school, go on to college, and complete college than are daughters of working-class families (Autor et al. 2016). Steven Davis and Till von Wachter (2011), using longitudinal Social Security records for men fifty years of age and younger with three or more years' job tenure, found that job loss from a mass layoff reduces the present discounted value of earnings by an estimated $77,557 over a twenty-year period. Losses are larger when unemployment rates are higher.

The evidence is clear: the earnings losses from this kind of job loss—from losing an established job—are high. This pattern holds particularly for less educated, long-tenure workers. The losses are larger for men than they are for women. For less skilled workers, the principal challenge is finding a job that pays similarly to the old one, when the old one was in manufacturing.

In the twenty-five years I have worked in this area, I have often worried that much of the economics profession has minimized trade-related job loss, and spent too much time quarreling over issues such as how good are our measures, how comfortable are we with the econometrics, and how certain are we of the magnitudes. A shared professional stake in protecting free trade likely contributed to a minimization of areas of agreement about the costs of trade-related job loss. By largely standing on the sidelines during debates about compensation, mainstream economists made a collective contribution to policy and program stasis. Workers have not been assisted well in navigating these difficult transitions. Whether or not this contributed to the Trump victory in November 2016, the result may be more protectionism. What is clear is that the results of the China shock research program should push aside skepticism about measuring and understanding the costs of trade-related job loss.

POLICY OPTIONS

The United States policy record to date is not impressive. Somewhat more optimistically, that record leaves much room for improvement and there is much to be done. Policy must start with the realization that globalization is costly for US workers who work in import-competing sectors or whose jobs otherwise depend on those sectors.[2] And policy makers, to my mind, have really failed to offer effective remediation, let alone to compensate workers who have lost their jobs.

---

[2] Manufacturing workers are the focus of this discussion. Workers employed in tradable services industries also face employment and earnings losses (see Jensen and Kletzer 2006).

Remediation would be a lower bar, but I do not believe we have met even the remediation bar.

Before turning to US policies targeted at trade-displaced workers, it is worthwhile to briefly describe the larger policy and program context.[3] Unemployment insurance (UI) is at the center of the suite of labor market adjustment policies and programs in the United States. Other programs for displaced workers include advance notice for major layoffs, mandated by the Worker Adjustment and Retraining Notification Act, and training and job search assistance, provided under the Workforce Investment Act. The United States is the only country that provides special assistance to workers who lose jobs due to increased imports and international shifts in production, as Trade Adjustment Assistance (TAA). But its social safety net is generally much sparser than those of other advanced economies, where other protections can substitute to some degree for dedicated assistance in the case of trade shocks.

Despite the array of US programs, there is considerable evidence that these labor market interventions are inadequate. Looking at UI (a program designed as a federal-state partnership), benefit amounts, benefit duration, and eligibility are all determined by the states, and because of this design, there is a great deal of regional variation in support. In 2015, only one in four unemployed workers received income-support assistance under the UI program (West et al. 2016). Most states continue to set a maximum benefit duration of twenty-six weeks, although a number of states have moved to considerably shorter maximum durations (e.g., Florida and North Carolina set a twelve-week maximum duration, Georgia set the duration at fourteen weeks, and Kansas set it at sixteen weeks) (Center on Budget and Policy Priorities 2018).

Because UI is meant to provide financial support to workers during a period of unemployment and is explicitly not designed to directly help workers find jobs, it is categorized as a passive labor market policy. The focus of active labor market policies is to increase the employability of unemployed workers. Active labor market policies generally fall into six categories: training programs, job search assistance, employment incentives, supported employment, direct job creation, and other policies. As discussed by Jun Nie and Ethan Struby (2011), training pro-

[3] This context-setting discussion borrows from Kletzer and Rosen 2005; Kletzer 2001.

grams accounted for an average of 28 percent of active labor market policy spending for the OECD countries, with employment incentives and job search assistance accounting for 16 and 11 percent, respectively. The level of spending on labor market policies differs widely across OECD countries. Denmark, Belgium, and Sweden typically top the list, at 3 to 4 percent of GDP, and the United States and United Kingdom occupy the bottom of the list, at 0.5 and 0.25 percent of GDP. US spending on labor market policies is not only low but also tilted heavily toward passive programs, such as UI. In the decade from 1998 to 2008, a full 70 percent of US labor market policy expenditures went to passive programs, while only 30 percent went to active ones. Outside the United States, in contrast, the average OECD country devoted 59 percent of labor market policy expenditures to passive programs and 41 percent to active ones (Nie and Struby 2011).

As noted above, the United States stands out among developed countries in its policy focus on trade-displaced workers, and from here the discussion will focus on these workers and US policy.[4]

TAA is the primary response to trade-related job loss. In various forms, it has been in place since the early 1960s, when it was legislated in parallel with the GATT's Kennedy Round of trade liberalization. A combination of weak labor market adjustment programs for all workers and the manner in which trade policy is conducted in the United States contributed to the establishment of TAA (see Kletzer and Rosen 2005). Practically speaking, Congress must temporarily transfer "trade promotion authority" to the president for the executive branch effectively to conduct trade negotiations. The facilitating legislation provides Congress with an opportunity to influence the negotiating agenda, and Congress has also used this opportunity to compensate US workers potentially adversely affected by changes in foreign competition.

TAA was most recently reauthorized in June 2015, in connection with negotiations over the TPP. To be eligible for TAA, a worker must be certified as having lost a job due to an increase in foreign competition. The certification process is handled by the Department of Labor, through the Employment and Training Administration. A petition is filed with the Employment and Training Administration by an eligible

---

[4] For a more comprehensive presentation of the range of labor market policies, active and passive, in the OECD, see IMF/WB/WTO 2017.

entity (a firm, union, or collection of workers), and the administration determines if the job losses were significantly caused by foreign competition. Eligible workers tend to be full time, long tenured, less educated, and generally live in nonmetropolitan areas with average earnings below the national average. Their pay is relatively high given their average education levels, and their jobs carry benefits (see D'Amico and Schochet 2012). TAA has active and passive assistance components, such as training, trade readjustment allowances (extended UI), and reemployment trade adjustment assistance (wage insurance, to be discussed further below). There are health coverage tax credits that were especially important before the passage of the Affordable Care Act. There is job search assistance, and in TAA's most recent reincarnation, in 2015, there is now individualized case management assistance.

Gordon Hanson's chapter this volume makes it clear that TAA has had little impact on import-sensitive communities. For a $1,000 per worker increase in imports from China during 1990–97, such communities saw a $57.73 increase in annual transfer receipts per capita. That $57.73 comprised $3.65 in UI and TAA benefits, compared with $8.40 in Social Security disability, $10 in Social Security retirement, and $18.27 in Medicaid. Communities experiencing this kind of labor market shock therefore cannot expect much from TAA. In fact, other benefits that workers receive swamp what they get from TAA.

The most recent evaluation of the TAA program was funded in 2004 in order to document program implementation and assess the program's ability to achieve its goal of helping participants rapidly find suitable reemployment. The evaluation was conducted jointly by Social Policy Research Associates and Mathematica Policy Research, over the study period 2004–11 (see D'Amico and Schochet 2012). The study period included the Great Recession of 2007–9, and therefore the measured effects have within them the associated damage to labor markets and the slow recovery. TAA participants were more likely to receive training (and of longer duration), career planning, and job search assistance. Participants were as likely to be employed or in training as were non-participants in the first two years. TAA participants had lower wages and were less likely to have access to fringe benefits on reemployment. Workers participating in TAA had lower incomes overall; the combined income support payments and earnings were lower for participants than for the comparison group. It is difficult to know whether this difference relates to the fact that TAA participants were less advantaged initially or is due to the special circumstances of the Great Recession. But there is certainly no evidence in this study to recommend TAA's effectiveness. Given how little is spent on TAA as well as other programs, and the limited coverage, perhaps mixed and minimal effectiveness is to be expected.

I will close with a brief discussion of wage insurance—an idea that resurfaced in the early 2000s (Kletzer and Litan 2001; Kletzer 2016). Wage insurance is an addition to income and transition support that is worth implementing, not just for workers who lose a job due to trade, but for all workers who lose a job through no fault of their own, including because of technology. The idea has been around since the days of optimal UI; wage insurance can help counteract the negative disincentives of UI because wage insurance is received only when the worker becomes reemployed. In this sense, wage insurance can be seen as an active labor market policy or a kind of employment subsidy. Essentially, wage insurance is a subsidy intended to cover some fraction of the difference between new and old job earnings. Wage insurance can support workers during a period of on-the-job training in a new job and help keep workers attached to the labor force. A narrow program of wage insurance was incorporated in an early 2000s' version of TAA and, as noted above, still exists (as reemployment TAA). The more general idea was revived in President Barack Obama's last State of the Union address in 2016. He proposed wage insurance for all workers who lose a job through no fault of their own, not just trade-displaced workers. A wage insurance program for all displaced workers acknowledges that it may be difficult in practice to separate out the cause of job loss.

Along with a coauthor, I (Kletzer and Litan 2001) proposed a version of wage insurance that could provide a 15 to 20 percent reduction in earnings losses over a two-year period. In another study, I (Kletzer 2004) discussed how the program might work. Eligible workers would receive some fraction, perhaps half, of the weekly earnings loss. The fraction could vary by age and the previous tenure of the worker. Payments begin only when a worker has a new (full-time) job and could continue for up to two years following the initial job loss, as long as the new job paid less than the old one. Annual payments could be capped at $10,000 per year. By "topping up" earnings if the new job pays less than the old one, and for a specified period, the program offers reemployment incentives, in contrast to the incentives in UI and training subsidies.

Continuing with the examples in my study (Kletzer 2004), if an eligible import-competing manufacturing worker made $600 per week on the old full-time job and found a new full-time job paying $520 (13 percent less), the supplemental payment would be $40 per week, for a total weekly earnings of $560.[5] At a 30 percent earnings loss, the new job would pay $420 per week, and the insurance payment would be $90, for weekly earnings of $510. In this case, the supplement could encourage a worker to take a job paying significantly less than the old one, yet with the supplement, the earnings loss is reduced by half.

The reemployment incentive in wage insurance is highlighted when compared with UI benefits. Generally, payments under UI are limited, replacing a little less than 50 percent of the average worker's previous earnings. In 1999, average weekly earnings for a production worker in wage and salary employment were $457, and the average weekly unemployment benefit was $212 (*Economic Report of the President* 2001, tables B-45, B-47). To summarize these examples:

Old job	New job	New job plus supplement	UI benefit
$600	$520	$560	$300
$600	$420	$510	$300
$600	$300	$450	$300

Wage insurance raises the return to job search, and more so for workers with greater reemployment earnings losses. A higher wage insurance replacement rate further increases the return to a job search, while it also reduces the worker's incentive to search for a different higher-paying job (but only during the eligibility period). If the supplement interval is fixed and limited—say, to two years—the present value of the supplement declines with the duration of unemployment and poses an incentive for a quicker return to work. Workers who have a more difficult time finding a job will receive a smaller supplement than workers with short unemployment spells.

[5] The amount of $600 per week coincides with the mean earnings on the prior job, in 1999 dollars, for a worker displaced from a highly import-competing industry, and the mean earnings change for this group was a loss of 13 percent.

High-tenure, lower-skill manufacturing workers will find the greatest value in wage insurance. These workers are not necessarily high wage, but they are earning a wage premium over their best alternatives. Clearly wage insurance is more valuable to these workers than it is to lower-wage workers. Lower-wage displaced workers will find it relatively easier to find an equivalent job and may be less likely to experience large earnings losses. This issue raises questions about fairness—such as that wage insurance helps displaced manufacturing workers preserve their rents for some period of time. Yet at the same time, there are workers who lose the value of their firm-specific human capital with the job loss, and these workers benefit from wage insurance, perhaps especially from the incentive created by the wage subsidy that encourages taking entry-level jobs that offer (new) firm-specific training.

There are some implications from restricting eligibility to full-time employment. Earnings losses are a product of changes in both hourly wages and hours. Either the hourly wage or hours, or both, could be lower on the new job. It is possible that for lower-skill workers, most readily available jobs will be part time, at lower hourly wages. Limiting benefits to those who find one of a limited supply of full-time jobs will end up rewarding winners. At the same time, if the earnings supplement is applied to earnings losses arising from changes in the hours worked, effective pay on the new part-time job could be quite high. For example, as noted by Donald Parsons (2000), if a particular worker's earnings loss arises solely from working part time on the new job, that worker can work half the hours (as compared to the old job) at three-quarters' pay. This level of subsidy could induce a sizable—and not socially desirable—shift to part-time work.

The reemployment incentive aspect of wage insurance gives rise to some standard questions. Will an earnings supplement encourage workers to look sooner or more intensely? Will it broaden the range of job offers considered? Will the supplement lower reservation wages, easing consideration of entry-level jobs in expanding industries—jobs that provide training in new skills and prospects for advancement?

Carl Davidson and Steven Matusz (2006) considered compensatory wage subsidies. The program of wage insurance described here, with a relatively short eligibility period starting on the date of job loss, creates a reemployment incentive and addresses some UI concerns, but it limits the compensatory nature of the program. What we know about the long-term nature of displaced worker earnings losses is that the losses persist five to six years after the job loss, not just two years (see Jacobson, LaLonde, and Sullivan 1993). That said, based on the findings of Davis and von Wachter (2011), wage insurance can make a substantial dent in reemployment earnings losses for two to three years after job loss (except in recessions).

CLOSING REMARKS

As seen recently, the failure to address the costs of globalization is itself costly. Over the past twenty years, many economists worried about demonizing trade by focusing on trade-related job loss and its costs. The appropriate policy was never not to do anything, and not doing anything (or much) likely contributed to the current situation, in which protectionism could run amok. Being caught up in structural economic change can be devastating for workers. Increasing imports is associated with job loss in competing sectors and for those who depend on them. Importantly, it is the job loss, not the circumstance that it may be linked to trade, that is the basic problem. Losing a job is costly. As we think ahead to the policies that we might put in place, we should not lose sight of the dignity and structure of work. We need to broaden the suite of policies that we have, strengthening UI, adding an expansive program of wage insurance, reinvigorating employer-based training, and educating the workforce of the future. This call for a stronger array of workforce policies is not just about trade; it is about supporting workers and communities bearing the costs of economic structural transformation.

REFERENCES

Autor, David H., David Dorn, and Gordon H. Hanson. 2016. "The China Shock: Learning from Labor Market Adjustment to Large Changes in Trade." *Annual Review of Economics* 8, no. 1 (October): 205–40.

Autor, David H., David Figlio, Krzysztof Karbownik, Jeffrey Roth, and Melanie Wasserman. 2016. "Family Disadvantage and the Gender Gap in Behavioral and Educational Outcomes." NBER Working Paper 22267. Cambridge, MA: National Bureau of Economic Research.

Center on Budget and Policy Priorities. 2018. "How Many Weeks of Unemployment Compensation Are Available?" Policy Basics. Washington, DC: Center on Budget and Policy Priorities.

D'Amico, Ronald, and Peter Z. Schochet. 2012. "The Evaluation of the Trade Adjustment Assistance Program: A Synthesis of Major Findings." Oakland, CA: Social Policy Research Associates.

Davidson, Carl, and Steven Matusz. 2006. "Trade Liberalization and Compensation." *International Economic Review* 45, no. 3 (August): 723–47.

Davis, Steven J., and Till M. von Wachter. 2011. "Recessions and the Cost of Job Loss." *Brookings Papers on Economic Activity*, Fall, 42: 1–72. Washington, DC: Brookings Institution.

Economic Report of the President. 2001. Washington, DC: Government Printing Office.

IMF/WB/WTO (International Monetary Fund, World Bank, and World Trade Organization). 2017. "Making Trade an Engine of Growth for All: The Case for Trade and for Policies to Facilitate Adjustment." Washington, DC: International Monetary Fund.

Jacobson, Louis, Robert LaLonde, and Daniel Sullivan. 1993. *The Costs of Worker Dislocation.* Kalamazoo, MI: W. E. Upjohn Institute for Employment Research.

Jensen, J. Bradford, and Lori G. Kletzer. 2006. "Tradable Services: Understanding the Scope and Impact of Services Offshoring." In *Brookings Trade Forum: 2005*, edited by Susan M. Collins and Lael Brainard, 75–134. Washington, DC: Brookings Institution Press.

Kletzer, Lori G. 2001. *Job Loss from Imports: Measuring the Costs.* Washington, DC: Institute for International Economics.

———. 2004. "Trade-Related Job Loss and Wage Insurance: A Synthetic Review." *Review of International Economics* 12, no. 5 (November): 724–48.

———. 2016. "Why the U.S. Needs Wage Insurance." *Harvard Business Review*, January 25. https://hbr.org/2016/01/why-the-u-s-needs-wage-insurance.

Kletzer, Lori G., and Robert E. Litan. 2001. "A Prescription to Relieve Worker Anxiety." International Economics Policy Brief PB01-2. Washington, DC: Institute for International Economics.

Krugman, Paul R., and Maurice Obstfeld. 2008. *International Economics: Theory and Policy.* 8th ed. New York: Pearson.

Kletzer, Lori G., and Howard Rosen. 2005. "Easing the Adjustment Burden on US Workers." In *The United States and the World Economy: Foreign Economic Policy for the Next Decade*, edited by C. Fred Bergsten, 313–42. Washington, DC: Institute for International Economics.

Nie, Jun, and Ethan Struby. 2011. "Would Active Labor Market Policies Help Combat High U.S. Unemployment?" *Federal Reserve Bank of Kansas Economic Review, Third Quarter*, 35–69.

Oreopoulos, Philip, Marianne Page, and Ann Stevens. 2008. "The Intergenerational Effects of Worker Displacement." *Journal of Labor Economics* 26, no. 3 (July): 455–83.

Parsons, Donald O. 2000. "Wage Insurance: A Policy Review." *Research in Employment Policy*, 2: 119–40. Greenwich, CT: JAI Press.

West, Rachel, Indivar Dutta-Gupta, Kali Grant, Melissa Boteach, Claire McKenna, and Judy Conti. 2016. "Strengthening Unemployment Protections in America: Modernizing Unemployment Insurance and Establishing a Jobseeker's Allowance." Washington, DC: Center for American Progress.

PART V

THE POLITICAL ECONOMY
OF TRADE BACKLASH

12

The Political Economy of the Globalization Backlash: Sources and Implications

JEFFRY FRIEDEN

For at least two decades, scholars and other observers have understood that international economic integration—globalization—has in the past, and could in the present, give rise to a backlash.[1] Over the past few years, in much of the advanced industrial world, we have gotten a sense of what that backlash looks like.

Political discontent has been central to the globalization backlash. Dissatisfaction has taken the form of large increases in voting for extremist political parties, the emergence of new parties and movements, and challenges from within existing parties. Large numbers of voters have rejected existing political institutions, parties, and politicians, often in favor of "populists" of the Right or Left whose common themes include skepticism about economic integration and resentment of ruling elites. In the United States, both Bernard Sanders and Donald Trump ran on programs that were openly hostile to international trade, investment, and finance; Trump also campaigned in favor of tighter controls on immigration. In Europe, the populist turn of the Right has largely centered on antagonism to European integration and immigration; the populism of the Left has mostly attacked austerity programs associated

[1] I want to thank the following for useful comments and suggestions on this chapter: Matilde Bombardini, Alessandra Casella, Andrew Coe, Lindsay Dolan, Chase Foster, Peter Hall, George Hoguet, Stephen Kaplan, Casey Kearney, Helen Milner, Stefanie Rickard, Ken Shepsle, Jack Snyder, David Stasavage, Dustin Tingley, and Stefanie Walter.

with the European Union's disastrous attempts to manage the eurozone debt crisis.

This chapter analyzes the sources of contemporary political discontent, with particular attention to the United States. I focus on the economic and political roots of the populist upsurge, leaving cultural and related issues to others. On the economic front, economic integration has had an adverse impact on many communities, and compensatory mechanisms have not addressed this impact effectively; there has been a *failure of compensation*. On the political front, large groups in the population have been alienated from mainstream political institutions, finding it hard to have their concerns taken seriously by existing political institutions; there has been a *failure of representation*. Both failures have been developing for decades, and there are many obstacles to overcoming them. I suggest some possible paths that politics may take in the current situation and their implications.

POLITICS AND THE DISTRIBUTIONAL EFFECTS OF ECONOMIC INTEGRATION

Increasing a country's ties to the international economy improves aggregate social welfare, but it also creates both winners and losers. A substantial and growing literature seeks to clarify how the distributional impact of globalization affects politics. The general conclusion is that groups and regions harmed by greater exposure to the international economy are more likely to vote for populist and extreme political parties and candidates as well as measures to reduce globalization. Most studies emphasize the impact of trade in manufactured products, especially with low-wage developing countries, for it is this trade that is expected, both theoretically and empirically, to have the most prominent negative effects on workers in North America and western Europe.[2]

Increased exposure to Chinese imports into western European countries is associated with more nationalistic voting and more votes for extreme right-wing parties (Colantone and Stanig, 2018b). In France specifically, regions more affected by low-wage import competition from developing countries were significantly more likely to vote for the

---

[2] Most of these studies use some variant of the China shock instrument first developed in Autor, Dorn, and Hanson 2013.

National Front, an extremist party hostile to both globalization and European integration, and this effect has grown over time. In the United Kingdom, exposure to Chinese import competition has been associated with a rise in authoritarian values, especially aggression born of frustration (Ballard-Rosa et al. 2017). Voting on the referendum to leave the European Union (dubbed Brexit) was also affected by susceptibility to trade. While some supporters of Brexit saw it as freeing the United Kingdom from the European Union's strictures on economic activity, surveys indicate that a substantial proportion of Brexit voters saw it as a way to limit economic ties with the rest of Europe, including immigration. In fact, areas harder hit by trade competition, in particular from China, were more likely to vote to leave the European Union (Colantone and Stanig 2018a).[3]

Many regions in the United States have experienced job losses and reduced wages due to the China shock, and more generally to low-wage imports from developing countries.[4] These regions have become more politically polarized since 2000 (Autor et al. 2016a). Their legislators have tended to vote in more protectionist directions (Feigenbaum and Hall 2015). And perhaps most strikingly, they were more likely to swing their votes toward Trump in the 2016 presidential election (Autor et al. 2016b; see also Jensen, Quinn, and Weymouth 2017). More generally, job losses due to trade have twice as large a negative impact on votes for incumbent politicians than do job losses for other reasons. This effect is stronger in midwestern industrial states; in some of them, the negative effect of trade-related job loss is greater than the difference in votes between incumbents and challengers (Margalit 2011).

Americans often blame globalization for job insecurity, due largely to the employment effects of low-wage foreign competition. It is also common for Americans to blame globalization for the increasing disparities between the middle class and the top 10 or 1 percent of US society. Bankers, corporate executives, and professionals in the

---

[3] Sascha Becker, Thiemo Fetzer, and Dennis Novy (2017) argue that the vote was more strongly affected by underlying socioeconomic characteristics of constituencies, and in particular by low income and education, high unemployment, and substantial employment in manufacturing.

[4] While I am not familiar with studies on the analogous distributional implications of the integration of capital markets, there are a few on the impact of foreign direct investment, or what's called offshoring. See especially Owen and Johnston 2017.

internationalized segments of the US economy are seen as having taken great advantage of their global ties, while leaving the middle and working classes behind.

There is no doubt that there are also noneconomic sources of the turn toward populism, including cultural bias and ethnic prejudice. I address one of these noneconomic sources below, but leave most to others. Similarly, the economic trends in question are not solely due to economic integration. Skill-biased technological change certainly has put downward pressure on the earnings of un- and semiskilled workers, and (probably fruitless) debates continue over the relative importance of trade and technological change. Nonetheless, technological change is not typically a policy variable, while trade and other international economic activities are; in addition, a focus on trade appeals to many— including many politicians—because it appears to make foreigners pay for some of the costs of globalization. For the purposes of this chapter, I focus on the economic sources of the populist backlash. I also, for both reasons of data availability and personal comparative advantage, draw most of my examples from the United States.

Two significant points are sometimes lost in current discussions. First, the broad trends that underlie present-day discontent are of long duration; they did not start when China joined the WTO. The first major wave of manufactured imports from low-wage developing countries began in the late 1960s, and accelerated through the 1970s and 1980s. As early as 1978, a year before China started opening up to the world economy, US manufactured imports from developing countries were at least 25 percent of the total, up from 13 percent ten years earlier (Grossman 1982, 272).[5] By 1990, when both the deindustrialization of the rust belt and "trade and wages" debate among economists were in full swing, developing countries accounted for 36 percent of the United States' manufactured imports; at that point, China was only fourth on the list of developing country exporters, well behind Taiwan, Mexico, and Korea.[6]

A second significant point is that these economic trends have a powerful impact on *communities* as well as individuals. This is a consequence of the historical geographic concentration of US manufacturing in the

[5] Another study (Sachs and Shatz 1994, 1) put the 1978 number at 29 percent.

[6] For a summary of the state of the debate on trade and deindustrialization since the 1990s, see Krugman 2008; and Krugman's chapter in this volume.

Midwest and parts of the South, and the fact that many of the industrial facilities hit hard by import competition are in towns or small cities. These communities have experienced a series of cascading effects of trade- and investment-related pressures on local manufacturing. The direct economic impact includes higher unemployment and lower wages in the short run, and eventually more underemployment, less labor force participation, and out-migration by the more mobile inhabitants. Over time there are *indirect* economic effects. As the local economy suffers, local income and property values fall, which leads to a decline in local government tax revenue and hence a deterioration of local public services.[7] The erosion of a community's economic base eventually has *social* effects, including a rise in alcoholism, opioid abuse, and suicidality (Pierce and Schott, forthcoming).

In the United States at least, there is substantial, albeit at this point only suggestive, evidence for this trajectory.[8] More recently, the extremely sharp and long recession that began in December 2007 severely aggravated ongoing trends, especially for those outside the top 25 percent of the income distribution. Median household wealth, for example, was still 34 percent below its 2007 levels ten years after the crisis began (Wolff 2017). This is, I believe, a major source of the political discontent that bubbled up, first with the Tea Party movement in 2010, and then with the candidacies of Sanders and Trump.

To identify economic integration as a significant source of political dissatisfaction is not to imply that voters have a clear notion of precisely how trade affects them. It is perfectly plausible—and indeed likely—that subjective perceptions of trade's impact are in many cases based on a broad sense of unease about current economic trends rather than on a clear analysis of the distributional impact of trade. Trade in particular and globalization more generally contributed to a general decline in the quality of life in many communities in the United States. Residents of these communities are aware of the decline, and although they may have no clear sense of its sources, one visible indicator is that local factories that used to provide decent-paying jobs have closed or moved abroad due to foreign competition. The generalized dissatisfaction that

[7] For a careful discussion and documentation of these effects, see Feler and Senses 2017.

[8] With colleagues, I am working to gather more systematic evidence about the process, and other scholars are engaged in similar enterprises.

results takes many forms, including a hostility to international economic engagement. Again, this is *not* to suggest that voters have a sophisticated model of the distributional impact of trade. It is to say that they know that their communities are doing poorly, trade probably played some role in the problem, and existing politicians have not done enough to halt the decline. This provides a foundation that populist political entrepreneurs can use for their own purposes—including fanning the flames of economic nationalism.

Indeed, in both the United States and Europe, the populist upsurge contains at least as much hostility toward political "elites" and traditional political institutions more broadly as it does toward globalization per se. It is difficult to separate the two strands of hostility: elites are blamed for having failed to manage globalization adequately, and globalization is blamed for having unduly rewarded elites. Nonetheless, in most of the contemporary populist political movements there is a strong strain of distrust in government itself. It is to this that I now turn.

POLITICS AND THE LOSS OF CONFIDENCE IN GOVERNMENT

Closely related to accelerating skepticism about globalization has been a loss of trust in the institutions of government. This has been apparent in US public opinion: after fluctuating over the course of the 1980s and 1990s, the proportion of Americans who say they trust the government in Washington, DC, all or most of the time has dropped continually from the vicinity of 50 percent around the year 2000 to below 20 percent today. There are differences among socioeconomic and partisan groups, but the decline in confidence in the government is universal. Not surprisingly, groups more likely to support Trump's candidacy were also less likely to trust the federal government; whites, older people, and those without a college degree all evince more distrust than blacks or Hispanics, younger people, and those with a college degree.[9]

European public opinion has undergone a similar evolution. In the case of Europe, the collapse in confidence began with the European debt crisis, and it takes the form of increased distrust of national governments, the institutions of the European Union, or both. Here too,

[9] For one comprehensive survey, see Pew Research Center 2015.

there are clear differences across countries and socioeconomic groups. People in the more crisis-affected debtor nations have lost much more confidence in the European Union and their national governments than have those in the less hard-hit creditor nations. Nonetheless, dissatisfaction with the functioning of traditional political institutions, parties, and politicians has grown in every country. The level of dissatisfaction as well as its growth have been greater among poorer and less educated Europeans than among wealthier and better-educated ones.[10]

Increased hostility to existing political parties, governments, and European institutions is clearly central to the populist upsurge. In both the United States and many European countries, those drawn to populism regard mainstream politicians and policy makers as indifferent to the concerns of common people. This does not necessarily mean that those voting for more extreme political parties share the views of the parties themselves. In fact, there is evidence in Europe that voters' ideological proclivities have not changed; what has changed has been their willingness to vote for more extreme candidates. The obvious implication is that at least some of the voting for more extreme, populist, political parties and candidates is classical "protest voting."

Nevertheless, it is clear that there have been substantial changes in the politics of globalization in much of Europe and North America. Important segments of the public are hostile to economic integration—international in the United States, and European in the European Union—while similarly important segments of the voting public are distrustful of traditional political parties and politicians. In what follows, I suggest that hostility to globalization is largely due to the failures of compensation, while distrust of political institutions is the result of the failures of representation.

THE FAILURES OF COMPENSATION

A basic principle of economics is that economic policies or trends that increase aggregate social welfare can be Pareto improvements with the right redistributive policies. Even if the policy or trend harms some, income can be reallocated from the beneficiaries to the losers in such

[10] For detailed, complementary data and analysis of these trends, see Algan et al. 2017; Dustmann et al. 2017; Frieden 2016; Foster and Frieden 2017.

a way as to make everyone better off. Any realistic model of trade, for example, posits that there will be winners and losers. But in principle, a compensatory scheme can be designed that addresses the costs to the losers without erasing the gains of the winners.

A basic principle of political economy, however, is that the winners from an economic policy or trend do not like having their gains taxed away in order to compensate the losers. This means that many Pareto improvements may not be politically feasible. If it is politically infeasible to compensate the losers from economic integration, the actual or potential losers are likely to react with hostility to both the political system and economic integration. To put it differently, a globalization backlash is likely to be mitigated by compensation mechanisms, and the absence of adequate compensation is likely to feed a globalization backlash.

The economic and social problems associated with the distributional impact of globalization have deep roots, and it will take substantial long-term policies to address these roots. Most advanced societies need to improve the quality of as well as access to education in order to help overcome the skills mismatch that has contributed to distress in some segments of the labor market and job shortages in others. Many countries are saddled with an outdated economic infrastructure, including in telecommunications, whose modernization will help bring more people and regions into the mainstream of economic life. But these reforms are for the long run, and are politically and economically difficult. More immediately pressing problems have fed the populist upsurge, and more immediate responses are necessary.

In this context, it is clear that governments in at least some countries have failed to provide compensation sufficient to overcome the concerns of those harmed by international economic integration. It is equally apparent—given the great variation in the appeal of populist antiglobalization movements among industrial countries—that the extent of this failure varies substantially among countries. This, then, suggests a question that is important both analytically and for policy makers: What explains why governments might be more or less likely to provide compensation for those harmed by international trade and investment?

There is long-standing evidence that small, open economies have developed more encompassing compensatory policies These policies are often associated with a substantial centralization of the institutions of both labor and management, and coordination between them and the government. The logic is that small, open economies have evolved to minimize the political costs of openness, inasmuch as their small size makes openness a necessity. In turn, political institutions in these countries have evolved so that major socioeconomic groups internalize the potential economic, social, and political costs of economic integration, and are willing to support compensatory policies. In the stylized picture of the political economies that fit this characterization, labor and management dependent on access to the world economy work together with government to cushion the impact of foreign competition with some combination of monetary transfers, retraining, mobility assistance, and related measures.[11]

The political economy of compensation is complicated, and varies from country to country. On the one hand, there is some evidence that even in the United States, export-oriented firms support compensation—as do those most negatively affected (Rickard 2015; Walter 2010). There are major differences, however, due to both variation in the causes and effects of the displacement, and among political systems (see, for example, Burgoon 2000; Menendez 2016).

Casual observation suggests that countries with broad and deep social safety nets that address many of the distributional effects of globalization have seen relatively small populist movements. On the other hand, the populist upsurge reflected in the campaigns of Sanders and Trump was particularly powerful in the United States, whose compensatory mechanisms and safety net are probably the least extensive among advanced countries.

The United States' principal compensation scheme, TAA, is small, politically contentious, and largely ineffective (see the chapters by Lori Kletzer and Gordon Hanson in this volume). It reaches few workers; indeed, trade-affected workers are far more likely to have recourse to disability benefits than TAA benefits. Perhaps more important, TAA is targeted at individuals, who must show direct harm from imports. This means that the program cannot address the broad effects of globalization on *communities* rather than specific workers—the main

---

[11] For early statements of this view, see Cameron 1977; Katzenstein 1985. For a work that systematizes and generalizes the argument, see Rodrik 1998.

channel for transmission of globalization discontent to the political system.

Compensation mechanisms vary across countries because policy makers supply them in line with the political incentives to do so. These incentives are a function of the organization of both groups representing potential beneficiaries of these social policies and those concerned to keep incipient opposition to economic integration at bay. The canonical examples are societies in which labor and management are extensively organized and centralized, and where they have a history of working together and with government to address potentially disruptive sociopolitical discontent. This pattern tends to be more prevalent in small, open economies, including Scandinavian social democracies, and the other developed northern European societies. At the other extreme are larger economies as well as societies in which labor and management are weakly organized, fragmented, or both, and in which there is little tradition of labor, management, and the government working together consensually to address social problems. The prototype of such a socioeconomic system is the United States. As noted, political support for compensation in the form of TAA is extremely limited—a fact reflected in its small budget and narrow reach.

Where socioeconomic structures and their political reflection give policy makers few incentives to attempt Pareto-improving social insurance or compensation, supply will lag demand—and this failure of compensation provides fertile ground for the rise of extremist opponents of both globalization and prevailing political institutions. Compensation failure thus can feed into a sense that the very foundations of representative government have failed as well. There are, in other words, clear connections between the failures of compensation and representation.

THE FAILURES OF REPRESENTATION

The widespread loss of confidence in government has expressed itself differently in different countries. In most, however, it has taken the form of opposing traditional, "mainstream" political institutions, parties, and politicians. As already mentioned, there is little, if any, indication that voters have actually become more extreme ideologically. But in many countries, they have shown a decided willingness to vote for extremist political parties, movements, and candidates within parties. Many voters appear to be looking for ways to indicate their displeasure with the political and policy status quo. Traditional, mainstream political parties and politicians have not brought many of these voters' concerns prominently enough to the political agenda. Such a failure of representation takes different forms in different political settings.

Some Western political systems have been dominated by two major parties (or coalitions) that have consensually supported the trend toward increased international economic integration—in some cases, without substantial compensation. In such "cartelized" political systems, those who feel ill treated and unrepresented by the dominant parties have only two choices: they can vote for either new political parties that challenge the trend or insurgent candidates within the existing parties. France's experience with the National Front seems closest to the former pattern; the US trajectories of the Sanders and Trump candidacies conform to the latter pattern. The United Kingdom experienced a similar phenomenon: given general agreement between the bulk of both major parties, disgruntled politicians and voters found a way to reject existing trends via Brexit. What ties all these instances together is that voters appear dissatisfied with the extent to which existing politicians represent their interests. When dissatisfied voters are given few options they like by the two dominant parties, they can react either by deserting traditional parties or voting to fundamentally transform them. On the Left, Syriza in Greece and Podemos in Spain would appear to fit into the category of creating a new force in what had been a largely two-party (or two-bloc) system.

Countries whose electoral systems give rise to multiple parties—typically with some form of proportional representation—present a different environment. Where new parties can enter easily or there is already a wide spectrum of views represented, unhappy voters have a protest option with a chance of being represented in the legislature. While some proportional representation systems have higher entry barriers, in many the degree of cartelization of the political system is lower than in systems dominated by two parties. This has made it possible, for example, for the extreme Left in Portugal to be both well represented in the legislature and effectively a part of the ruling coalition, while the extreme Right in Austria is an official coalition partner in government. The rise of Alternative für Deutschland and similar right-wing populist movements in northern Europe is similar: electoral protest has taken the form of voting for small extreme parties. Italy, with its mixed electoral system, is a bit of a hybrid: the right-wing, populist Northern League and new antiestablishment Five Star Movement supplanted the more established center Left and center Right.

Whatever one may think of the presence of Communists and neo-fascists in parliament, the fact that disgruntled voters have an opportunity to express their dissatisfaction may act as something of an escape valve for the pressures that contributed to the victory of Trump in the United States and Brexit in the United Kingdom. In countries like the United States, the sense on the part of many people that they had no political voice was a serious enough failure of representation to play a major role in Trump's rise. The presence of parties like Alternative für Deutschland in Germany and the Communists in Portugal provides an outlet for those who feel they lack true representation. These mechanisms may help explain the different course that the rise of populist and antiglobalization sentiment has taken in different countries.

IMPLICATIONS FOR THE FUTURE

It is not difficult to project the continuation of these trends into the future: populist candidates will win more elections, and there will be a turn toward more economically nationalist policies in some countries, which encourages others to move in the same direction. International economic cooperation will begin to break down, while traditional centrist political parties will find it more difficult to sustain the domestic and international commitments that have dominated the post–World War II period.

While this downward spiral is certainly plausible, it is also possible to imagine forces that counteract it. There are powerful interests, especially in the business community, that stand to lose a great deal if international trade, finance, and investment are impeded by increasingly nationalistic and protectionist governments. Yet given the powerful populist sentiments in many countries—not least in the United States—it is not clear that the opposition of big business would be sufficient to slow the turn toward more nationalist and protectionist policies. An alternative possibility is that internationalist businesses, and the social classes that rely on them, accept that part of the cost of their access to the world economy is paying for much more generous compensation for people and regions that have not shared in globalization-fed prosperity.

The notion that the United States' globalization winners might accept redistribution toward its losers may seem improbable. To some extent, however, this was precisely the arrangement that structured the construction of the Bretton Woods order in the aftermath of World War II: an agreement that both economic openness and the welfare state were reasonable goals (Ruggie 1982). Indeed, few would have anticipated that the Great Depression of the 1930s would create a Democratic Party coalition that included southern segregationists, northern business and labor, and northern blacks—and yet that coalition dominated both national politics and the building of the postwar world order for decades. By the same token, the farmer-labor entente that was the core of many postwar European political alliances came after decades of bitter conflict between the two groups (Luebbert 1991).

It may be the case that until recently, most politicians in the United States and Europe felt little need to represent the concerns of those people and communities hard hit by globalization, but in the current environment they have strong incentives to take notice. Trump and Marine Le Pen are hardly the only politicians to have recognized trends in public opinion, and we can expect that there will be a new generation of politicians attempting to ride the populist wave. Some of them may see the possibility of different coalitions, given national socioeconomic and political conditions. Any observer of US politics is struck by the spectacle of the Democratic Party's attempts to recraft and repackage itself in this new environment. The fact that so far it has been unsuccessful does not mean that success is impossible.

There is also an international dimension to the dynamic. If country after country turns inward, the incentives of the remaining nations to maintain strong international economic ties declines. This was the downward spiral that characterized international economic relations in the early 1930s. If, however, some of the major powers are able to make purposive steps in the direction of sustaining economic cooperation, the incentives to turn inward are weakened. The domestic political economy of international cooperation interacts with its international politics: the stronger domestic political support is for international engagement, the easier is cooperation, and the more successful is cooperation, the stronger is domestic political support.

CONCLUSION

The industrialized world is being swept by a wave of popular sentiment skeptical of economic integration and hostile to the political institutions that have encouraged it. The economic sources of this populist upsurge are of long duration, and are both broad and deep.

Populist skepticism about globalization and European integration largely grows out of the failures of compensation: the weakness of mechanisms to address the social costs of international trade, investment, and immigration. Populist distrust of existing political institutions largely reflects the failures of representation: the unwillingness or inability of mainstream political parties and politicians to address the concerns of those who feel they have been left behind by the galloping pace of economic change.

The growing success of these populist movements may signal a turn away from the world economy, at least for some countries. If the trend gathers enough momentum, it could substantially reverse the past several decades of economic integration and international cooperation.

Yet there is nothing inevitable about the inadequacy of compensation and defects of representation that have provoked the strongest movements against international economic integration since the 1930s. Socioeconomic interests, political parties, and politicians created the conditions that have spawned the current trends. They can create the conditions for an effective response to these trends—one that does not unravel the social and economic gains of the past fifty years, and instead makes them more inclusive and expansive.

REFERENCES

Algan, Yann, Sergei Guriev, Elias Papaioannou, and Evgenia Passari. 2017. "The European Trust Crisis and the Rise of Populism." Brookings Papers on Economic Activity Conference Draft, September 7–8. Washington, DC: Brookings Institution.

Autor, David H., David Dorn, and Gordon H. Hanson. 2013. "The China Syndrome: Local Labor Market Effects of Import Competition in the United States. *American Economic Review* 103, no. 6 (October): 2121–68.

Autor, David H., David Dorn, Gordon H. Hanson, and Kaveh Majlesi. 2016a. "Importing Political Polarization? The Electoral Consequences of Rising Trade Exposure." NBER Working Paper 22637. Cambridge, MA: National Bureau of Economic Research.

———. 2016b. "A Note on the Effect of Rising Trade Exposure on the 2016 Presidential Election." Unpublished manuscript, November.

Ballard-Rosa, Cameron, Mashail Malik, Stephanie Rickard, and Kenneth Scheve. 2017. "The Economic Origins of Authoritarian Values: Evidence from Local Trade Shocks in the United Kingdom." Working paper, October.

Becker, Sascha, Thiemo Fetzer, and Dennis Novy. 2017. "Who Voted for Brexit? A Comprehensive District-Level Analysis." *Economic Policy* 32, 92 (October): 601–50.

Burgoon, Brian. 2001. "Globalization and Welfare Compensation: Disentangling the Ties That Bind." *International Organization* 55, no. 3: 509–51.

Cameron, David R. 1978. "The Expansion of the Public Economy: A Comparative Analysis." *American Political Science Review* 72 (May): 1243–61.

Colantone, Italo, and Piero Stanig. 2018a. "Global Competition and Brexit." *American Political Science Review* 112, no. 2: 201–18.

———. 2018b. "The Trade Origins of Economic Nationalism: Import Competition and Voting Behavior in Western Europe." *American Journal of Political Science* 62, no. 4 (October): 936–53.

Dustmann, Christian, Barry Eichengreen, Sebastian Otten, André Sapir, Guido Tabellini, and Gylfi Zoega. 2017. *Europe's Trust Deficit: Causes and Remedies.* London: CEPR Press.

Feigenbaum, James, and Andrew Hall. 2015. "How Legislators Respond to Localized Economic Shocks: Evidence from Chinese Import Competition." *Journal of Politics* 77, no. 4 (October): 1012–30.

Feler, Leo, and Mine Z. Senses. 2017. "Trade Shocks and the Provision of Local Public Goods." *American Economic Journal: Economic Policy* 9, no. 4 (October): 101–43.

Foster, Chase, and Jeffry Frieden. 2017. "Crisis of Trust: Socio-economic Determinants of Europeans' Confidence in Government." *European Union Politics* 18, no. 4 (April): 511–35.

Frieden, Jeffry. 2016. "The Crisis, the Public, and the Future of European Integration." In *After the Crisis: Reform, Recovery, and Growth in Europe*, edited by Francesco Caselli, Mario Centeno, and Jose Albuquerque Tavares, 146–70. Oxford: Oxford University Press.

Grossman, Gene M. 1982. "Import Competition from Developed and Developing Countries." *Review of Economics and Statistics* 64, no. 2 (May): 271–81.

Jensen, J. Bradford, Dennis Quinn, and Stephen Weymouth. 2017. "Winners and Losers in International Trade: The Effects on U.S. Presidential Voting." *International Organization* 71, no. 3 (Summer): 423–57.

Katzenstein, Peter J. 1985. *Small States in World Markets: Industrial Policy in Europe.* Ithaca, NY: Cornell University Press.

Krugman, Paul. 2008. "Trade and Wages, Reconsidered." *Brookings Papers on Economic Activity* 1, (Spring): 103–54.

Luebbert, Gregory M. 1991. *Liberalism, Fascism, or Social Democracy: Social Classes and the Political Origins of Regimes in Interwar Europe.* Oxford: Oxford University Press.

Margalit, Yotam. 2011. "Costly Jobs: Trade-Related Layoffs, Government Compensation, and Voting in U.S. Elections." *American Political Science Review* 105, no. 1 (February): 166–88.

Menendez, Irene. 2016. "Globalization and Welfare Spending: How Geography and Electoral Institutions Condition Compensation." *International Studies Quarterly* 60, no. 4 (August): 665–76.

Owen, Erica, and Noel P. Johnston. 2017. "Occupation and the Political Economy of Trade: Job Routineness, Offshorability, and Protectionist Sentiment." *International Organization* 71, no. 4 (Fall): 665–99.

Pew Research Center. 2015. *Beyond Distrust: How Americans View Their Government*. Washington, DC: Pew Research Center.

Pierce, Justin R., and Peter K. Schott. Forthcoming. "Trade Liberalization and Mortality: Evidence from U.S. Counties." *American Economic Review: Insights*.

Rickard, Stephanie J. 2015. "Compensating the Losers: An Examination of Congressional Votes on Trade Adjustment Assistance." *International Interactions* 41, no. 1 (January): 46–60.

Rodrik, Dani. 1998. "Why Do More Open Economies Have Bigger Governments?" *Journal of Political Economy* 106, no. 5 (October): 997–1032.

Ruggie, John G. 1982. "International Regimes, Transactions, and Change: Embedded Liberalism in the Postwar Economic Order." *International Organization* 36: 379–415.

Sachs, Jeffrey, and Howard Shatz. 1994. "Trade and Jobs in U.S. Manufacturing." *Brookings Papers on Economic Activity*, 1: 1–69. Washington, DC: Brookings Institution.

Walter, Stefanie. 2010. "Globalization and the Welfare State: Testing the Microfoundations of the Compensation Hypothesis." *International Studies Quarterly* 54, no. 2 (June): 403–26.

Wolff, Edward N. 2017. "Household Wealth Trends in the United States, 1962 to 2016: Has Middle Class Wealth Recovered?" NBER Working Paper 24085. Cambridge, MA: National Bureau of Economic Research.

13

Roots and Offshoots of Current US Trade Policy

EDWARD ALDEN

In the first twenty months of his presidency, Trump threatened to rip up NAFTA with Canada and Mexico, slapped tariffs on imports of steel, aluminum, solar panels, and washing machines, and imposed new duties on nearly half of all imports from China. He walked away from the TPP, a regional trade agreement that would have modernized economic rules for 40 percent of the global economy, and turned his back on the multilateral rules of the WTO in favor of bilateral deals in which the United States could throw around its economic weight against smaller partners. The moves upended the long-standing position of the United States as a champion of global, liberal trade and raised the specter of trade wars of the sort the world has not seen since the 1930s.

Whether Trump carries through on all his threats, or is kept in check by farmers, manufacturers, and Wall Street traders wary of disruption, there is little doubt that the United States has forced the world into a new era on trade. Trump has a long-standing, consistent view on trade: the rest of the world is winning, and the United States is losing. In the 2016 election, he brought just enough of the country along with him, and quickly took US trade policy in new and often-unpredictable directions. But his goal is clear: he no longer wants the United States to be the guardian of a system of global trade rules; instead, he wants a country that pursues more narrowly self-interested measures that he hopes will make the United States a "winner" in global trade. For a trading system that was built and sustained under US leadership, the implications of this new approach are enormous—and the impact will depend as much on how other countries respond as on the actions taken by the United States.

Trump's views on US trade policy are not newly formed and are far more developed than on virtually any other issue. During his first flirtation with running for president, in 1987, the then real estate developer took out full-page ads in the *New York Times*, *Washington Post*, and *Boston Globe* in the form of "an open letter to the American people." In the ads, he attacked Japan for relying on the United States to defend it militarily while building "a strong and vibrant economy with unprecedented surpluses," and keeping the yen weak to boost exports (Kruse 2016). Trump was referring here, of course, to Japan's large trade surplus with the United States, and has maintained his fixation with bilateral trade deficits as the scorecard for which nations are winning and losing on trade.

During the entire 2016 election campaign, Trump gave only one truly substantive policy speech—in June 2016 in the former steel town of Monessen, Pennsylvania, in which he laid out his trade policy plans. Monessen is the sort of place that Trump had in mind when he spoke in his dark inaugural address of "the rusted-out factories scattered like tombstones across the landscape of our nation" (Trump 2017). In the 1960s, Monessen had been a bustling town of close to twenty thousand, with two large steel plants; by 2016, the population had shrunk to seventy-five hundred, academic achievement ranked 475th out of 500 school districts in Pennsylvania, and the closest thing to a steel plant was a recycler of crushed aluminum cans that served as the backdrop for Trump's speech. In that speech, the future president blamed trade for the loss of well-paid manufacturing jobs. He promised to quit the TPP agreement with Japan and ten other Asia-Pacific countries—a deal that had been pursued energetically by both the Bush and Obama administrations. Trump said he would force a renegotiation of the 1994 NAFTA with Canada and Mexico. He pledged to declare China a currency manipulator, and use the full panoply of largely dormant trade enforcement tools against China and other offenders, including Section 232 of the Trade Expansion Act of 1962 along with Sections 201 and 301 of the Trade Act of 1974.[1] Except for China's currency practices—

[1] For a transcription of Trump's June 28, 2016, campaign speech in Monessen, see https://www.politico.com/story/2016/06/full-transcript-trump-job-plan-speech-224891.

on which he appears to have relented in the face of contrary evidence that China is no longer pursuing an artificially weak renminbi—his administration has moved forward on each of these promises (Swanson and Paletta 2017).

Trump's message on trade had a lot of resonance during the election campaign and was a big reason for his electoral victory. Gordon Hanson's pathbreaking work with David Autor and David Dorn has helped bring to light some of the concentrated costs of trade opening in those parts of the country that were most exposed to import competition from China (Autor, Dorn, and Hanson 2012, 2016; chapter 7 in this volume). Trump won the election in closely contested states like Pennsylvania, Ohio, Michigan, North Carolina, and Wisconsin—all places that saw some of the sharpest reductions in manufacturing employment in the 2000s in no small part because of import competition.[2]

So if it is your core belief that the United States has been a loser from trade, what can you do as president? One possibility, as others in this volume have argued, and as I contend in part in my book *Failure to Adjust*, is that the United States should look inward at the various things it could be doing to adjust more effectively to global economic competition and spread the benefits of trade more evenly—through more career-focused education, less wasteful health spending, effective retraining programs, progressive tax reform, and more extensive investment in infrastructure, including in broadband for schools and rural areas (Alden 2017). If you look at labor market adjustment measures in particular, the United States does far less than any other advanced economy to help those who lose jobs find their way back into the labor market.[3]

This is certainly not President Trump's approach. Indeed, his first proposed budgets would have slashed spending on most forms of retraining and support for the unemployed, and the tax-cutting bill he signed in December 2017 will largely profit the wealthiest and reduce tax revenues available to help the "losers" from trade. Trump's approach should instead be understood in light of what the political scientist

---

[2] For manufacturing job losses by state, see Scott 2015. For the debate over trade versus technology as a cause of lost manufacturing employment, see Houseman 2018.

[3] For data on labor market adjustment spending in the advanced economies, see OECD 2017. See also the chapters by Lori Kletzer and Laura Tyson in this volume.

Robert Keohane (1978) wrote back in the late 1970s, when the scale of the economic challenge from Japan was just starting to be appreciated by US policy makers: "The politics of foreign economic policy center around the question of which states will bear the major costs of adjusting to change. Each state seeks to impose unwanted costs on others, rather than inflicting them on their own citizens." This is the heart of Trump's approach to trade. He wants to impose more of the costs of trade on other countries and capture more of the benefits for the United States. Trump wants to use the leverage provided by the large US market to persuade companies to locate more of their production in the United States and less in other countries (Alden 2018). Unlike every president going back to Franklin Delano Roosevelt, Trump is not looking for a set of trade policies that will expand the global pie. Instead, he is focused only on seizing a bigger share for the United States.

A RADICAL NEW TRADE PHILOSOPHY

Let me offer three examples of this new approach, emphasizing how radically different it is from previous US administrations for most of the past century.

Let's start with the NAFTA renegotiation. Every trade negotiation going back at least to the first round of the GATT in 1947 has started from the same premise, which is how to expand mutual gains for the participating countries through trade. To be sure, there were often bitter fights over the distribution of those gains, and which sectors would win and lose. In the Uruguay Round of the GATT negotiations, for instance, US holders of patents and copyrights such as drug companies and filmmakers emerged as big winners from the new protections of intellectual property rights, while developing country textile and apparel makers were winners from the elimination of import quotas in the advanced economies. The losers were generic drug makers in the poorer countries as well as textile and apparel workers in the wealthier countries. But the agreed-on goal among negotiators from different countries was always to find some mutually acceptable balance of concessions.

The NAFTA renegotiation demanded by the Trump administration started from a wholly different place. If you believe, as Trump does, that the United States has been a loser from trade, then the purpose of renegotiating NAFTA was not to achieve some new, mutually beneficial balance of concessions. The goal was to "rebalance" the agreement so it favored the United States more, and Canada and Mexico less. Indeed, the administration was quite specific about its intentions, and backed them up with aggressive actions by imposing tariffs on Canadian and Mexican steel and aluminum exports, and threatening to do the same on cars. After the contentious fourth round of the negotiations, US trade representative Robert Lighthizer (2017a) concluded with a statement that NAFTA had become "very lopsided" and lamented that "we have seen no indication that our partners are willing to make any changes that will result in a rebalancing and a reduction in these huge trade deficits." Wilbur Ross, the commerce secretary, was even blunter: "We're asking two countries to give up some privileges that they have enjoyed for 22 years, and we're not in a position to offer anything in return" (Wingrove and Martin 2017).

This approach was at the heart of the controversial proposals that the United States put forward in the talks as well as the somewhat-shocked response from Canada and Mexico. Among the Trump administration's initial goals, for example, were:

- A "US-only" content requirement for automobiles to avoid tariffs.
- Expansion of "Buy America" procurement policies—with no commensurate expansion of "Buy Canada" or "Buy Mexico" policies.
- The elimination of binding dispute settlement provisions, which were seen as favoring the two smaller countries over the United States.
- A sunset clause requiring new approval of the deal every five years, so that the United States could regularly reassess whether it was winning under the new arrangements or not.

In the form originally presented, these positions were all essentially nonnegotiable from the Canadian and Mexican perspective, because each would have required political leaders from those countries to try to sell an agreement that was explicitly understood as one-sidedly in favor of the United States. One of the ironies of NAFTA is that publics in each of the three countries believe that the other two were the bigger winners from NAFTA and their own country was the loser.[4] Not surprisingly, negotiating over these proposals proved tremendously difficult; NAFTA's so-called modernization chapters, which promised mutual gains in sectors like telecommunications and e-commerce, were fairly easy to conclude, but the "rebalancing" provisions were strongly resisted by Canada and Mexico.

In the end, the three countries were able to reach a deal in part because of economic necessity—Canada and Mexico each send more than 75 percent of their exports to the United States—and in part because the Trump administration was willing to negotiate back from its most extreme proposals. The final deal included a sixteen-year sunset clause rather than a five-year one, weakened but did not eliminate the dispute settlement mechanisms, and offered a creative compromise on autos intended to push a bit more of the production to "high-wage" countries, including the United States and Canada. While Canada and Mexico emerged from the talks relieved, neither was particularly happy with the outcome, nor with the aggressive way that the Trump administration had approached the negotiations. Mexico's incoming secretary of state said that Mexico "did what was possible, not what was desirable," and noted drily that "it seems to me it's better to have a NAFTA 0.8 than not to have a NAFTA" (Blackwell 2018).

A second example of the Trump administration's new approach to trade is its suspicion of binding trade dispute settlement. The WTO dispute settlement system was the crowning achievement of the 1995 Uruguay Round agreement, and it was among the top priorities for the United States during the negotiations. The goal was not just to improve the effectiveness of trade enforcement but also to enhance its legitimacy by imposing the same rules and procedures for all countries, large or small. And for many years it has functioned quite well. The United States has initiated and won more WTO cases than any other country, and wins about 85 percent of the cases it brings (Mayeda 2017). It has lost its share of cases too and most times complied fairly readily, even where it was politically difficult to do so.[5] There are certainly legitimate

[4] See the presentation by Gerardo Esquivel, El Colegio de Mexico, in "The Future of NAFTA and North American Economic Integration Conference," Georgetown University, October 6, 2017, https://www.law.georgetown.edu/carola/news-events/past-events/the-future-of-nafta-conference.

[5] Among the politically difficult WTO losses for the United States have been the

criticisms of the WTO dispute process, in particular its challenges in containing China's trade distortions. Scholars such as Harvard Law's Mark Wu (2016) have argued that China's economy has developed in a way that many of its market distortions are not easily remedied through the enforcement of WTO rules.

But the Trump administration believes that binding dispute settlement is not in the interests of a big country like the United States. Lighthizer (2010) has been quite explicit in asserting that the United States was better off back in the pre-WTO days when it could use its market size and threaten retaliatory tariffs against others, especially Japan. Under WTO rules, that option is mostly unavailable; the United States, like any other country, must appeal to the WTO and wait for a ruling in its favor before imposing new tariffs. While the Trump administration is not overtly trying to eliminate the WTO dispute system, it has been slowly strangling the dispute resolution process by refusing to allow the appointment of new judges to the WTO's Appellate Body, the court of final appeal (Elsig, Pollack, and Shaffer 2017). Moreover, it has been willing to act outside the WTO dispute process—including imposing new tariffs without WTO authorization—to go after what it considers unfair trading practices by China in particular, but also against allies in Europe, Japan, Canada, and elsewhere. The administration has not abandoned the WTO disputes proces and indeed has continued to file cases. But it has clearly abandoned the principle embraced by previous administrations that most trade differences should be resolved within the WTO's rules and procedures.

The third example of this new approach is the administration's stated preference for bilateral over multilateral trade negotiations, which Trump (2017) has called "a whole big mash pot" of international agreements "that tie us up and bind us down." If the goal in trade is to maximize mutual gains, then there is a pretty strong consensus in the economics profession that the bigger the deal, the better. Economist Jagdish Bhagwati (2008) has called these various bilateral agreements "termites in the trading system" that do little to expand trade, but instead serve mostly to redistribute it. The United States has long fa-

---

successful EU challenge to the foreign sales corporate tax rebate for manufacturers, the successful challenge from the European Union, Japan, Brazil, India, and others to the US Continued Dumping and Subsidization Offset Act of 2000, and the successful challenge by Canada to country-of-origin labeling for beef and pork products.

vored multilateral liberalization, primarily through the eight rounds of the GATT negotiations. When it began to negotiate smaller bilateral and regional deals in earnest during the 2000s, it did so reluctantly and pursued a strategy of "competitive liberalization" (Bergsten 1996). The idea was not that regional and bilateral trade agreements were better than a multilateral agreement—from a trade-enhancing perspective, they were clearly worse—but rather that these deals would help put pressure on countries to agree to multilateral liberalization. At the very least, they would offer some way forward if global negotiations were hopelessly stalled, as they mostly have been for the past two decades.

The Trump administration does not agree with any of this—again for the same logic: the United States still has the biggest economy and therefore can bully its way into better deals bilaterally than it could if more countries were involved. In the larger deals involving many countries, the relative size and power of the United States can be diminished, but in bilateral talks with smaller countries, the United States mostly gets what it wants. As Lighthizer (2017b) has put it, "The working assumption is that if you have an $18 trillion economy, you can do better negotiating individually." So far the administration has had some success in pursuing this bilateral strategy. In addition to the new NAFTA, the administration renegotiated parts of the US trade agreement with South Korea, and is now trying to pursue similar bilateral deals with Japan and Europe.

THE REACTION FROM TRADING PARTNERS

The new Trump approach on trade has already been highly disruptive—and could prove fatally damaging—to the system of trade rules built up over the last seventy-five years that has contributed to the fastest growth in trade in the history of the planet and greatest alleviation of the poverty the world has ever seen. While there is merit to the president's claim that the United States has sometimes got the short end of certain trade deals, the larger truth is that the promotion of an open, global trading system has unquestionably served US interests. As Alan Wolff (2017), a former senior US trade official and now deputy director general of the WTO, has argued, the embrace of open trading rules was an "expression of enlightened self-interest created in reaction to and flight from the severe, self-absorbed and self-destructive protection-ist policies of the 1930s." But that has changed profoundly with the Trump administration, he said, noting that "the country that was in-dispensable to the creation of the international trading system has opted out of its leadership role, and the date and nature of its return to any-thing like its former position is completely uncertain."

What that means is that for the near future at least, the preservation and advancement of the trading system will be largely in the hands of other countries. Those countries must find a way to work, both indi-vidually and collectively, to preserve the gains from the trading system while waiting, hopefully, for the United States to settle on a less myopic course. I would offer three suggestions for how other nations might fill the vacuum left by the United States.

First, whatever one thinks of the claim that the United States has been a big loser from trade, the president's complaints have some merit. The United States has run large and persistent trade deficits for many years, caused mostly by its own domestic choices, but also in part by the economic choices, including mercantilist approaches, of other na-tions. Where those approaches have served to deepen trade imbalances, other countries would be advised to revisit them, not as a favor to the United States, but in their own longer-run self-interest.

Second, as difficult as it will be, international cooperation and co-ordination have never mattered more than they do now. If you look at previous trade policy crises—the Nixon administration's abrogation of the Bretton Woods agreements and its temporary import surcharge, or the fierce battles with Japan during the Reagan administration—they were resolved at the end of the day by cooperation among the major economic powers. And those deals did involve, to be sure, concessions to the United States that acknowledged that trade imbalances were indeed a problem and coordinated steps were needed to correct them. The G20 and G7 may provide the best forums for such conversations, but the WTO and IMF will also have critical roles to play.

Finally, other countries should resist simply capitalizing on the US withdrawal for their own narrow economic advantage. Whether it is the proliferation of bilateral trade deals led by the European Union or China's efforts to consolidate a trading bloc in Asia, the short-term gains from such initiatives could be more than offset by the damages to the larger global trading system. The United States for many years was willing, at least at times, to subordinate its own short-term economic interests to build a stronger trading system. Other countries must now step up and do some of the same. The decision by the remaining members of the TPP, led by Japan and Canada, to move ahead with completion of the TPP-11 was encouraging in that regard. In particular, the remaining members have offered an open door to the United States should it wish to reconsider and rejoin the agreement. Also encouraging are the various efforts by the European Union, Canada, and others to offer proposals aimed at addressing some of the US concerns with WTO reform. Other countries, including reluctant ones like China and India, should also consider how reengaging in WTO negotiations would serve their long-term interests rather than playing the system for shorter-term economic advantages.

The trading system is in a perilous moment. It will need leaders from many countries cooperating to preserve the gains that have been made from trade during the era of US leadership. That era has ended, and what comes next will be especially challenging.

REFERENCES

Alden, Edward. 2017. *Failure to Adjust: How Americans Got Left Behind in the Global Economy.* Lanham, MD: Rowman and Littlefield.

———. 2018. "The Real Game Trump Is Playing on NAFTA." *Politico Magazine,* February 26. https://www.politico.com/magazine/story/2018/02/26/donald-trump-nafta-negotiations-217085.

Autor, David H., David Dorn, and Gordon H. Hanson. 2012. "The China Syndrome: Local Labor Market Effects of Import Competition in the United States." NBER Working Paper 18054. Cambridge, MA: National Bureau of Economic Research.

———. 2016. "The China Shock: Learning from Labor Market Adjustment to Large Changes in Trade." NBER Working Paper 21906. Cambridge, MA: National Bureau of Economic Research.

Bergsten, C. Fred. 1996. "Competitive Liberalization and Global Free Trade: A Vision for the Early 21st Century." Institute for International Economics Working Paper 96-15. Washington, DC: Institute for International Economics.

Bhagwati, Jagdish. 2008. *Termites in the Trading System: How Preferential Agreements Undermine Free Trade.* New York: Oxford University Press.

Blackwell, Tom. 2018. "NAFTA Deadline Looms, But Canada Sets Itself Apart from Mexico, Resists Pressure for Quick Deal." *National Post,* September 17. https://nationalpost.com/news/deadline-looms-but-canada-sets-itself-apart-from-mexico-and-resists-pressure-for-quick-nafta-deal.

Elsig, Manfred, Mark Pollack, and Gregory Shaffer. 2017. "Trump Is Fighting an Open War on Trade. His Stealth War on Trade May Be Even More Important." *Washington Post,* September 27. https://www.washingtonpost.com/news/monkey

-cage/wp/2017/09/27/trump-is-fighting-an-open-war-on-trade-his-stealth-war
-on-trade-may-be-even-more-important/?utm_term=.f331672d2879.

Houseman, Susan N. 2018. "Understanding the Decline of U.S. Manufacturing Employment." Upjohn Institute Working Paper 18-287. Kalamazoo, MI: W. E. Upjohn Institute for Employment Research.

Keohane, Robert O. 1978. "American Policy and the Trade-Growth Struggle." *International Security* 3, no. 2 (Fall): 20–43.

Kruse, Michael. 2016. "The True Story of Donald Trump's First Campaign Speech—in 1987." *Politico Magazine*, February 5. https://www.politico.com/magazine/story/2016/02/donald-trump-first-campaign-speech-new-hampshire-1987-213595.

Lighthizer, Robert E. 2010. "Evaluating China's Role in the World Trade Organization over the Past Decade." Testimony before the US-China Economic Security Review Commission, June 9. https://www.uscc.gov/sites/default/files/transcripts/6.9.10HearingTranscript.pdf.

———. 2017a. "Closing Statement of USTR Robert Lighthizer at the Fourth Round of NAFTA Renegotiations." Office of the United States Trade Representative, October 17. https://ustr.gov/about-us/policy-offices/press-office/press-releases/2017/october/closing-statement-ustr-robert.

———. 2017b. "U.S. Trade Policy Priorities: Robert Lighthizer, United States Trade Representative." Center for Strategic and International Studies, September 18. https://www.csis.org/analysis/us-trade-policy-priorities-robert-lighthizer-united-states-trade-representative.

Mayeda, Andrew. 2017. "America Wins Often with Trade Referee That Trump Wants to Avoid." *Bloomberg*, March 27. https://www.bloomberg.com/news/articles/2017-03-27/trump-isn-t-a-fan-of-the-wto-but-u-s-lawyers-often-win-there.

OECD (Organization of Economic Cooperation and Development). 2017. *Employment Outlook*. Paris: Organization for Economic Cooperation and Development.

Scott, Robert E. 2015. "The Manufacturing Footprint and the Importance of U.S. Manufacturing Jobs." Economic Policy Institute Briefing Paper 388. Washington, DC: Economic Policy Institute.Error! Hyperlink reference not valid.

Swanson, Ana, and Damien Paletta. 2017. "Trump Says He Will Not Label China Currency Manipulator, Reversing Campaign Promise." *Washington Post*, April 12. https://www.washingtonpost.com/news/wonk/wp/2017/04/12/trump-says-he-will-not-label-china-currency-manipulator-reversing-campaign-promise/?utm_term=.c08db5c312f7.

Trump, Donald J. 2017 "Remarks of President Donald J. Trump, as Prepared for Delivery, Inaugural Address, Friday, January 20, 2017, Washington, D.C." https://www.whitehouse.gov/briefings-statements/the-inaugural-address/.

Wingrove, Josh, and Eric Martin. 2017. "Canada Warns NAFTA Talks Can't Be 'Winner Takes All.'" *Bloomberg*, October 26. https://www.bloomberg.com/news/articles/2017-10-26/canada-says-nafta-can-t-be-winner-take-all-after-ross-comments.

Wolff, Alan. 2017. "There Is Enormous Potential for Forward Progress in Global Trading System." Second Wenger Annual Distinguished Lecture on Trade, American University, November 8. https://www.wto.org/english/news_e/news17_e/ddgra_08nov17_e.htm.

Wu, Mark. 2016. "The China Inc. Challenge to Global Trade Governance." *Harvard International Law Journal* 57, no. 2 (Spring): 1001–63.

The Fracturing of the Postwar, Free Trade Consensus: The Challenges of Constructing a New Consensus

MICHAEL TREBILCOCK

While the *Economist* magazine in a cover story of July 30, 2016, describes a new political divide, where political contests are not left versus right, but open versus closed (drawbridges down or up), free trade (and by extension, immigration policy) has always provoked controversies, from the ancient Greeks onward, as masterfully described by Douglas Irwin (1996). Even in more recent decades, from the 1990s onward, international trade has engendered a series of controversies, in many cases reflecting critiques from the Left rather than the Right that are reflected in contemporary forms of economic nationalism. Examples include:

- Controversies from the 1990s onward (exemplified dramatically in the "Battle of Seattle" in fall 1999) relating inter alia to the relationship between trade and the environment (reflected in a firestorm of criticism by environmental groups to the GATT decisions in the early 1990s in the Tuna-Dolphin cases).[1]

[1] The GATT was a legal international agreement whose overall purpose was to promote international trade by reducing or eliminating trade barriers such as tariffs or quotas. It was first discussed during the UN Conference on Trade and Employment, and was signed by 23 nations in 1947, taking effect on January 1, 1948. It remained in effect until it was revised and signed by 123 nations in Marrakesh, on

- Opposition to a number of the Uruguay Round special agreements, especially the TRIPS agreement, which critics have argued imposed Western intellectual property standards on developing countries and in particular impeded their access to essential medicines.[2]
- The Agreement on the Application of Sanitary and Phytosanitary Measures, which critics assert has inhibited countries from setting standards for food products that reflect their domestic risk preferences.
- The General Agreement on Trade in Services, which critics contend unduly constrains governments from regulating domestic service markets or providing services directly to their citizens.
- Concerns over adherence to basic or core labor standards as a precondition to international trade in goods.
- Criticisms of the proliferation of bilateral investment treaties that provide special protections to foreign direct investors against policy changes in host countries, especially developing ones.
- Controversies surrounding international trade in agriculture and food products in particular, following sharp spikes in food prices in 2007–8.
- Debates surrounding the regulation of cross-border financial flows following the global financial crisis in 2007–8.

Few of these controversies centrally challenged the virtues of a relatively liberal international trading regime, and could for the most part be accommodated with refinements to that regime. Contemporary manifestations of economic nationalism, with which the *Economist* is concerned in its description and critique of the new political divide, more squarely challenge the central premises of a liberal international

---

April 14, 1994, during the Uruguay Round agreements, which established the WTO on January 1, 1995. The WTO (now with 164 members) is a successor to GATT, and the original GATT provisions are still in effect under the WTO framework, as discussed below.

[2] The TRIPS agreement was signed by all the member nations of the WTO, setting minimum standards for the regulation by national governments of many forms of intellectual property. The agreement was negotiated at the end of the Uruguay Round of the GATT in 1994 and is under the WTO's purview.

trading regime by resurrecting previously discredited claims about the virtues of economic autarky, such as keeping economic production and the related jobs at home. More benignly, they can be interpreted as an assertion of a much more aggressive form of reciprocity (however much disparaged by many economists as an economically illiterate form of mercantilism) in order to better manage the politics of trade policy domestically by reconfiguring constellations of winners and losers.

BUILT-IN TRANSITION COST MITIGATION MECHANISMS

I would like to focus the balance of my comments on the contemporary challenges to the premises of a liberal international trading regime. I would note at the outset that the GATT/WTO multilateral trading regime, from its inception in 1947, was not insensitive to the transition costs associated with trade liberalization. In my (Trebilcock 2014) book *Dealing with Losers: The Political Economy of Policy Transitions*, one of the seven case studies that I present of policy transitions and the challenges of addressing the losers, even where the transitions are on balance socially beneficial, is trade liberalization in the postwar era. Here I point out three features of the GATT/WTO regime that have squarely addressed the challenge of moderating transition costs.

First, the regime espoused a strategy of *gradualism*, where tariffs and other border restrictions on trade were reduced gradually over time, both within and across negotiating rounds. Accordingly, tariffs on industrial goods fell from almost 50 percent on average in 1947 to less than 5 percent on average today, but this outcome was not achieved overnight. Instead, it took nine negotiating rounds and many decades.

Second, *reciprocity in the form of an exchange of concessions by negotiating partners* been central to postwar trade liberalization efforts. Through the exchange of concessions, export-oriented industries could be enlisted as a political counterweight to import-impacted domestic industries in advancing the trade liberalization agenda. Moreover, this strategy provided the potential for moderating transition costs as resources (including jobs) gravitated over time from contracting import-impacted sectors to expanding export-oriented sectors.

Third, the GATT/WTO regime recognized from the outset the importance of *reversibility* if commitments made by signatories (for example, tariff reduction commitments) led to an unexpected surge in imports that caused severe dislocation costs to domestic industries and their workforces. Hence, the safeguard regime in the GATT's Article XIX, now elaborated in the Uruguay Round Agreement on Safeguards, provides a form of force majeure relief from prior trade commitments, even though such measures are often costly to consumers relative to the value of jobs saved. Regrettably, restrictive interpretations of these provisions by the Appellate Body of the WTO have made invocation of safeguard measures increasingly problematic.

Notwithstanding their sensitivity to the transition costs associated with trade liberalization, these provisions have obviously not sufficed to assuage contemporary manifestations of economic nationalism (or tendencies to autarky). This failure leads me (and many other commentators) to ask the question, What more should be done to moderate the transition costs associated with a liberal trading regime (and globalization more generally)? I first address contemporary concerns that seek to distinguish *fair* from *free* trade. I then outline two, more general policy directions—one internationally focused and one domestically focused—that I believe are imperative for muting the contemporary rise of economic nationalism.

FAIR VERSUS FREE TRADE

It is often argued that some forms of international trade may constitute a form of "unfair" trade or competition, and hence economic dislocations induced by unfair trade may be normatively unacceptable (see generally Bhagwati and Hudec 1996). First, trade deficits are frequently cited as evidence of unbalanced trade commitments. Such concerns are often misplaced, however, with empirical evidence revealing that trade deficits typically rise with a booming domestic economy where consumers have more resources to spend on imports. Moreover, as Irwin points out, if a foreign country is exporting more than it imports from another country, the overall balance of payments is divided between the current account and financial account, which includes all portfolio and direct investments. Foreign countries can either use their export earnings to purchase imports, or invest the surplus in acquiring assets or investments in the country with which they are running a trade surplus (e.g., China's investment in US Treasury bills and other securities). As Irwin

(2015, 162) explains, "If the US adopted protectionist measures to reduce the trade deficit, then capital inflows from abroad would necessarily have to fall (i.e., China would no longer buy Treasury bills and the renminbi would appreciate and the dollar would depreciate), and domestic investment would have to be financed by domestic savings, implying higher interest rates, which would reduce the number of jobs created by business investment. In the end, the positive impact of a lower trade deficit on employment might be offset by the negative impact of lower domestic investment and higher interest rates."

Beyond the issue of trade deficits, unfair trade concerns frequently focus on claims that foreign exporters are deliberately manipulating their currencies to induce an undervaluation, and hence render their exports cheaper and their imports costlier. It is difficult to evaluate as an analytic matter the "true" value of a country's currency, but in any event, in the case of the principal target of such complaints in this millennium—China—it now seems widely accepted that China has allowed its currency (the renminbi) to appreciate significantly in recent years and that it may no longer be significantly undervalued, if at all.

A related complaint of unfair trade concerns the foreign subsidization of exports, which renders them artificially competitive in importing countries' markets and may lead to job displacement in these markets. This is again a difficult complaint to evaluate analytically, especially in the case of economies in transition from command to market economies (like China's), with large numbers of state-owned enterprises as well as the extensive use of regulated or directed pricing (Wu 2016). But as with currency manipulation, it is a complaint that cannot be dismissed out of hand, and is subject to detailed disciplines in the WTO's Agreement on Subsidies and Countervailing Measures. Yet there are legitimate concerns over the appropriateness and enforceability of a number of these disciplines, nor do they address at all the increasingly salient issue of tax and subsidy competition among host jurisdictions to attract foreign direct investment (see, for example, Horlick and Clarke 2010).

A further complaint is that foreign exporters often "dump" goods in the markets of importing countries at lower prices than prevail in their home markets. While antidumping actions are usually initiated by importing countries on this or related bases, beyond the narrow category of cases involving predatory pricing by foreign exporters, most dumping cases lack any coherent economic rationale and simply reflect geographic price discrimination (see, for example, Trebilcock 2015, 70–75). Nevertheless, antidumping actions have proliferated around the world in recent years and have frequently become the protectionist instrument of choice, despite their lack of any convincing economic rationale in most cases, and dominate by several orders of magnitude the other two principal trade remedy regimes: safeguards and countervailing duties, both of which have more plausible economic rationales.

A further claim of unfair trade relates to foreign countries that improperly appropriate the intellectual property of firms based in other countries through either lax laws or the lax enforcement of them, thus conferring on them an artificial comparative advantage in international trade as well as unfairly prejudicing these firms and their workforces. While TRIPS, negotiated during the Uruguay Round, seeks to address many of these concerns, there may still be legitimate concerns relating to the lax enforcement of these commitments. Moreover, TRIPS does not apply to the controversial practice—routine in China— of imposing technology-sharing agreements as a condition of inward foreign investment.

A further set of "unfair" trade complaints relates to lax labor or environmental laws in foreign countries that enable them to reduce costs unfairly, rendering their products artificially competitive in international trade. With respect to concerns over lax labor standards, it may well be the case that there are compelling noneconomic rationales for insisting that all trading countries adhere to core labor standards such as those promulgated by the International Labor Organization in its 1998 Declaration on Fundamental Principles and Rights at Work—that is, freedom of association along with the elimination of forced labor, child labor, and discrimination in employment (and perhaps also basic workplace safety standards). Nevertheless it is important to recognize (as the International Labor Organization does) that lower wage levels in some foreign countries (especially developing ones) are not a source of unfair trade but indeed a key source of their comparative advantage (taking into account the differences in labor productivity across countries) (Singer 2016, 16–68). Similarly, lax environmental standards in some foreign countries may be a legitimate concern for other countries where these involve transboundary externalities or threats to the global commons (such as climate change) and justify trade sanctions (Singer 2016, chapter 2), but where their effects are purely local it is not nearly as obvious that other countries have any legitimate basis for insisting on adherence to their own environmental standards as a precondition to international trade.

PROVIDING MORE FLEXIBILITY IN THE MULTILATERAL TRADING SYSTEM

In terms of the international economic architecture, the one-size-fits-all, all-or-nothing negotiating modality adopted during the Uruguay Round, particularly in addressing a wide range of nontariff barriers to trade in goods and services that implicate idiosyncratic features of many countries' internal domestic policies, seriously discounts the widely divergent states of development, economic particularities, and political and economic philosophies of the 164 WTO member countries (see Rodrik 2011, 2017). In part that approach is responsible for the proliferation of preferential trade agreements over the past twenty-five years (paralleling the proliferation of bilateral investment treaties over the same period). The proliferation of preferential trade agreements risks serious fragmentation of the international trading system and an abandonment of the ideal of the key framers of the Bretton Woods agreement in 1944 out of which the GATT emerged, where in principle every country in the world would trade with every other country under a common set of ground rules, mitigating the tendency to economic factionalism that many commentators believe was a contributing factor to the outbreak of World War II and ensuring that comparative advantage is undistorted by discriminatory trade rules.

This vision of the postwar international economic architecture, however, while noble in many respects, was insensitive to the distinctive needs of many newly independent developing countries and emerging economies. While some accommodations for the special needs of developing countries were made in the mid-1950s and mid-1960s through the adoption of special dispensations for them on both the import (infant industry protection) and export sides (nonreciprocal trade preferences by developed countries)—often referred to compendiously as special and differential treatment—the Uruguay Round all-or-nothing negotiating modality seriously derogated from the spirit of these accommodations. Instead, I believe there should be much greater scope within the multilateral system for plurilateral agreements among "coalitions of the willing" that would be open over time to accession by other members on a conditional most favored nation basis, and could accommodate quite ambitious multicountry agreements and would invoke the widely respected dispute settlement regime of the WTO in the interpretation and enforcement of such agreements. This has a strong precedent in the Tokyo Round nontariff barriers codes.

The present WTO rule requiring the consensus of all members for the incorporation of plurilateral agreements into the WTO needs to be repealed or relaxed. This seems preferable to attempting to unlock the immobilizing consensus rule of decision making within the WTO by moving to some form of majority voting, where large trading blocs would routinely be outvoted by aggregations of smaller countries, or alternatively trade-weighted voting regimes, where smaller countries would be routinely outvoted by large trading bloc. Neither state of affairs would be acceptable to the membership as a whole.

Providing greater scope for plurilateral agreements within the GATT/WTO regime would offer something of a intermediate option between strict multilateralism where all countries operate under the same set of international trading rules, and one-on-one preferential trading agreements and the concomitant risk of international trade degenerating into a "spaghetti bowl" of sui generis rules governing every trading relationship along with the attendant increase in transaction costs that such rules would engender (Bhagwati 2008). In addition, there are serious concerns about asymmetrical bargaining power inherent in many one-on-one bilateral trade negotiations, which are mitigated by coalition bargaining within the multilateral regime. While some commentators are skeptical of the virtues of a multispeed multilateral system, I argue that it has many virtues compared to the alternatives: one-size-fits all multilateralism, bilateralism, and (worst of all) unilateralism with the concomitant risk of a trade war and global recession.

THE IMPORTANCE OF ACTIVE LABOR MARKET ADJUSTMENT POLICIES

The second policy priority that I think commands urgent attention is strengthening active labor market policies in many developed countries, especially in the United States, which relative to many other developed countries, spends a paltry amount of resources on active labor market policies. In a recent paper, my coauthor and I (Trebilcock and Wong 2018) review comparative experience with labor market adjustment policies across many developed countries, and it is clear that some developed countries have done much better than others in actively assisting displaced workers to reengage with the labor force. In this respect, it is crucial to acknowledge the fact highlighted by Anne Krueger and LauraTyson in this volume (see chapters 10 and 16, respectively) that while the United States and other developed economies have experienced a substantial decline in manufacturing employment in recent years, only a small percentage of such job losses (estimates range from 15 to 25 percent) is attributable to trade. Notwithstanding the dramatic expansion of imports from China and other low-wage countries, the bulk of such job displacements are attributable instead to technology and, related to the latter, the substitution of capital for labor due to a generally declining price of investment goods. Indeed, in the United States, manufacturing output in real terms has increased over the past decade or so, while employment has declined substantially (WTO 2017). Yet it should be acknowledged that disentangling the effects of trade and technology on labor markets is complex in that the two are sometimes complements and sometimes substitutes; for example, technology has enabled trade through containerization as well as information and communications technologies in orchestrating global supply chains, while in other contexts it substitutes for trade (Baldwin 2016).

One implication of the dominant role of technology is that labor market adjustment policies that are tied to the impact of international trade on local labor markets (such as the US TAA program initiated following the Kennedy Round of GATT negotiations in the 1960s) are seriously misconceived. US experience with the TAA suggests that it is practically impossible to determine whether particular workers are being displaced by trade or technology, and even if this were practically possible, it is ethically difficult to defend more generous treatment of workers displaced by trade relative to those displaced by technology (although trade policy is a policy variable, while technology is not) (Alden 2017, 107–26). Moreover, recent empirical studies show that TAA benefits play a relatively inconsequential role in moderating the impacts of job displacement, whether caused by trade or technology (see Gordon Hanson's and Lori Kletzer's chapters in this volume).

Without a much more concerted emphasis on labor market adjustment policies in general and active labor market adjustment policies in particular, we should recognize the serious risk that drawbridges up will become the default option. In my view, the temptation to scapegoat the "barbarians at our gates" with foreign faces from foreign places (e.g., foreign traders, investors, and immigrants) rather than faceless forces within our gates (especially technology) for all sources of stress on our labor markets and social safety nets is almost certainly a recipe for serious policy misdiagnosis as well as misprescription. While as a matter of political economy generous labor market adjustment policies may not fully mute demands for protectionism by trade-impacted sectors, they provide a principled basis for other constituencies to resist these demands by demonstrating a commitment to taking seriously the losers from economic transitions more generally.

CONCLUDING REMARKS

In the postwar period, three central features of the global trading system—gradualism, reciprocity, and reversibility—sustained a broad free trade consensus by moderating the transition costs associated with trade liberalization. In order to reinvigorate the multilateral system and moderate the tendency to fragmentation through a proliferation of preferential trade agreements, more scope needs to be provided within the multilateral system for open-ended plurilateral agreements, while aggressive forms of reciprocity might well focus on weaknesses or omissions in existing multilateral subsidy and intellectual property disciplines, and revisiting the appropriate scope and conditions of the safeguards regime. Beyond these international initiatives, domestic policy needs to focus much more centrally on developing active labor market policies to assist displaced workers to reengage with the workforce (whatever the cause of their displacement).

REFERENCES

Alden, Edward. 2017. *Failure to Adjust: How Americans Got Left Behind in the Global Economy.* Lanham MD: Rowman and Littlefield.
Baldwin, Richard. 2016. *The Great Convergence: Information Technology and the New Globalization.* Cambridge, MA: Harvard University Press.

Bhagwati, Jagdish. 2008. *Termites in the Trading System: How Preferential Trade Agreements Undermine Free Trade.* Oxford: Oxford University Press.

Bhagwati, Jagdish, and Robert Hudec, eds. 1996. *Free Trade and Harmonization: Prerequisites for Free Trade?* Cambridge, MA: MIT Press.

Horlick, Gary, and Peggy Clarke. 2010. "WTO Subsidies Disciplines during and after the Crisis." *Journal of International Economic Law* 13, no. 3 (September): 859–74.

Irwin, Douglas. 1996. *Against the Tide: An Intellectual History of Free Trade.* Princeton, NJ: Princeton University Press.

———. 2015. *Free Trade under Fire.* Princeton, NJ: Princeton University Press.

Rodrik, Dani. 2011. *The Globalization Paradox: Democracy and the Future of the World Economy.* New York: W. W. Norton.

———. 2017. *Straight Talk on Trade: Ideas for a Sane World Economy.* Princeton, NJ: Princeton University Press.

Singer, Peter. 2016. *One World Now: The Ethics of Globalization.* New Haven, CT: Yale University Press.

Trebilcock, Michael. 2014. *Dealing with Losers: The Political Economy of Policy Transitions.* Oxford: Oxford University Press.

———. 2015. *Advanced Introduction to International Trade Law.* Cheltenham, UK: Edward Elgar.

Trebilcock, Michael, and Sally Wong. 2018. "Trade, Technology, and Transitions: Trampolines or Safety Nets for Displaced Workers?" *Journal of International Economic Law* 21, no. 3 (September): 509–45.

WTO (World Trade Organization). 2017. *Trade, Technology, and Jobs.* World Trade Report. Geneva: World Trade Organization.

Wu, Mark. 2016. "The China Inc. Challenge to Global Trade Governance." *Harvard International Law Journal* 57: 1001–63.

PART VI

CHALLENGES AHEAD

15

Globalization and Health in the United States

ANGUS DEATON

I want to start with something that Christine Lagarde said in her opening remarks to the IMF's Meeting Globalization's Challenges conference on October 11, 2017. She reminded us that what we have seen over the last seventy years and especially over the last forty years is something wonderful, something that has never before happened in human history: an extraordinary reduction in global poverty accompanied by an extraordinary increase in life spans around the world. It is inconceivable that we would have seen this unprecedented, simultaneous improvement in living standards and the length of life without globalization in one of its forms.

One of my favorite statistics is that there is not a country in the world today whose infant mortality rate is higher than it was fifty years ago. Infant mortality in India today is lower than it was in Scotland when I was born there in 1945. This explosion in the very opportunity of having a life was brought about by taking ideas from one place to another, bringing the germ theory and techniques that go with it—antibiotics, vaccinations, clean water, pest control, and sanitation—from the countries where the ideas and techniques were invented to the rest of the world. The reduction in poverty, in the Asian tigers, and then in China and India, could not have happened without opening up trade. If we turn our back on globalization, which we are under threat of doing, we are risking catastrophe. And even if it were to benefit us—

North Americans or Europeans—which it will not, we cannot turn away from those whose lives have been so greatly improved and who are so still so much worse off than we are.

WHAT HAS GONE WRONG?

Let me focus on the United States, where globalization has taken some of the blame for the bad things that are happening. Certainly, these bad things are bad indeed. Median real wages have been stagnant for almost fifty years; for those without a university degree, wages have done worse still. These findings can be challenged, such as by questioning the price indexes that are used to calculate real wages, and perhaps after correction, there has been meaningful progress. Yet as my work with Anne Case (Case and Deaton 2017, 2020) has shown, one important indicator of progress—the rate of mortality in the United States—has stopped its century-long decline and has begun to rise.

It is important to be precise about who is and is not affected. Middle-aged white non-Hispanics have seen no mortality decline since the beginning of the twenty-first century, and among them, those without a bachelor's degree are seeing an *increase* in mortality. Hispanic mortality—already lower than white mortality—continues to decline at its long-established rate, which is similar to rates of decline in Europe. Mortality among US blacks has been declining even more rapidly, though blacks continue to have higher mortality rates than either whites or Hispanics. Mortality rates among the elderly in the United States continue to fall, at least for the time being. Those who are suffering are members of the white working class (or perhaps the middle class, for those who do not think there is a working class in the United States). Native Americans appear to do the worst of all groups—worse than white non-Hispanics, both in mortality levels and their rate of increase.

The opioid epidemic is a big part of the problem, but it is not all of it. Suicides are rising, and so are deaths from cirrhosis and alcohol-related liver disease. Most recently, the fall in mortality from heart disease, which has been the main driver of the increase in life expectancy in the United States over the last forty years, has stalled and begun to reverse. Heart disease is the leading cause of death in the United States, so that changes in the mortality rate from heart disease can have large effects on the overall mortality. Many commentators blame increasing obesity for the turnaround, though we do not yet have definitive evidence. If obesity is indeed the culprit, then, along with suicide, alcohol, and drugs, we have another category to add to the list.

We tend to think of all these deaths as suicides in some sense; all are self-inflicted, with the means sometimes operating slowly, and sometimes quickly. That they are rising so rapidly suggests that something is wrong in people's lives. Case and I have used the label "deaths of despair" to suggest that they reflect a loss of meaning and purpose in life—that people who kill themselves quickly or slowly are in despair about how their lives are going.

Despair runs deeper than unhappiness about earnings or job prospects, though we think that both are involved. Despair comes from failing marriages, failing relationships with children, the failure of religion to support people, increasing social isolation, and for many people, persistent and intractable physical pain. Indeed, the story that we are suggesting involves the slow and cumulative erosion of the meaning and substance of working-class life in the United States. We think of this as having started in the late 1960s and early 1970s, and worsening ever since. It is not so much the stagnation (and decline for those without a college degree) of median wages that has gone on for almost half a century but more the other, more important deterioration in lives that accompanied it and were in part caused by it. The China shock is part of the story, but only a part. While the educated elite have flourished and minorities have made progress in social inclusion, if not so much in incomes, less educated whites have been left behind, socially and physically as well as economically.

We see this in many measures of well-being, not only in stagnant or falling wages, but in decreasing attachment to the labor force—there is a long-term decline in the fraction of men in the workforce, which has more recently spread to women—falling marriage rates, and increasing births out of wedlock. A majority of less educated white mothers in the United States have had at least one child out of wedlock. Cohabitation is becoming more common, and these nonmarital relationships tend not to last, though they often produce children. As a result, there are many middle-aged fathers who do not live with and perhaps do not even know their children, and who are living without their children or with other men, and there are many middle-aged women who are living with a man who is not the father of at least one of their children.

The private sector unions that used to help raise the wages of their members are largely gone. Unions also gave workers some measure of control over their working conditions; they represented their members in local and national politics, and sometimes provided a route for talented workers to rise to national prominence in politics. In many towns, social and associational activities were promoted by or centered on unions.

As earnings declined and good jobs were replaced by less desirable jobs, health began to deteriorate. People in midlife reported more physical pain, such as lower-back pain, neck pain, and sciatica. At the same time, levels of self-reported pain were falling among the elderly and well educated. The same is true for self-reports of social isolation.

The divide between people with and without a bachelor of arts degree is not just for those in middle age but is also spreading down to younger people. For each later-born age cohort, a host of indicators—marriage, divorce, pain, workforce participation, wages, social isolation, and deaths of despair themselves—are worse at every age than for those in previous cohorts, and the rate at which each indicator worsens with age is faster the younger the cohort.

TAKING THE CON OUT OF GLOBALIZATION

The question is whether this is the inevitable consequence of technical progress and globalization. Is this the price that people in the United States must pay so that hundreds of millions of people in China and India can be better off? I think the answer is no. And it is immensely important to understand just why.

One reason we know that globalization and technical change are not the cause is that both of them are, well, *global*. Britain, Germany, France, and Sweden live in the same world that we do, and face the same challenges. Yet there are no (or many fewer) deaths of despair in those countries, nor in other rich countries in the world. Something is happening in the United States that is not happening elsewhere. Of course, globalization and technical change play a part, but the key difference is how those forces are handled in the United States, and how the US policy environment somehow fails to prevent the suffering that is prevented elsewhere.

Globalization and technical progress are good things. They render the *possibility* that life could be better for everyone, including the people of the United States. That is what economists have known for a long time. So if we don't manage to make it happen, it is not because it's the inevitable consequence of globalization but rather because we're handling it wrong. It is because policy is wrong.

This is a positive message compared with an "us" or "them" narrative, such as either Chinese and Indians die, or we die. Policies can be changed, and there are lots of policies that have helped undermine working-class life in the United States or have made the consequences of globalization much worse than they might have been. There is no good reason why people in the United States *and* China cannot benefit together from globalization.

I do not have space here to work through all the relevant policies, let alone rank their importance, or which are most urgent to change; that work remains to be done. Yet I want to point out a few of the possibilities.

Health care is a great disaster for working-class people in the United States. Not only has it played a role in the iatrogenic medicine that helped ignite the opioid epidemic. At least as serious is its role in holding down wages. The United States spends 18 percent of GDP on health care, compared with around 12 percent for our nearest competitors. Six percent of GDP is a trillion dollars a year. That trillion dollars a year is not improving our life expectancy but instead helping to reduce it. What the health care system *is* effective at doing is transferring money upward, from wages and taxes, to hospitals, physicians, device manufacturers, and pharmaceutical companies. The prices for the goods and services provided by each of these groups are much higher than in other countries, and it is prices, not quantities, that account for higher spending in the United States.

I am no expert on the difficult process of how we get from where we are to some better place, but it is clear from looking at other rich countries that there are a range of alternative, less costly financing schemes. If we could move from the most expensive to the second most expensive system, we could recoup $8,000 per household per year, with no loss in health outcomes. A good deal of today's spending on health care comes out of wages, because so much of health insurance is provided by employers to their employees.

Another difference between western Europe and the United States is the extent of the social safety net. Income taxes rates differ by relatively little, but Europeans have a value-added tax that because it is included in the price of goods, is relatively invisible compared with income taxes, which likely makes it easier to collect. The US safety net is much less generous than European safety nets. It should perhaps be noted that the fraction of white non-Hispanics without a university degree who are below the US poverty line is smaller than the fraction of less educated blacks below the line. As a result, blacks in the United States have more access to welfare programs than do whites, though it is hard to see why this would differentially protect them given that they have lower incomes in the first place. The literature does, however, suggest that this differential access is sometimes associated with resentment against minorities by whites. I also note that welfare schemes that impose work requirements, such as the earned income tax credit (and perhaps Medicaid in the future), may do much good, but they also reduce wages below what they would have been without the work requirements.

US industries, including hospitals, are becoming more consolidated. The lack of competition has raised margins and hurt workers, not only through higher prices, but because monopolists produce less and so hire less labor, and because some employers have monopsony power over wages. It is *real* wages that we care about, so it is not just nominal wages that matter but the prices of the goods and services that they buy too. The benefits of globalization that show up in lower prices, such as goods imported from China, are being undermined by the decreasing competitiveness of domestic firms. The share of labor in GDP is falling while the share of capital is rising—something that economists long thought would never happen.

There are other examples. The federal minimum wage has not been raised in nominal terms for a decade. Noncompete contracts, which used to be designed for people who knew trade secrets, are now applied even to some fast-food workers. Consumers and employees are increasingly forced to settle disputes with firms through arbitration using arbitrators who nearly always decide in favor of the firms. Employees are being replaced by outside contractors, who are cheaper, but have fewer benefits, less security of tenure, and fewer possibilities for promotion; they also lose the sense and meaningfulness that comes from belonging to a common enterprise. The gig economy has provided employment to people who were previously unemployed as well as finding a productive use for time and assets that were previously idle. But it has also undercut any remaining rents that were shared by workers in the service industries where they operate.

Let me say once again that all the forces that are making these changes possible—the internet, cheap goods from abroad, and information technology more generally—operate in Europe just as they do here. Yet their harshest effects have been avoided in Europe.

All the mechanisms that I have listed are tipping the scales against workers and toward capital. They raise the share of income going to capital and redistribute income upward. My guess is that it is these policies, in a time of globalization and technical change, that have slowly destroyed the way that the US working class used to live. Changing policies to be more favorable to labor will improve matters, but because the process has been going on so long, it is not easily or quickly reversible. If we are to dig ourselves out, though, it is these policies that must change. We need to construct an economy that is more favorable to labor even as it is less favorable to capital.

None of this gainsays the importance of tackling the opioid epidemic in the short run, even though that is itself no easy task. But even if opioid addiction were to be eliminated, the underlying problems and other deaths would still be there.

FINAL REMARKS

Returning to the main theme of this volume, I want to say again that globalization is certainly part of the story. But it is a mistake to think that you have to fix the consequences of trade through restricting trade, through protectionism, or via any trade-related policy. Nor is it a simple matter of redistributing so that the gainers from globalization and technical change are made to compensate the losers. I think that this is too narrow a view. The central point is that we need to create an economic environment in which the benefits to globalization and technical change are more widely shared—meaning an environment in which real wages for the less educated in the United States can rise. That will require safety nets that are not only more extensive but also do not put downward pressure on wages. We need to enforce antitrust law more rigorously and rethink antitrust policy for the tech titans. These measures give us a much broader palate to work with than just trade-related policies.

I also believe that general redistribution is not the answer, even if it were more politically feasible than it currently is. The United States needs to tackle the root causes of the rising pretax inequality, rent seeking, excessive patenting, consolidation of industry, and the disgrace that is our health care system. Stopping redistribution upward would take us a long way toward a fairer and healthier United States.

REFERENCES

Case, Anne, and Angus Deaton. 2017. "Mortality and Morbidity in the 21st Century." *Brookings Papers on Economic Activity*, Spring, 397–476. Washington, DC: Brookings Institution.
———. forthcoming. *Deaths of Despair and the Future of Capitalism*. Princeton, NJ: Princeton University Press.

16

Trade and Policy Adjustment to Automation Challenges

LAURA D. TYSON

Globalization is at a crossroads.[1] The 2008 financial crisis and ensuing global recession ended the very rapid growth in cross-border financial flows and in the trade of goods and services that the global economy experienced since the mid-1990s—a period often referred to as the era of hyperglobalization. During this period, global exports and imports as well as cross-border capital flows hit historic highs as shares of global GDP, making the world more connected than ever before. In sharp contrast, during the next ten years since the 2008 crisis, global trade has stagnated as a share of global GDP and global financial flows have fallen by more than two-thirds. More worryingly, the threat of an all-out trade war, following actual and threatened hikes in tariff rates by the United States and the vows of retaliation by China and other countries, has increased the risk of a major setback to the global trading system rebuilt after its collapse during the Great Depression of the 1930s and World War II.

These developments reflect a major shift of public attitudes in advanced countries—notably in the United States, which was long a champion of globalization. In those countries, the political conversation about trade has shifted from a focus on its benefits for economic growth, efficiency, and competition to a focus on its negative side effects, including job loss, dislocation, deindustrialization, and income

[1] For a further discussion of the background trends, see Lund and Tyson 2018.

inequality. Technological changes that have enabled increasing trade between countries at quite-different development and wage levels, and that have enabled the creation of global supply chains based on labor arbitrage, have intensified these negative impacts on a growing number of workers, businesses, and communities. The key questions at stake are:

1. To what extent have these dislocations been due to trade versus technology, and will they continue and intensify?
2. What can and should policy makers do to ease their costs?

TRADE, TECHNOLOGY, AND JOB DISLOCATION

Economists have long recognized that there are both benefits and losses from trade, arguing that on net, the benefits exceed the costs and can be distributed to compensate the losers. But economists have both underestimated the losses and overestimated the willingness of the winners from trade to compensate those who are harmed. Policy responses to achieve the redistribution of trade's net benefits and compensate the losers have been woefully lacking, undermining political support for globalization, and fueling a rise of nationalist populism in the United States, the United Kingdom, and many other (mostly advanced) countries.

Although trade, driven by labor arbitrage, has played a role, labor-saving and skill-biased technological change has been a much more significant factor behind the loss of manufacturing jobs, the polarization of labor markets, and growing income inequality in developed economies. The IMF estimates that about half the thirty-year decline in labor's share of national income in the developed economies reflects the impact of technology, with trade contributing about half as much (IMF 2017). The consensus among economists is that about 80 percent of manufacturing job losses in the United States have been the result of technology, with trade a distant second (DeLong 2017). And the skill-biased nature of technological change has fueled polarization in both employment and wages, with median workers facing stagnating real wages, and noncollege-educated workers suffering a significant decline in their real earnings, while workers with a college education or higher have enjoyed a substantial wage premium. The resulting inequality in wage income in turn has been a key driver of increasing inequality in overall income (Tyson and Spence 2017).

In fact, it is difficult to distinguish between the effects of technology and effects of globalization on employment, wages, and income inequality because technology has enlarged trade based on differences in labor costs. Nonetheless, trade has borne the brunt of the blame by workers and voters, creating a powerful backlash against globalization in the developed countries.

Recently, fears about the effects of technological change on jobs, skills, and wages have been intensifying as the pace of labor-saving and skill-biased technological change has accelerated, and gains in artificial intelligence and robot capabilities have outpaced predictions. Feeding these fears are recent studies finding that large shares of the work done by human labor in both developed and developing countries are "susceptible to automation" even with currently demonstrated technologies.

The widely cited study by Oxford University professors Carl Benedikt Frey and Michael Osborne (2013), for example, concludes that 47 percent of US occupations and on average 57 percent of occupations in OECD countries are at high risk of automation over the next two decades. A more recent study by the McKinsey Global Institute (2017a), which covers forty-six countries and 80 percent of the global labor force, finds that while less than 5 percent of existing occupations could be fully automated, 30 percent or more of the constituent tasks of 60 percent of these occupations could be automated. Both studies find that automation risks are greatest for routine cognitive tasks like data collection and data processing, and routine manual and physical tasks in structured predictable environments such as production line jobs in manufacturing. Large shares of workers in the developed economies have jobs consisting of such routine cognitive and manual tasks.

Both studies also find a negative correlation between the skill levels and wages of occupations/tasks and their potential for automation. These conclusions are evidence of the skill-biased nature of automation and artificial intelligence; on balance, these technologies reduce the demand for low- and middle-skill labor in routine tasks and jobs while increasing the demand for high-skill labor performing abstract tasks that require technical and problem-solving skills. The skill-biased nature of technological change is reflected in both widening educational wage differentials and widening overall wage inequality in most developed countries, albeit to differing degrees. According to a recent survey, the majority of people in the United States fear that automation will increase income inequality. As Michael Spence and I (Tyson and Spencer 2017) conclude in a recent paper, the history of the last forty years indicates that these concerns are warranted.

The fact that large shares of existing tasks and occupations are at risk of automation is fanning fears of widespread technological unemployment as human labor is replaced by intelligent machines. Most economists believe that such fears are unwarranted. According to traditional economic logic, confirmed by historical evidence, technological change fuels productivity gains, which in turn fuel income gains, boosting the demand for goods and services as well as the human labor to produce them. In the long run, technology affects the composition of employment but not the level of unemployment. So far, the specter of technological unemployment raised by John Maynard Keynes nearly a century ago has not become a reality. But in the short to medium run, the changes in the sectoral, occupational, and skill mix of tasks and occupations resulting from automation as well as the dislocation costs of such changes are likely to be substantial. And if the workers displaced by automation are unable to acquire the skills necessary for new jobs or find and move to those jobs quickly, both frictional and structural unemployment can rise, with negative macro effects on growth and potential output.

Another recent study by the McKinsey Global Institute (2017b) concludes that under a moderate scenario for the speed and breadth of automation, about 15 percent of the global workforce—four hundred million workers—could be displaced by technology between now and 2030. The good news is that as a result of projected increases in the demand for goods and services—driven primarily by rising incomes, the growing health care needs of aging populations, investment in infrastructure and energy efficiency, and the marketization of unpaid care—enough jobs can be created to offset job losses in individual countries. In some countries like the United States and Mexico, this outcome will depend on a "step up" relative to current trends in both infrastructure and energy investment as well as the marketization of care, while in other countries like Germany and China, enough new jobs are likely to be created at the current trends to offset the effects of automation and decline in the labor force.

Regardless of the country, the scale of labor market dislocation caused by automation will be substantial. According to McKinsey Global Institute (2017b) estimates, depending on the pace of automation, 75 to 375 million workers, or 3 to 14 percent of the global workforce, will need to change occupational categories by 2030. Moreover, the new jobs will differ significantly from the ones displaced by automation in terms of tasks, educational and skill requirements, and location. In the United States and the other developed countries where automation is likely to be more rapid as cheaper intelligent machines displace costlier human labor, 9 to 32 percent of the workforce may need to change occupational categories and the skills/education associated with them. In these countries, jobs in high-employment occupational categories like production and office support, and jobs requiring a high school education or less, are likely to decline, while jobs in occupational categories such as health care provision, education, construction, and management, along with other jobs requiring a college or advanced degree, will increase. Overall, inequality in wage income is likely to continue as growth in high-wage occupations outpaces growth in middle- and low-wage occupations. In China and other emerging economies, in contrast, middle-income occupations such as service and construction jobs are likely to experience the strongest net job growth.

POLICIES

Like trade, technological change causes structural changes in the composition of output and employment, and these changes impose painful dislocation costs on businesses, workers, and communities. Policy makers can do many things to mitigate these costs. Fiscal and monetary policies to sustain high employment levels of aggregate demand are critical. Policies to expand investment in infrastructure, alternative energy, and paid care for the young and aging can expand demand for workers in jobs and occupations likely to be augmented rather than displaced by automation. Policies to help those displaced by automation—including retraining programs, income support and social safety nets, and portable health, retirement and childcare benefits—are essential. Such policies must have a broader reach than past adjustment policies that attempted to target trade dislocations per se and have had a poor track record (see Anne Krueger's and Lori Kletzer's chapters in this volume).

Lifelong learning needs to become a reality, requiring changes at all levels of education and the redesign of workforce training programs. OECD countries must reverse their widespread two-decades decline in public spending on worker training and active labor market policies that promote participation in the labor force and match employment opportunities with job seekers (McKinsey Global Institute 2017b). Economic theory, confirmed by empirical research, shows that such policies help workers in finding new jobs or acquiring new skills to boost their productivity and earnings, with benefits for the whole economy (Council of Economic Advisers 2016). In the United States, both the expansion of publicly funded high school education to the entire population in the early twentieth century and the GI Bill, which dramatically expanded college education after World War II, were sizable investments in human capital that yielded robust aggregate returns in the form of rising productivity and incomes.

For workers already in the labor market, training that is measured in weeks and months, not years, will be necessary, as will financial support to undertake such training. Apprenticeship programs, such as those in Switzerland and Germany that combine classroom training and work, and enable workers to earn wages while learning, can be redesigned to apply to displaced workers. The SkillsFuture program in Singapore provides another possible model. This program supplies all Singaporeans over the age of twenty-five with an annual credit to pay for approved courses for skill development. By the end of 2016, more than 4 percent of the Singaporean resident population had used the program's credits to take courses.

Denmark's active labor market and training policies—its "flexicurity" system—is another model to be considered. Flexicurity rests on three pillars: the ease of hiring and firing, a generous social safety net encompassing both unemployment insurance and social assistance, and so-called activation policies to train workers and link them to available jobs quickly. With its flexicurity policies, Denmark has achieved strong labor market performance; compared to the rest of Europe, the United Kingdom, and the United States, Denmark has low unemployment rates, high labor force participation rates, and high labor force mobility as measured by high turnover rates.

Automation, like trade, boosts productivity and produces economy-wide benefits. But like trade, it also creates winners and losers. As already noted, trade adjustment assistance programs and other measures to ease the dislocation costs from trade and redistribute its net benefits have been ineffective as well as inadequate. As a result, popular support for trade has declined in many countries, replaced in some by inward-looking populism and nationalism.

How will policy makers respond to the transition costs and income inequalities resulting from the coming wave of automation? Who will bear the dislocation costs on the path to an automated future? Will the benefits of intelligent machines be widely shared or captured by a small share of the population? How will they affect the future of jobs and the future of livelihoods? The answers to these questions depend not on the design of these machines but rather the design of intelligent policies to reap their benefits and share them broadly across society.

REFERENCES

Council of Economic Advisers. 2016. "Active Labor Market Policies: Theory and Evidence for What Works." Issues Brief, December. Washington, DC: Council of Economic Advisers.

DeLong, J. Bradford. 2017. "Where US Manufacturing Jobs Really Went." Project Syndicate, May. https://www.project-syndicate.org/commentary/manufacturing-jobs-share-of-us-economy-by-j--bradford-delong-2017-05?barrier=accessreg.

Frey, Carl Benedikt, and Michael A. Osborne. 2013. "The Future of Employment: How Susceptible Are Jobs to Computerization?" Unpublished manuscript, Oxford University.

IMF (International Monetary Fund). 2017. "Understanding the Downward Trend in Labour Income Shares." In *World Economic Outlook*, chapter 3. Washington, DC: International Monetary Fund.

Lund, Susan, and Laura D. Tyson. 2018. "Globalization Is Not in Retreat." *Foreign Affairs*, May–June. https://www.foreignaffairs.com/articles/world/2018-04-16/globalization-not-retreat.

McKinsey Global Institute. 2017a. "A Future That Works: Automation, Employment, and Productivity." McKinsey and Company, January. https://www.mckinsey.com/~/media/McKinsey/Global%20Themes/Digital%20Disruption/Harnessing%20automation%20for%20a%20future%20that%20works/MGI-A-future-that-works-Executive-summary.ashx.

———. 2017b. "Jobs Lost, Jobs Gained: Workforce Transitions in a Time of Automation." McKinsey and Company, December. https://www.mckinsey.com/~/media/mckinsey/featured%20insights/Future%20of%20Organizations/What%20the%20future%20of%20work%20will%20mean%20for%20jobs%20skills%20and%20wages/MGI-Jobs-Lost-Jobs-Gained-Report-December-6-2017.ashx.

Tyson, Laura D., and Michael Spence. 2017. "Exploring the Effects of Technology on Income and Wealth Inequality." In *After Piketty: The Agenda for Economics and Inequality*, edited by Heather Boushey, J. Bradford DeLong, and Marshall Steinbaum, 170–208. Cambridge, MA: Harvard University Press.

17

The "Elites" against "the People":
The Crisis of Democratic Capitalism

MARTIN WOLF

> Democracy, national sovereignty and global economic integration are mutually incompatible: we can combine any two of the three, but never have all three simultaneously and in full."
>
> —*Dani Rodrik, "The Inescapable Trilemma of the World Economy," 2007*

> μηδὲν ἄγαν (never in excess).
> —*Temple of Apollo, Delphi, Greece*

Until the global financial crises, which originated in the high-income countries of the North Atlantic in 2007, a march toward both globalization and democracy characterized our world. Globalization—the integration of markets for goods, services, capital, and albeit to a more limited and controversial extent, labor—increasingly became the world's dominant economic system. Democracy—the legitimization of power through contestable and regular elections—became an increasingly widespread political system. Since the crisis, however, both have faced backlashes—ones that have affected not just new democracies with recently opened economies but also well-established Western democracies with entrenched market systems. Battered by a huge financial crisis, slow economic growth, rising inequality, and unwelcome pressures from migration, the Western world is losing confidence in its governing elites as well as its political and economic institutions.

What, then, has been happening? Why has the relationship between democracy and today's global capitalism become so fraught? Where might these trends end? These are the questions to be addressed below.

GLOBALIZATION AND DEMOCRACY IN MODERN HISTORY

Let us start with the record and then consider the nature of this complex relationship.

Ups and Downs of Globalization and Democracy

Between 1977 and 2008, the proportion of the world's countries with democratic regimes—ones characterized by competitive elections, participatory politics, and checks on executive power—soared from 24 to 57 percent.[1] The ratio of world trade (exports plus imports) to global output also soared from 22 percent in 1968 to 60 percent in 2008, where it has more or less remained (Ortiz-Ospina, Beltekian, and Roser 2014).[2] Never before in history was such a large proportion of the world's political regimes democratic and never before was the world economy so open. The age of globalization was also an age of democratization.

Something not so dissimilar happened in the nineteenth and early twentieth centuries. This earlier period is sometimes known as the "first globalization" to distinguish it from contemporary globalization, which began in about 1960 (Baldwin and Martin 1999). In that earlier period too, the world economy grew more open (as shown by the spliced Klasing and Millions and the Penn World Table indicators measured along the left axis of figure 17.1). At the same time, the proportion of democracies rose (as shown by the Polity-IV indicator measured along the right axis of figure 17.1), although democratic systems remained far rarer in sovereign states in the earlier period than today. These democracies also fell well short of current standards; in only four small countries—New Zealand, Australia, Finland, and Norway (in that chronological order)—did women have the vote prior to

---

[1] These data are from the Polity IV Project database, http://www.systemicpeace .org/polityproject.html.

[2] These data are drawn from Penn World Tables Version 8.1.

Figure 17.1. Globalization and Democracy

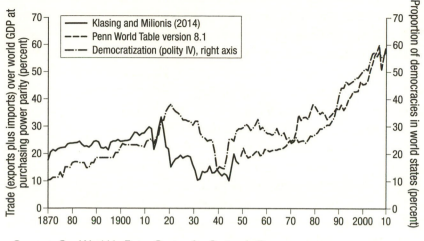

Sources: Our World in Data; Center for Systemic Peace.

World War I. Moreover, a substantial proportion of humanity then still lived in colonial empires.

The proportion of democracies then fell sharply between the two world wars of the first half of the twentieth century, from a peak immediately after the end of World War I. This period was marked, in addition, by a collapse in world trade, as the Great Depression and protectionism worked their evil magic. The nadir for both democracy and openness was reached in the Second World War.

Not coincidentally, the globalization of finance and migration of people show much the same historical pattern as trade. Capital markets achieved far greater integration in the nineteenth century. Gross foreign assets peaked relative to world output before World War I at close to 20 percent, but collapsed between 1914 and 1945. They surpassed pre–World War I ratios, once again, in the early 1980s, but then exploded upward, reaching 185 percent of the global gross output in 2007. Since then these ratios have roughly stabilized.[3] The story of migration is not so dissimilar. Migration ran at a high rate in the late

[3] For the data for the years before the Second World War, see Crafts 2000. For the data for the postwar era up to 2000, see Obstfeld and Taylor 2003, 143, figure. For data after 2000, see Lund et al. 2017, 7, exhibit. See also Lane and Milesi-Ferretti 2007, 223–50; King 2017, 72.

nineteenth century, mainly to the Americas and Australasia. It fell between 1914 and 1945. More recently, it has once again risen sharply, but this time also to Western Europe (see Lindert and Williamson 2001; Hirst and Thompson 1999, 23; O'Rourke 2002, 73).

The globalization of the nineteenth and early twentieth centuries was different in many ways from that of the current era. The earlier period was one of colonial empires; the more recent one was one of sovereign states and international institutions. The earlier period was one of national companies, interindustry trade, and rapid income divergence between the richest and poorest countries; the more recent one was of intraindustry trade, cross-border unbundling of supply chains, global companies, and at least conditional income convergence, particularly between a few large poor and populous countries and their richer peers (Baldwin 2016).[4] The earlier period was one of large, mostly unidirectional flows of capital from rich to emerging economies; the more recent one is of great financial complexity, huge two-way capital flows, and surprisingly large net flows from some emerging to high-income countries. The earlier period was one of vast flows of people to the relatively empty lands of new settlement; the more recent one is characterized, in addition, by large-scale migration to already densely populated European countries.

Technology has always been a powerful driver of globalization and democratization. The railway, steamship, telegraph and newspaper drove economic and political changes during the pre–World War I era. Civil aviation, the container ship, the communications revolution, and advances in digital technologies, notably the internet, drove the economic and political changes of the post–World War II era. But technology unaided does not determine economic or political outcomes. Policy is also vital. Technology largely continued to improve opportunities for global economic integration between 1914 and 1945. Yet policy and politics stopped it from happening. The two eras of globalization were driven, respectively, by the laissez-faire policies of the nineteenth century and conscious economic liberalization after World War II, starting with

---

[4] The convergence of life expectancy and infant mortality has been even more dramatic than in incomes. See Max Roser, "Life Expectancy," Our World in Data, https://ourworldindata.org/life-expectancy; Max Roser, "Child Mortality," Our World in Data, https://ourworldindata.org/child-mortality.

the European and Asian allies of the United States, and then spreading worldwide, above all via China's opening under Deng Xiaoping in 1978.

The imperialism, globalization, and nascent democratization of the nineteenth and early twentieth centuries created powerful countervailing forces. Nationalism, xenophobia, protectionism, militarism, and communism surged. Huge changes undermined the domestic and global social and political orders. Mass industrialisation and urbanization were among the most important aspects of these domestic changes. The economic ascents of the United States, Germany, and Russia were among the most significant changes in international relations. Between 1914 and 1945, these countervailing forces took hold, inflicting a series of political and economic catastrophes. War, financial crisis, and protectionism killed globalization while driving democracy into retreat. Imperialism lingered on, finally dying after World War II.

History does not repeat itself, but it rhymes.[5] A backlash is now emerging that looks similar, at least in some ways, to that of the late nineteenth and early twentieth centuries. While revolutionary socialism is in abeyance for the moment, we see upheavals that bear a marked resemblance to those of a century ago. Nationalism, authoritarianism, populism, xenophobia, and protectionism are on the march. The rise of such ideologies is, once again, driven by the inability of contemporary elites' conventional wisdom to address, let alone redress, today's economic and social changes, coupled with its evident failures in the eyes of the wider public, notably including people in long-established, high-income democracies.

Larry Diamond (2015, 144) of Stanford's Hoover Institution, and an academic expert on democracy, argued in 2015 that "the world has been in a mild but protracted democratic recession since 2006." In its 2018 report, the think tank Freedom House went much further, stating baldly that "democracy is in crisis. The values it embodies—particularly the right to choose leaders in free and fair elections, freedom of the press, and the rule of law—are under assault and in retreat globally." It added that "for the 12th consecutive year . . . , countries that suffered democratic setbacks outnumbered those that registered gains. States that a decade ago seemed like promising success stories—Turkey

---

[5] This remark is attributed to Mark Twain, but appears to be apocryphal. See https://quoteinvestigator.com/2014/01/12/history-rhymes/.

and Hungary, for example—are sliding into authoritarian rule. . . . Meanwhile, the world's most powerful democracies are mired in seemingly intractable problems at home, including social and economic disparities, partisan fragmentation, terrorist attacks, and an influx of refugees that has strained alliances and increased fears of the 'other' " (Abramowitz 2018). The democratic recession is indeed reaching even into established Western democracies.

As in the late nineteenth and early twentieth centuries, the rapid shifts in the relative economic size of countries—this time the rise of China, above all—have destabilized geopolitics. Again, just as in that earlier era, mutual suspicion characterizes relations between the rising and established power. Graham Allison (2017) of Harvard describes this as the "Thucydides trap," after the analysis by the great Athenian historian of relations between Athens and Sparta in the fifth century BC.

Globalization is in recession too, albeit so far a mild one, arguably even a surprisingly mild one. Cross-border capital flows have shrunk sharply since the crisis, but most analysts would agree that this was a reasonable correction from grossly excessive levels (Lund et al. 2017, 1). The regulation of finance has also tightened sharply, but for evident reasons. The backlash against flows of people seems to be becoming ever more vicious on both sides of the Atlantic. Yet migration continues. The growth of trade has fallen sharply relative to world output (Hufbauer and Jung 2016; IMF 2016, 63–119. Nevertheless, there has been no shrinkage of trade relative to world output. A big question is whether this will continue to be the case. In his inaugural address, Trump (2017) asserted that "protection will lead to great prosperity and strength." This might herald the reversal of the entire post–World War II effort at liberalization. Subsequent US actions and presidential rhetoric show this was no idle threat. Even the flow of ideas is endangered, notably behind the great internet wall of China.

Complex Relationship between Globalization and Democracy

In sum, eras of globalization have tended to be ones of prosperity or at least the promise of it, while eras of de-globalization, such as the 1930s, have been periods of economic breakdown. Again, eras of prosperity, such as the 1950s and 1960s in the Western world, tended to strengthen democracy, while eras of economic misery foment the politics of fear and suspicion. Harvard's Benjamin Friedman (2005) has documented just such a positive relationship between prosperity and democracy. But mismanaged, globalization may fail to produce prosperity—especially widely shared prosperity. It may instead sow the seeds of economic downfall (see Kuttner 2018). This is the danger today, even in the established democracies.

The connection between democracy and global capitalism is not just complex in practice. It is also complex in theory. These political and economic systems share an ideal of equality: everybody is entitled to do the best they can in the market, regardless of social status, and similarly, everybody is entitled to a voice in public affairs, again regardless of social status. Democracy depends on the rule of law, and so does global capitalism (see Olson 2000). Yet we can also identify clear conflicts between these political and economic systems. Democratic politics rest on the notion of a shared public weal; capitalism is driven by the pursuit of individual, not social, gain. Democracy is territorial; capitalism is global. Electorates desire security; capitalism is prone to crises. Democracy gives citizens voice; markets rest on the threat of exit (see Hirschman 1972). Perhaps most important, citizenship rests on loyalty; markets are transactional.

Notwithstanding these tensions, today's high-income countries are democracies. Under Xi Jinping, China is trying to pioneer an alternative: a market economy governed by a resurgent Communist Party state (Wolf 2018b). Yet for all its successes, that rising superpower remains relatively poor, with real incomes per head still only about a third of those of the United States (IMF 2018). Even so, established democracies cannot be complacent about the way their political and economic systems are working. The relationship between democracy and global capitalism may go terribly wrong, perhaps because the economy founders, the benefits of economic progress are too narrowly shared, or the globalization of business clashes too much with the voters' insistence on their right to come first in economic decision making. "America First" might be viewed as no more than a call to both companies and country to put "Us First." Financial crises are particularly dangerous in this regard because being so dramatic, they destroy both prosperity and trust in elites overnight. If big parts of the body politic ceases to trust elites and those on the other side of the political divide to use power competently as well as honorably, democracy may perish altogether. Would-be despots are extremely good at cultivating and exploiting such mistrust. This was true in the 1930s. It is, alas, true today.

GROWING ANXIETY AND LOSS OF TRUST

The evidence shows that there has indeed been a loss of trust in elites, democratic institutions, and the global market economy in the established high-income democracies. This erosion has shown itself in populist politics, protectionist rhetoric (and more recently practice), and hostility toward immigration. What is the root of these shifts?

Cultural versus Economic Change

The answer below will be divided into longer-term and more recent developments. It will not, however, be divided into cultural and economic causes. This is so for two reasons. First, lack of space and professional competence dictate a focus on the economic changes. Second, the distinction between cultural and economic changes seems rather unproductive, since the two are so interrelated and, in most cases, economic change underlies cultural shifts. Certainly, many of the great cultural shifts of our era seem to have economic roots.

Thus, prosperity underlies the urge toward self-realization characteristic of our era. That impulse was inconceivable in a society in which most people were permanently on the margins of survival. Collapsing infant mortality, huge reductions in the time and work demands of household labor, the declining significance of physical strength as a productive attribute, and the rise of the service economy help explain the remarkable transformation in the social and political role of women. The huge gaps in wealth between rich and poor societies along with the declining costs of transport and information help explain the upsurge in migration. At the same time, the political impact of migration in the high-income recipient countries would surely have been far smaller if real wages had been rising consistently and strongly in these countries.

A particularly important economic change is the relative decline in the position of less educated men. This shift followed the period in the mid-twentieth century when this group of people enjoyed high employment, stable jobs, and significant social status. The reduction in their economic position is due to a complex mixture of technological change and global competition. Not surprisingly, this relative decline has led to "status anxiety" and a strong political backlash. According to Noam Gidron and Peter Hall (2017), "Exit polls indicate that 64 per cent of manual workers voted for Brexit compared to 43 per cent of managers or professionals; 37 per cent voted for Marine Le Pen in the first round of the French presidential elections compared to 14 per cent of managers or professionals; and white Americans without a college degree voted for Donald Trump by a margin of almost 20 per cent over Hillary Clinton." Similarly, the "deaths of despair" among less educated white people associated with the soaring consumption of opioids is also a reflection of economic woes, as discussed in Angus Deaton's chapter in this volume (see Case and Deaton 2017).

Longer-Term Economic Changes

The most fundamental economic change is the globalization of capitalism. This development has several significant consequences. Businesses have become increasingly global, thereby eroding their sense of responsibility to any given country or any national group of workers. Moreover, it is easier for businesses than workers to "exit" from a given location or country, in whole or part, thus greatly increasing their bargaining power—with governments as well as workers. An important change in this context is the rise of global value chains: foreign value added has, for example, become an increasingly crucial share of gross exports (OECD 2017, 90). The impact of business mobility on corporate revenue as a share of GDP in the high-income countries has been surprisingly small, however, presumably because base widening has offset declining corporate tax rates (OECD 2018). But perhaps the most significant aspect of the globalization of capitalism is the creation of a global financial system, which was ineffectively managed (leading to the global financial crisis) and in its present form might even be unmanageable (Wolf 2015; Bayoumi 2017; Kuttner 2018).

With the globalization of capitalism has come the globalization of economic governance. This was both inevitable and desirable. It began in 1944 with the Bretton Woods conference, which led to the birth of the IMF in 1945 and Havana Charter in 1948, creating the GATT and ultimately WTO in 1995. Also important was the creation in 1957 of the European Economic Community, which ultimately led to the

European Union in 1993. The creation of these institutions recognized the twin realities that prosperity depends on international commerce, especially trade, and this requires access to other countries' markets and at least some agreement on regulatory standards, including in finance. Furthermore, in open economies with free movement of capital and skilled labor, countries need to cooperate against tax avoidance and evasion. In all these ways, therefore, institutionalized cooperation is a natural consequence of globalization itself. Yet as Dani Rodrik (2007) notes, these developments (however natural and appropriate) can be seen to create conflicts with the notion of democratic sovereignty—conflicts that exploded in recent years, in the referendum on Brexit in 2016, election of Trump that same year, and rise of populism across the European Union, notably including hostility to the rules of the eurozone.

A dominant feature of the period since the early 1980s has been a tendency toward increasing inequality in both wealth and incomes (pre- and posttax) in many countries—despite great diversity of trends, as discussed in Francois Bourguignon's chapter in this volume (see Piketty 2013). In terms of household disposable incomes, the United Kingdom and United States are now the most unequal of the established high-income countries. Indeed, the latter is almost in a class of its own (see figure 17.2). Combined with smaller labor market programs relative to those other advanced countries (cf. figure I.8), rising inequality may help explain the rise of populism in these two countries. Among other large high-income countries, inequality in Italy is also relatively high, and there too, populism is markedly on the rise (Mayer 2016). The OECD (2019) has recently noted that "income inequality in OECD countries is at its highest level for the past half century." It also points out that "the economic crisis has added urgency to the need to address inequality. Uncertainty and fears of social decline and exclusion have reached the middle classes in many societies."

The combination of rising inequality with modest real growth has over lengthy periods has also meant stagnant real incomes for large parts of the population. In the United States notably, real median household disposable incomes in 2016 were much the same as they had been in 1999 and 2007 (see figure 17.3).

A further significant trend was deindustrialization, or more precisely, the rapid decline in the share of employment in industry. Interestingly,

Figure 17.2. Inequality of Household Disposable Incomes 2014 (Gini Coefficient)

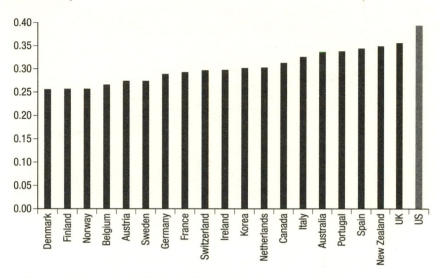

Source: Organization for Economic Cooperation and Development.

Figure 17.3. Mean and Median Real Household Disposable Incomes in the United States (1984 = 100)

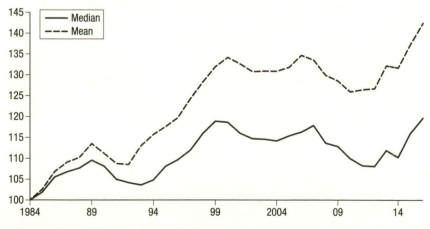

Source: Federal Reserve Economic Data.

Figure 17.4. Share of Total Employment in Industry

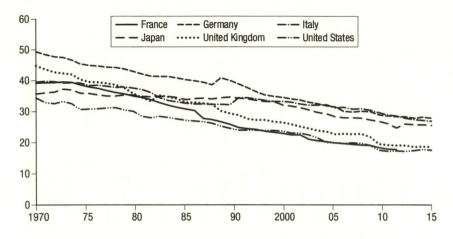

the trends in Germany and the United States are much the same, although the former has had a consistently higher share of manufacturing employment (see figure 17.4). This difference reflects Germany's large and persistent trade surpluses in manufacturing, and the large and persistent trade deficits of the United States. Industry used to generate a large number of relatively highly paid and secure jobs for less educated men. One reason for the high pay was unionization. This was, in turn, supported by the relative ease of organizing large workforces concentrated in huge plants, which had the capacity to inflict damage on the profitability of these correspondingly capital-intensive businesses. The fact that the decline in the share of manufacturing in employment was substantial even in Germany, despite its growing trade surpluses, suggests that the principal cause of the trend decline in the share of manufacturing in employment has been rising productivity. But such increases in productivity are, in turn, partly due to the loss from high-income countries of relatively low-skilled jobs within supply chains that increasingly cross international borders (see Coco 2016).

The final and perhaps politically most important longer-term change has been immigration. In virtually all high-income countries, the share of the foreign born in the population has risen. In 2013, the countries with the highest shares of foreign born in their populations were Switzerland, Australia, New Zealand, Canada, Austria, and Ireland (see figure 17.5). Yet only in Austria do we currently see a big backlash,

Figure 17.5. Foreign-Born as Share of Population

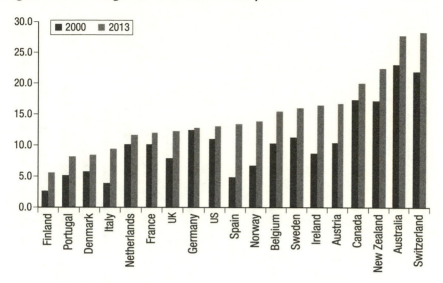

Source: Organization for Economic Cooperation and Development.

though Australia experienced a backlash in the early 2000s. Again, the countries with the largest increases in the proportion of foreign born between 2000 and 2013 were Spain, Ireland, Norway, Switzerland, Austria, and Italy. Only in the last two was the backlash considerable. The increase in the proportion of foreign born has certainly been socially and politically significant. Some analysts would even argue that it was the most important factor in explaining the vote in favor of Brexit in the June 2016 British referendum (Goodhart 2017, 122–27). The vote in favor of Trump in 2016 is partially attributed to immigration too. But interestingly, the increase in the proportion of foreign born in the United States between 2000 and 2013 was among the lowest in high-income countries (see figure 17.6).

The link between immigration and popular hostility is a complex one. Whether someone is foreign born will not tell one enough about popular attitudes. The ethnic origins of the native-born members of long-established communities may also be a factor, while foreign-born people may create few problems if they are viewed as being ethnically or culturally similar to the native population. The economics of immigration are complex and controversial too. Yet there is little doubt that many citizens resent high levels of immigration for cultural, social,

Figure 17.6. Change in the Proportion of Foreign Born in the Population, 2000–13

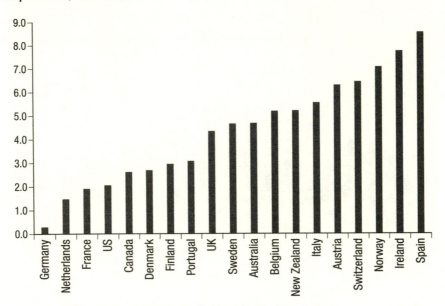

Source: Organization for Economic Cooperation and Development.

or economic reasons. In economic terms, many see high levels of immigration as eroding the value of what is, for many citizens of high-income societies, the most valuable asset they own: their citizenship.

Impact of the Crisis

Long-term trends have created important economic divisions in the high-income democracies. But probably even more devastating was the crisis that emanated from the core of the global financial system in 2007 and 2008, and proceeded to devastate the world economy. It is now clear that the crisis has had a powerful impact on the political economy of the high-income democracies along several dimensions.

The most obvious legacy is the impact on real incomes. Of the group of seven leading high-income countries, plus Spain, only Germany experienced no shortfall in GDP per head relative to what would have been expected if the precrisis trend had continued. Elsewhere, the shortfalls are enormous (see figure 17.7). In the UK case, for example, the postcrisis shortfall in real GDP per head (compared with the precrisis trend) represents, at least to this point, a substantially bigger loss in

Figure 17.7. Deviation of GDP per Head from 1980 to 2007 Trend (Actual, Less Exponential Trend Line, as Percent of Trend)

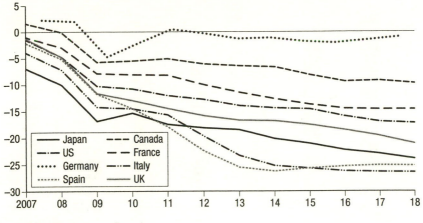

Source: Conference Board.

aggregate output than that imposed by either of the two world wars or Great Depression. Maybe this will reverse with a burst of faster productivity growth, but no sign of that yet can be seen.

The stagnation in real GDP per head has naturally had a powerfully negative effect on household incomes. A study by the McKinsey Global Institute (2016) showed that on average, between 65 and 70 percent of all households in high-income countries had flat or falling real incomes from wages and capital between 2005 and 2014—that is, before redistribution by governments. In hard-hit Italy the proportion was 97 percent, in the United States it was 81 percent, and in the United Kingdom it was 70 percent. This stagnation of household incomes is partly the result of longer-term trends. But it has much to do with the crisis too (see figure 17.8).

The crisis also had significant effects, in some cases temporary and in other cases relatively permanent, on unemployment. In the United States, for example, the unemployment rate jumped from 4.4 percent in March 2007 to a peak of 10 percent in October 2009. In the eurozone, it rose from 7.3 percent in late 2007 to a peak of 12.1 percent in early 2013 after a substantially lengthier crisis than in the United States. Unemployment fell back to low levels fairly quickly in the United Kingdom and United States, and remained low throughout in Japan and Germany. In some other large countries, unemployment reached high

Figure 17.8. Proportion of Households with Flat or Falling Real Incomes from Wages and Capital, 2005–14

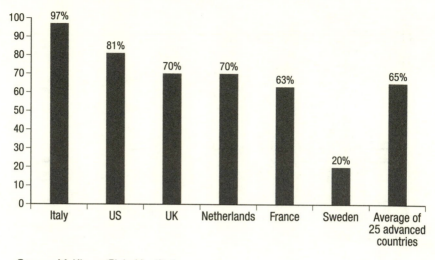

Source: McKinsey Global Institute.

or even very high levels, and then stayed quite high. In Italy, for instance, the unemployment rate peaked at 13.1 percent in November 2014 (from a precrisis low of 5.8 percent in April 2007), but was still 11.2 percent in April 2018.

Yet the unemployment rate is an imperfect indicator of what is happening in the labor market. The participation rate also matters, because many people may be discouraged even from seeking work. Socially, detachment from the labor market is most significant when the people who have withdrawn are prime-age adults—those who bear the main responsibility for the upbringing of the next generation. Remarkably, the US participation rate for adults aged twenty-five to fifty-four was among the lowest reported by the OECD in 2017, at a mere 81.7 percent (see figure 17.9).

Another important economic impact of the crisis was on the fiscal positions of affected countries. The recession and subsequent weak recovery led to higher spending and a permanent reduction in revenue relative to precrisis expectations. Revenue loss from the previously buoyant financial sector was especially important in some countries, notably the United Kingdom. If we look at the members of the group of seven leading high-income countries, we find that they all imposed

Figure 17.9. Labor Force Participation Rates, 2017, for People Aged Twenty-Five to Fifty-Four

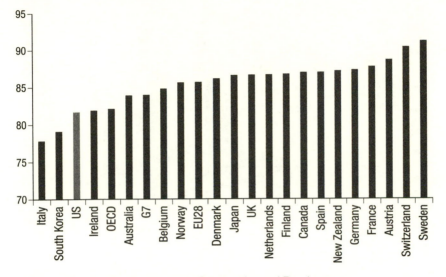

Source: Organization for Economic Cooperation and Development.

significant structural fiscal tightening between 2010 and 2017, but the tightening was biggest in the United States and United Kingdom (see figure 17.10).

The crisis shook trust in the wisdom and probity of those running the affected countries' financial, economic, and political systems. It did so in four ways. First, the voting public at large realized that those in charge did not really have a clue about the risks they were allowing the financial sector to run. The emperors really were naked. Prior to this, the public might have taken their competence on trust, but such trust inevitably disappeared as a result of the crisis. Second, many members of the public came to believe that these failings were the result not just of stupidity but also the corruption of decision makers and opinion formers at all levels—in the financial sector, the regulatory bodies, academia, the media, and politics. Third, members of the public saw the resources of the state being used to rescue both banks and bankers, the architects, as they saw it, of the disaster, while they (and those they loved) suffered large immediate losses through unemployment, or a prolonged period of stagnant or falling real wages (or both), together with the consequences of fiscal retrenchment. Finally, they saw that

Figure 17.10. Tightening of General Government Structural Fiscal Deficit

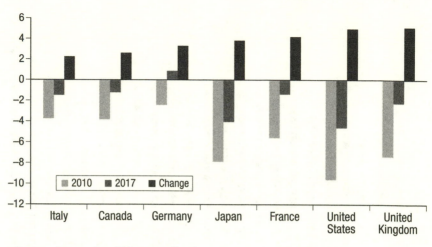

Source: International Monetary Fund.

while institutions may have been forced to pay large fines, nobody (or nobody of any importance) was punished for what had happened.

Assessment

Significant long-term economic changes undermined the relative economic and, to a great extent, social positions of important parts of the body politic of high-income countries, especially less skilled male workers. This outcome had multiple causes. But the key point is that little was done to alleviate the difficulties in many countries. Then came the crisis, which was a severe shock; it changed everything, including most notably politics.

RISE OF POPULISM

A modern democracy rests on a tacit contract between ruling elites (whose existence is unavoidable in a complex society) and the people at large. The former ensure the reasonably smooth running of the economy and polity, from which all benefit. The latter, in turn, accept the authority of the former, while choosing the leaders they prefer. This contract has broken down with the erosion of trust and thus the consent on which a democracy is based. The general result is fragility: anything can happen. The specific result is the rise of a new sort of politics (or more exactly, the return of an old form of politics): populism.

Populism can be viewed as nothing more sinister than a desire of voters to choose leaders whom they see as better aligned with their interests. This form of populism would, in light of recent experience, be reasonable. The elites have indeed been discredited. Their replacement by other politicians would be perfectly understandable and potentially even beneficial, provided those new politicians put relevant reforms in place. Some US analysts write from this perspective, influenced no doubt by the previous experience of their country with populist uprisings. The US journalist John Judis (2016) uses this perspective to explain what is presently happening on both sides of the Atlantic.

Unfortunately this view of populism looks too benign today. There is a more compelling and relevant conception of populism rooted in the far darker history of Europe, but now relevant to the United States under Trump. This is one of a subversion of democratic norms by populist movements that morph into dictatorships. Princeton University's Jan-Werner Müller (2016), who is of German origin, explored this form of populism in an important recent book. It is impossible to read his book without recognizing crucial features of today's politics.

What are the features of this form of populism? They are a condemnation of elites as corrupt and treacherous; a distrust of established institutions, especially ones that check the "will of the people," such as courts and independent media; a distrust of "experts" and expertise; a fevered enthusiasm for conspiracy theories; and a hostility toward those not viewed as part of "the real people" and, frequently, desire for direct action, often including violence.

Left-wing populists think of workers and the poor as "the people," identify the rich as the enemy, and favor public ownership and a tightly controlled economy. Right-wing populists think of established ethnic groups as "the people," identify foreigners and intellectuals as the enemy, support "traditional" social values, and are xenophobic and nationalistic—in politics and economics alike. Right-wing populists also tend to replace lost confidence in established elites and institutions with trust in a charismatic leader who can do no wrong. That leader will then seek to throw off constitutional and political constraints, emerging as an autocrat. The tendency of both forms of populism is toward protectionism, fiscal irresponsibility, and authoritarianism. Both forms tend to be hostile toward independent media, globalization, and especially in the case of right-wing populism, treaty-based international cooperation. Both forms of populism are ultimately incompatible with liberal democracy—that is, a democratic order protected by entrenched individual freedoms and institutional protections, notably protections of the rights of political minorities.

To varying degrees, these populist ideas, especially right-wing populism, can be seen in many Western democracies today. They have already seized power in Hungary and Poland. They are a marked feature of the rule of Trump in the United States. Some of the attitudes of right-wing populism have marked the Brexit campaign, especially the headline on a front page of the *Daily Mail*, which scandalously described the British High Court as "enemies of the people" (Slack 2016).

US right-wing populism is particularly remarkable, since the policies of the Trump administration—especially massive tax cuts—are so obviously devoted to the interests not of the mass of his white voters but rather to those of a plutocratic elite. How has this happened? The answer lies in what I call "pluto-populism." These are the politics of highly conservative billionaires whose aims are low taxes, minimal social spending, and high inequality. But how can they achieve these aims in a universal suffrage democracy characterized by the ills already discussed above? The answer is through propaganda in favor of "trickle-down" economics, splitting the less well off on cultural and racial lines, gerrymandering, and voter suppression. Trump is a perfectly logical outcome of these perverse politics. He gives rich people what they desire, while offering the nationalism and protections wanted by the Republican base (Wolf 2018a).

Adding to all this, no doubt, is the transformation of media. In truth, it is hard to evaluate the roles of the rise of social media, end of broadcasting hegemonies, and arrival of new niche media that cater to relatively narrow groups. But politicians who are good at exploiting new media, including Obama and Trump, have proved remarkably successful in shaping the political environment for their own ends. Equally striking, however, is what is not so new. The charge of lying laid against opponents by those who have themselves turned lying into an art was the foundation of the Nazi propaganda factory. Thus did the US Office of Strategic Services describe Adolf Hitler during World War II: "His primary rules were: never allow the public to cool off;

never admit a fault or wrong; never concede that there may be some good in your enemy; never leave room for alternatives; never accept blame; concentrate on one enemy at a time and blame him for everything that goes wrong; people will believe a big lie sooner than a little one; and if you repeat it frequently enough people will sooner or later believe it."[6] Does this sound familiar? By now it should.

WHERE ARE THE HIGH-INCOME LIBERAL DEMOCRACIES HEADED?

So where does this leave us? The short answer is that it leaves us in a crisis of the political and economic systems of the high-income countries, which are still, despite the rise of the Asian emerging economies, the core of the world economy. It might be liberal democracy as we know it that disappears. It might be global capitalism that disappears. It might be both. It might, with a burst of creative policy making, be neither. The future is unknown. It is ours to shape.

Two things, however, seem evident.

First, it is impossible for us to retreat into our tribal caves. The world has become not only economically globalized but globalized in even deeper ways too. For the first time, humanity has the capacity to ruin the entire planet. It is hard, given this, to see any rational basis for withdrawing from the task of a shared system of global governance. The populist tide as it is now advancing, especially on the Right, seems likely to make such governance impossible. That is a serious threat to the world.

Second, there is a case for reconsidering the balance of the current relationship between the global economic rules, on the one hand, and domestic policy, on the other. Nevertheless, the way that Rodrik (2007) frames these trade-offs is unpersuasive. He argues that if a country is to be both democratic and sovereign, it must abjure deep economic integration. Yes, there are trade-offs. But they are far from simple ones. An industrial policy that does not come with access to the global economy is, for all but the largest economies, an illusion. That is to say, economic integration makes such a sovereign choice more, not less, effective. The case for the global trade rules is that it makes the relevant policy choices more effective, not less.

[6] "Big Lie," Wikipedia, https://en.wikipedia.org/wiki/Big_lie.

The same point applies in other areas. Raising tax from corporations requires stronger cooperation among national authorities; so, for many countries, will managing immigration, which is not a purely national decision, especially in continental Europe. Again, the regulation of finance cannot easily be achieved at a purely national level, unless one is prepared to cut one's country off from the global financial system altogether, which would impose its own costs. Again and again, countries find that international rules are part of making domestic choices more effective, not less.

Moreover, the constraints of globalization must not be exaggerated. The high-income countries all faced rather-similar challenges from trade, for example. But the impact in terms of rising inequality, falling labor force participation, and other social ills varied enormously. The evidence indicates that highly open economies—the Nordics being a notable example—are able to tax and thus provide the benefits that their voters demand. Too often, globalization is used as a scapegoat for wider policy failures.

The right way to think about this challenge is as one of getting the correct balance among sovereignty, democracy, and international integration. This balance may need to be adjusted from time to time. But "corner solutions" are never likely to be optimal. "Never in excess" is surely the right motto. The backlash against the developments of the period between 1980 and 2007 is understandable, especially in the wake of the financial crisis that followed. But the xenophobic populism we are seeing is most definitely not the solution. Democratic reformers must find a way to use the policy autonomy that they possess to introduce reforms, at both the domestic and global levels, that maintain the advances we have made and rectify the failures. No reasonable alternative exists. If we do not adopt that approach, we will end up with the unreasonable alternatives.

REFERENCES

Abramowitz, Michael J. 2018. "Democracy in Crisis." Freedom House. https://freedomhouse.org/report/freedom-world/freedom-world-2018.

Allison, Graham. 2017. *Destined for War: Can America and China Escape Thucydides's Trap?* Boston: Houghton Mifflin Harcourt.

Baldwin, Richard E. 2016. *The Great Convergence: Information Technology and the New Globalization.* Cambridge, MA: Belknap Press.

Baldwin, Richard E., and Philippe Martin. 1999. "Two Waves of Globalisation: Superficial Similarities, Fundamental Differences." NBER Working Paper 6904. Cambridge, MA: National Bureau of Economic Research.

Bayoumi, Tamim. 2017. *Unfinished Business: The Unexplored Causes of the Financial Crisis and the Lessons Yet to Be Learned.* New Haven, CT: Yale University Press.

Case, Anne, and Angus Deaton. 2017. "Mortality and Morbidity in the 21st Century." *Brookings Papers on Economic Activity*, Spring, 397–476. Washington, DC: Brookings Institution.

Coco, Federica. 2016. "Most US Manufacturing Jobs Lost to Technology, Not Trade." *Financial Times*, December 2. https://www.ft.com/content/dec677c0-b7e6-11e6-ba85-95d1533d9a62.

Crafts, Nicholas. 2000. "Globalisation and Growth in the Twentieth Century." *IMF Working Paper WP/00/44.* Washington, DC: International Monetary Fund.

Diamond, Larry. 2015. "Facing Up to the Democratic Recession." *Journal of Democracy* 26, no. 1 (January): 141–55.

Friedman, Benjamin. 2005. *The Moral Consequences of Economic Growth.* New York: Vintage Press.

Gidron, Noam, and Peter A. Hall. 2017. "The Politics of Social Status: Economic and Cultural Roots of the Populist Right." *British Journal of Sociology* (November): 1–25.

Goodhart, David. 2017. *The Road to Somewhere.* London: Penguin Random House.

Hufbauer, Gary Clyde, and Euijin Jung. 2016. "Why Has Trade Stopped Growing? Not Much Liberalizaton and Lots of Micro-Protection." Peterson Institute for International Economics, March 23. https://piie.com/blogs/trade-investment-policy-watch/why-has-trade-stopped-growing-not-much-liberalization-and-lots.

Hirst, Paul, and Grahame Thompson. 1999. *Globalisation in Question: The International Economy and the Possibilities of Governance*, 2nd ed. Cambridge, UK: Polity Press.

Hirschman, Albert O. 1972. *Exit, Voice, and Loyalty: Responses to Decline in Firms, Organizations, and States.* Cambridge, MA: Harvard University Press.

IMF (International Monetary Fund). 2016. *World Economic Outlook*, October. Washington, DC: International Monetary Fund.

———. 2018. "World Economic Outlook Database." https://www.imf.org/external/pubs/ft/weo/2018/01/weodata/index.aspx.

Judis, John B. 2016. *The Populist Explosion: How the Great Recession Transformed American and European Politics.* New York: Columbia Global Reports.

King, Stephen D. 2017. *Grave New World: The End of Globalization and the Return of History.* New Haven, CT: Yale University Press.

Klasing, Mariko, and Petros Milionis. 2014. "Quantifying the Evolution of World Trade, 1970–1949." *Journal of International Economics* 92, no. 1 (January): 185–97.

Kuttner, Robert. 2018. *Can Democracy Survive Global Capitalism?* New York: W. W. Norton.

Lane, Philip R., and Gian M. Milesi-Ferretti. 2007. "The External Wealth of Nations Mark II: Revised and Extended Estimates of Foreign Assets and Liabilities, 1970–2004." *Journal of International Economics* 73, no. 2 (November): 223–50.

Lindert, Peter H., and Jeffrey G. Williamson. 2001. "Globalization and Inequality: A Long History," Paper prepared for the World Bank Annual Conference on Development Economics—Europe, Barcelona, June 25–27.

Lund, Susan, Eckart Windhagen, James Manyika, Philipp Härle, Jonathan Woetzel, and Diana Goldshtein. 2017. *The New Dynamics of Financial Globalization*. New York: McKinsey and Company.

Mayer, Jane. 2016. *Dark Money: The Hidden History of the Billionaires behind the Rise of the Radical Right*. New York: Anchor Books.

McKinsey Global Institute. 2016. "Poorer Than Their Parents? Flat or Falling Incomes in Advanced Countries." https://www.mckinsey.com/featured-insights /employment-and-growth/poorer-than-their-parents-a-new-perspective-on -income-inequality.

Müller, Jan-Werner. 2016. *What Is Populism?* Philadelphia: University of Pennsylvania Press.

Obstfeld, Maurice, and Alan M. Taylor. 2003. "Globalization and Capital Markets." *In Globalization in Historical Perspective*, edited by Michael D. Bordo, Alan M. Taylor, and Jeffrey G. Williamson, 121–87. Chicago: University of Chicago Press.

Olson, Mancur. 2000. *Power and Prosperity: Outgrowing Communist and Capitalist Dictatorships*. New York: Basic Books.

OECD (Organization for Economic Cooperation and Development). 2017. *Employment Outlook*. Paris: Organization for Economic Cooperation and Development.

———. 2018. "Tax on Corporate Profits." https://data.oecd.org/tax/tax-on -corporate-profits.htm.

———. 2019. "Inequality." http://www.oecd.org/social/inequality.htm.

O'Rourke, Kevin. 2002. "Europe and the Causes of Globalization, 1790 to 2000." In *From Europeanization of the Globe to the Globalization of Europe*, edited by Henryk Kierzkowski, 64–86. London: Palgrave.

Ortiz-Ospina, Esteban, Diana Beltekian, and Max Roser. 2014. "Trade and Globalization." Our World in Data. https://ourworldindata.org/international-trade.

Piketty, Thomas. 2013. *Capital in the Twenty-First Century*. Translated by Arthur Goldhammer. Cambridge, MA: Harvard University Press.

Rodrik, Dani. 2007. "The Inescapable Trilemma of the World Economy." Dani Rodrik's weblog, June 27. https://rodrik.typepad.com/dani_rodriks_weblog/2007 /06/the-inescapable.html.

Slack, James. 2016. "Enemies of the People: Fury over 'Out of Touch' Judges Who Have 'Declared War on Democracy' by Defying 17.4M Brexit Voters and Who Could Trigger Constitutional Crisis." *Daily Mail*, November 3. http://www .dailymail.co.uk/news/article-3903436/Enemies-people-Fury-touch-judges -defied-17-4m-Brexit-voters-trigger-constitutional-crisis.html.

Trump, Donald J. 2017 "Remarks of President Donald J. Trump, as Prepared for Delivery, Inaugural Address, Friday, January 20, 2017, Washington, D.C." https://www.whitehouse.gov/briefings-statements/the-inaugural-address/.

Wolf, Martin. 2015. *The Shifts and the Shocks: What We've Learned—and Still Have to Learn—from the Financial Crisis*. London: Penguin Allen Lane.

———. 2018a. "How We Lost America to Greed and Envy." *Financial Times*, July 17. https://www.ft.com/content/3aea8668-88e2-11e8-bf9e-8771d5404543.

———. 2018b. "Xi's Power Grab Means China Is Vulnerable to the Whims of One Man." *Financial Times*, February 27. https://www.ft.com/content/38996858 -1af0-11e8-956a-43db76e69936.

18

Meeting Challenges or Matching Challengers?

ERNESTO ZEDILLO

The title of this volume is highly suggestive of how defensive even the strong proponents of globalization have become in this debate in recent years. Speaking of "meeting globalization's challenges" rather than "challenging globalization's challengers" transmits a certain sense of admission of guilt about the downsides reputedly brought about by the process of increasing international economic integration. This twist of the language could project a most welcome intellectual humility on the part of globalization's proponents. But it could also be interpreted as signaling a weaker conviction about the benefits of globalization on their part, liable to misuse or abuse by its recalcitrant opponents.

The proponents' current flimsy stand, if prudently influenced by a careful assessment of the accumulated evidence, also seems to be a defensive response to the globalization backlash or even "globaliphobia" that has been intensifying particularly since the great crisis of 2008–9 and its aftermath. On the one hand, globaliphobia is driven by reasons of ideology and political convenience. On the other hand, it is rooted in faulty economic analysis that goes back to the time when sheer mercantilism ruled the world of the now-developed countries, or in the case of developing countries, import substitution strategies were seen as the panacea for achieving industrialization and development. Unfortunately, the backlash is also fed by biased or partial interpretations of highly respectable research on the consequences of freer international trade and investment.

In any case, the backlash against contemporary globalization seems to be approaching an all-time high in many places including, remarkably, the United States. Part of the backlash may be attributable to the simple fact that world GDP as well as nominal wage growth—even accounting for the healthier rates of 2017 and 2018—are still below what they were in most advanced and emerging market countries in the five years prior to the 2008–9 crisis. Globaliphobia is also nurtured by the increase in income inequality and the so-called middle-class squeeze in the rich countries, along with the anxiety caused by automation, which is bound to affect the structure of these countries' labor markets (as discussed in Laura Tyson's chapter in this volume). It is in fact quite in vogue, on the one hand, to blame globalization for any number of things that have gone wrong in the world, and on the other hand, dismiss the benefits that it has helped to bring about, not least of which is what Angus Deaton (2013) has called "the Great Escape": the exit of a good chunk of humanity from poverty.

The tendency to impute a range of ills to globalization is of course not a new one. Open markets, for a host of reasons, are always contentious. But making globalization the preferred culprit to explain all kinds of unsavory situations with the intensity reached lately could be consequential for the continuity of the process, causing great damage to its potential to provide vast development opportunities.

More subtly, but equally negative, such a tendency entails deflecting responsibility away from domestic policies and toward external forces as the cause of problems actually caused by those policies themselves. Blaming the various dimensions of globalization—trade, finance, and migration—for phenomena such as insufficient GDP growth, stagnant wages, inequality, and unemployment always seems to be preferable for governments, rather than admitting their failure to deliver on their own responsibilities.

As observed repeatedly, the most extreme cases of such a deflection of responsibility are found among populist politicians. More than any other kind, the populist politician has a marked tendency to blame others for their country's problems and failings. Foreigners, who invest in, export to, or migrate to their country, are the populist's favorite targets to explain almost every domestic problem. That is why restrictions, including draconian ones, on trade, investment, and migration are an essential part of the populist's policy arsenal. The populist praises isolationism and avoids international engagement, except with foreign populist cronies. The "full package" of populism frequently includes antimarket economics, xenophobic and autarkic nationalism, contempt for multilateral rules and institutions, and authoritarian politics.

Only exceptionally, individual cases of populist experiments may become a serious threat to the process of global interdependence. When countries have toyed, democratically or not, with populist leadership, the damage has been largely self-inflicted, with any spillover effects limited to their immediate neighbors. For example, Latin America is a place where populism has been at times pervasive. Yet most of the hardship that populism caused has been contained within the countries suffering the populist maladies. Unfortunately, a major exception to the rule of contained spillovers may be the current case of the United States, where a president with an evident antiglobalization populist platform, along the lines noted above, came into office in early 2017. As mentioned by Edward Alden earlier in this book, unlike every US president since at least Franklin Delano Roosevelt, Trump's trade policies are aimed not at expanding the global economic pie but rather seizing a bigger share for the United States. Given the United States' sheer weight in the global economy and its role as the key founder of the multilateral trading system that has operated with great success over the more than seventy years since World War II, it should not be surprising that the spillovers of a neomercantilist US stance are bound to be widespread.

In what follows, I will first delve into some policy implications of this return to a neomercantilist policy outlook and then take on other main critiques of globalization that, albeit much more analytically sound and intellectually respectable, are otherwise also flawed in some important respects.

THE NEW NEOMERCANTILISM, NAFTA, AND BEYOND

Even in October 2017 when the IMF conference inspiring this volume took place, there was still hope that the trade platform that Trump advanced in order to be elected might not survive the checks imposed by both domestic economic self-interest and the rules emanating from the international system—a system propelled in the first place by the

United States itself. By mid-2018, however, such hopes could be discarded as simple wishful thinking, as the US government already had provided ample evidence of its staunch intention to pursue its trade goals unilaterally through aggressive restrictive measures.

There was, of course, the early decision to withdraw from the TPP—an action never really satisfactorily justified by Trump or any member of his cabinet. The decision proved rather ironic given that the TPP was an agreement molded to a great extent to please US interests, not only on trade, but on matters such as intellectual property rights, investor-state arbitration, and labor standards.

There was also the action to initiate the renegotiation of NAFTA on false—or at best wrongheaded—premises. In May 2017, when the formal announcement to start the renegotiation process was made, the US trade representative argued that the quarter-century-old agreement no longer reflected the standards warranted by changes in the economy. This may have sounded plausible before noticing that the to-do list to update the agreement had already been addressed in the discarded TPP, of which both Mexico and Canada were a part. If NAFTA had been modernized in practice through the TPP, why call for renegotiation of the former while trashing the latter?

The worst fears about the US government's intent for NAFTA started to be confirmed when the US trade representative published—as required by law—the objectives for the renegotiation. That document falsely associated NAFTA with the explosion of US trade deficits, closure of thousands of factories, and abandonment of millions of US workers.

In retrospect, the Mexican and Canadian governments should not even have sat down at the negotiating table without first receiving some apologetic explanation from their US counterparts about those unwarranted arguments. Accepting to negotiate on deceptive premises might help to explain why so little progress had been made after almost one year of talks.

Betting in mid-July 2018 on a conclusion of the renegotiation of NAFTA within the targeted time frame would have looked like an overwhelmingly losing proposition. After seven rounds of negotiation, the last one having taken place as far back as February 2018 with little or no progress, and then followed by several months of deadlock and even rhetorical confrontation, things started to change positively as August approached.

The deadlock was quite understandable. The US trade representatives had not moved a single inch from their most outlandish demands, giving credence to the idea that what they were seeking was to get a deal that far from promoting trade and investment among the NAFTA partners, would have destroyed it.

Fortunately, the Mexican and Canadian governments did not cave to the US government's pretension. Repeatedly those countries' chief negotiators expressed firmly and credibly that they would rather take the unilateral termination of NAFTA by the United States than sign an agreement that would have the same practical consequence. Probably we will never know what motivated the US government to move away from most of the recalcitrant positions it had held for almost a year. The important fact is that it did, leading to a deal in 2018 first with Mexico on August 27, and then with Canada in the last hours of September 30.

There was the US insistence on a sunset clause that would automatically end the new trade agreement every five years unless the three governments agreed otherwise—a feature that would have precluded the certainty for investors that these deals are supposed to provide. They settled for a rather-convoluted formula that avoids the sudden death of the agreement and makes possible—and practically certain—an extended life for it.

The US negotiators had demanded to make the NAFTA investor-state dispute settlement procedure optional for the United States, with a view to deny such protection to its own companies, thus discouraging them from investing in the NAFTA partners. This demand was rejected all along by Mexico on the correct basis that it is important to give foreign investors every assurance that they would not be subject to discriminatory or arbitrary actions if they decided to invest in the country. The US trade representative was never shy about his dislike for the NAFTA investment rules, including sometimes even questioning why it was a good policy of the US government to encourage investment in Mexico. There are of course many good answers to his question, not least that by investing in Mexico, US firms, in order to do some part of their fabrication processes at a lower cost, get to be more competitive not only in the entire region but also globally, allowing them to preserve and enhance job opportunities for their US workers. Consequently, it is good for the two countries that the mechanism to protect US investments in Mexico was preserved despite the US negotiators' originally declared intentions.

By the same token, the United States had sought to eliminate the dispute resolution procedure that protects exporters against the unfair application of domestic laws on antidumping and countervailing duties. This was a deal breaker for Canada, where there is the sentiment that the United States has in the past abused the application of such measures against Canadian exporters. Canada's perseverance paid off, and its exporters will have recourse to the dispute settlement system as it is in NAFTA.

The US side had also been stubborn about getting the Mexican side to accept a special mechanism in the new deal by which the United States could easily apply antidumping tariffs on the Mexican exports of seasonal fruits and vegetables. Mexico would not assent to the inclusion of this mechanism, and in the end, the new agreement will not contain this US negotiators' request—to the benefit of both US consumers and Mexican producers. Similarly, it is to the benefit of Canadian consumers and US exporters of dairy products that Canada ultimately accepted a US request for at least a modest opening of such a market.

The only significant US demand accommodated by Mexico and Canada was in the automotive sector, where more restrictive and cumbersome rules of origin are to be adopted. It has been agreed that 75 percent of a car or truck should have components from North America to qualify for tariff-free imports, up from the current level of 62.5 percent. Furthermore, 70 percent of the steel and aluminum used in that sector must be produced in North America, and 40 percent of a car or truck would have to be made by workers earning at least US$16 per hour—a measure obviously calculated to put a dent in Mexico's comparative advantage. Fortunately, the destructive effects of the new rules of origin for trade and investment could be mitigated in the case of cars by the provision that vehicles failing to fulfill those rules would simply pay the low, most-favored-nation tariff of 2.5 percent as long as the total exports do not exceed an agreed-on reasonable number of vehicles.

Other things being equal, however, it is clear that the new regime will reduce both the regional and global competitiveness of the North

American automotive industry—a result that will not be good for US, Mexican, or Canadian workers. Of course, other things may not be equal if the US government decides to impose tariffs, as it has threatened to do, on vehicles produced by European or Asian companies. If the US government were to impose those tariffs, the burden of the new regime would fall disproportionately on the US consumer.

As purported from day one, the trade agreement will be subject to an update on a number of topics such as digital trade, intellectual property rights, environmental policies, and labor practices. Interestingly, the agreed-on new provisions really are a "cut and paste" of what was contained in the TPP, which was discarded early on by the Trump administration in a decision so damaging to US interests that it will always be a mystery for economic and political historians.

NAFTA aside, trade hostilities by the United States generally escalated significantly in 2018. In January, safeguard tariffs on solar panels and washing machines were announced. Next, invoking national security arguments (Section 232 of the Trade Expansion Act of 1962), an implausible assertion for commodity metals, the US government imposed high tariffs on imports of steel and aluminum from China (effective in March 2018) as well as the European Union, Japan, Turkey, Canada, and Mexico (effective early July 2018). Predictably, all the affected trade partners responded at once by announcing their own retaliatory trade actions.

The confrontation with China intensified with the announcement (effective in early July 2018) of tariffs on US imports from that country worth $34 billion. The stated rationale was unfair trade practices (under Section 301 of the Trade Act of 1974). By September 2018, the total value of Chinese imports subject to US Section 301 tariffs had risen to $250 billion, with tariffs on a further $236 billion threatened.

It did not take long—in fact only a few hours—for China to respond in kind to the US action. At the time of this writing, the Trump administration is vowing to react with even more tariffs on imports from countries challenging its arbitrary actions. The latter could well mark the beginning of a trade war that as history well teaches, will inflict substantial suffering on all involved.

It is hard to know whether the US administration really believes that sooner rather than later the targeted countries will succumb to the United States' outlandish demands, and thus deliver Trump a win in the still-incipient confrontation. If this were the assumption—most likely a wrong one—the trade war could reach epic proportions, with rather-irreversible damage. Even worse, however, the US authorities could be envisioning a scenario in which the affected parties implement recourse to the WTO, and this is taken as an excuse to withdraw from that institution, as Trump has sometimes threatened to do.

This episode of US neomercantilism can hardly have a happy ending simply because it has been launched on wrong premises and with questionable objectives. The US government's ongoing policy not only ignores the notion of comparative advantage and its modern incarnation into complex supply chains but also the essential insight from open economy macroeconomics that the difference between an economy's national income and its expenditure is what drives its current account and trade balances. Playing with trade policy without looking at the underlying variables of income and expenditure is bound to be futile and counterproductive. Furthermore, focusing on bilateral balances to fix the aggregate balances makes the undertaking even more pointless.

The short summary is that it is hard to track down any serious intellectual underpinnings in the globaliphobia being practiced by the current US government—underpinnings that admittedly none of its members claim to have, including the US president himself. Their assertions against trade and other expressions of contemporary globalization have never been accompanied by any supporting empirical evidence or conceptual argument.

WHY GLOBALIZATION IS NOT INCOMPATIBLE WITH SOVEREIGNTY AND DEMOCRACY

The case of sheer populist mercantilism stands in contrast to that of other doubters who purport to challenge globalization, or at least some aspects of it, from a platform of serious scholarship. Highly respectable researchers have over time produced work that is used by themselves or misused by others to weaken the intellectual as well as practical case for economic interdependence. Giving serious consideration to the arguments advanced by those challengers is justified not only because they raise a number of valid points but also because of their influence on policy.

It is well beyond the scope of this chapter to offer a comprehensive survey of the globalization-skeptic research produced by highly respectable scholars. I will limit my succinct comments here to the work of Dani Rodrik since for nearly two decades now, it has been influential in dampening observers' cheeriness about globalization. Singling out his writings is appropriate in light of three important contributions that he has made to the public debate on the costs and benefits of globalization. The first contribution is that of developing a critique of globalization within an orthodox neoclassical paradigm, enabling it to speak to a wider audience that includes mainstream economists and promarket policy makers. The second contribution of Rodrik's work lies in its prescience: in his monograph titled *Has Globalization Gone Too Far?*, published more than twenty years ago, and thus before the recent wave of nationalism and populism rose up in the United States and Europe, he pointed to the possibility of "a political backlash against trade" stemming from "a deep fault line between groups who have the skills and mobility to flourish in global markets and those who either don't have these advantages or perceive the expansion of unregulated markets as inimical to social stability and deeply held norms" (Rodrik's 1997, 2). Third and no less important, Rodrik's (2011) more recent work claims the existence of a trilemma linking globalization, democracy, and sovereignty such that that no country can benefit from all three potentially desirable goals at the same time.

Having disagreed with commentators who thought of modern globalization as ineluctably advancing—because in their view, driven essentially by irreversible technological progress—I found myself in full accord with Rodrik when he expressed the view that continued globalization should not be taken for granted and a retreat is always possible. Likewise, I also agree on highlighting the threat of social disintegration, which encompasses various worrisome phenomena such as the stagnation of wages among different categories of employees in developed countries and worsening of the income distribution—trends that at the time were far less entrenched, but were firmly confirmed over the next twenty years.

That said, I will argue in the remainder of this chapter that we should not jump from the above considerations to the conclusion that globalization was the cause of the social disintegration threat that may halt or reverse altogether the globalization clock. More specifically, Rodrik's argumentation—as well as that of some other globalization challengers—does not start with a hypothesis to be rigorously tested but rather with a strong prior (even if sometimes backed by selective evidence) that the identified social tensions are being generated primarily by globalization, including through its effects on technology and constraints on policies that favor redistribution of the gains from trade. Insufficient credence is given to other forces and circumstances that could have been at the root of the ills that Rodrik presciently identified, some of which were already at play long before hyperglobalization, making more inclusive growth also elusive in many countries in the past.

Cast within this (arguably biased) mind-set, the simultaneous occurrence (or correlation) of globalization and social bads can easily become tantamount to strong causality from the first to the second. It thus becomes just a matter of imagination to identify numerous unequivocal relations between globalization and socially unjust outcomes. Indeed, as globalization deepened, and some of the social trends highlighted early on by Rodrik were also reaffirmed, the author's original critique of globalization not only has been reiterated but actually enlarged too—as have his prescriptions to deal with the issues at hand.

In this context, and to go straight to the heart of the matter, it is worth revisiting here the premises, factual underpinnings, and policy implications of the postulated trilemma among democracy, national sovereignty, and globalization. If true, it would imply that the options for countries are to restrict democracy in the interest of pursuing globalization, limit globalization in the pursuit of building domestic democratic legitimacy, or globalize democracy at the cost of national sovereignty. That such a trilemma has acquired credence among some scholars and students of the social sciences is intriguing for somebody (like me) who has been or still is directly involved in policy making with a commitment to promote the tripod of democracy, free trade, and a rules-based international system sustained by sovereign nations.

It is intriguing for three main reasons.

First, international covenants and institutions, however imperfect they may be, are the best vehicle that weak and emerging countries have to defend themselves from the arbitrary exercise of economic as well as geopolitical force by the most powerful countries' governments and commercial interests. Thus global governance, far from being a threat to countries' sovereignty, can be its protector.

Second, I question whether globalization conspires against domestic democratic legitimacy. The latter, hard to achieve and even harder to sustain, ultimately depends on widely delivering the benefits of prosperity—something historically more likely to happen in open than in closed economies. Consequently, it is not true that for countries to pursue democracy, it is necessary for them to somehow disengage from globalization. This would be valid only under the Rodrik basic premise that globalization *by itself* explains a significant number of the maladies present in the world. Any country, in the South or North, can be democratic, economically open, and engaged in the multilateral rules-based system while simultaneously exercising its sovereignty—with the latter being understood, of course, in the modern sense of the word. That sovereignty could include decisions to offset through domestic policies some of the undesired side effects of globalization.

It is also important to note that much of this critique was developed (as in Rodrik 1997, 2011) when globalization, undeservedly in my view, was suffering a black eye, in the first case just a few months before the Asian crisis, and in the second, when the sequel of the 2008–9 financial crisis was still hitting Europe severely. The recent rise of isolationist populism in the most unusual places—of most concern, in the United States—has given leeway to the possibility of a third charge against globalization. Specifically, that charge is that the populist backlash was largely predictable, with economic globalization being the ultimate culprit in the emergence of populism, not only in the systemically dangerous US case, but in previous episodes in various parts of the world, including Latin America (see Rodrik 2018).

Yet reading about this association between populism and economic interdependence, those of us from Latin America who have studied, opposed, and even suffered from populism, and think of Juan Perón, Getúlio Vargas, and Hugo Chávez, to name just a few from our long list of homegrown populist strongmen, are tempted to ask, as Jagdish Bhagwati, paraphrasing a pop song, famously wrote, What's globalization got to do with it? My concern is that by focusing on globalization and downplaying what he calls the other forces at play, Rodrik and other critics may be aiming at a straw argument and missing more important targets, thereby drawing erroneous policy prescriptions. In my view, a glance at some of Rodrik's proposals should suffice to justify this concern.

Finally, my third concern pertains to the implications for the multilateral trade system. Although Rodrik's (1997) contribution claims not to be prescriptive, it actually went so far as to call for multilateral rules on how countries can depart from multilateral rules. It advocated—barely three years after the formal start of the WTO—finding new ways for countries to disengage selectively from multilateral disciplines. In particular, Rodrik submitted that the WTO escape clause (the safeguard mechanism discussed in the chapter by Michael Trebilcock in this volume) should be changed to give countries even more latitude to deviate from their trade liberalization commitments in order to pursue other domestic policy objectives. This proposal therefore suggested a radical shift from market access to domestic policy space as the core matter for multilateral negotiations. With this change, countries would be allowed to suspend their WTO commitments, arguably to pursue their development priorities. In an earlier review of the book, I claimed and still do, that if adopted, Rodrik's formula would be a safe bet not only for perpetual conflict but also for regression into autarky (Zedillo 2011).

By now it should be clear that the Trump administration would have been most pleased with a trading system reformed along the lines of the Rodrik criteria. An unruly trading system rather than the present rules-based one would have given the United States license to carry on with its protectionist agenda in an even more expeditious fashion. The unreformed WTO safeguard provisions, which Rodrik faults for being too stringent, fortunately have proven sufficiently so to force the US administration to rely not on those provisions but instead on a bizarre appeal to national security to justify some of its most egregious trade policy threats and decisions.

FINAL REMARKS

Advocacy of greater space for national policy making is not wrong in principle. What is questionable is to call for that margin so that countries can erect trade barriers anew under the misguided premise that they will serve to fix the economic, social, and political cleavages that rightly concern Rodrik. Those cleavages are first and foremost the consequence of domestic policies, both in the recent and far past, and therefore ultimately reflect political choices by those who have held political power over time.

As argued elsewhere in this volume (see, for example, the chapters by François Bourguignon, Edward Alden, and Angus Deaton), regressive tax and expenditure policies, hollow social safety nets, bad educational systems particularly for the poor, rejection of universal health care, and laws unduly segmenting the labor market, not to mention perennial public underinvestment—along with flawed design in programs to support workers to adapt to and overcome shifts in labor markets due to technological change and trade—are not policy features mandated inescapably by open markets and globalization. Rather, they are inherent to policies that tend to perpetuate polarization in societies and protect the power of those at the top of the income distribution.

REFERENCES

Deaton, Angus. 2013. *The Great Escape: Health, Wealth, and the Origins of Inequality.* Princeton, NJ: Princeton University Press.

Rodrik, Dani. 1997. *Has Globalization Gone Too Far?* Washington, DC: Institute for International Economics.

———. 2011. *The Globalization Paradox: Democracy and the Future of the World Economy.* New York: W. W. Norton.

———. 2018. "Populism and the Economics of Globalization." *Journal of International Business Policy* 1, no. 1–2 (June): 12–33.

Zedillo, Ernesto. 2011. "The Globalization Paradox: Democracy and the Future of the World Economy by Dani Rodrik." *Journal of Economic Literature* 49, no. 4 (December): 1269–71.

Index